DOMESDAY BOOK

Bedfordshire

History from the Sources

DOMESDAY BOOK

A Survey of the Counties of England

LIBER DE WINTONIA

Compiled by direction of

KING WILLIAM I

Winchester
1086

DOMESDAY BOOK

text and translation edited by

JOHN MORRIS

20

Bedfordshire

edited from a draft translation prepared by

Veronica Sankaran and David Sherlock

PHILLIMORE
Chichester
1977

1977

Published by

PHILLIMORE & Co. Ltd.,

London and Chichester

Head Office: Shopwyke Hall,
Chichester, Sussex, England

© John Morris 1977

ISBN 0 85033 149 8 (case)
ISBN 0 85033 150 1 (limp)

Printed and bound in Great Britain by
Redwood Books, Trowbridge, Wiltshire

BEDFORDSHIRE

Introduction

The Domesday Survey of Bedfordshire

History from the Sources
General Editor: John Morris

The series aims to publish history
written directly from the sources
for all interested readers, both
specialists and others. The first
priority is to publish important
texts which should be widely
available, but are not.

DOMESDAY BOOK

The contents, with the folio on which each county begins, are:

Domesday Book is termed *Liber de Wintonia* (The Book of Winchester) in column 332c

INTRODUCTION

The Domesday Survey

In 1066 Duke William of Normandy conquered England. He was crowned King, and most of the lands of the English nobility were soon granted to his followers. Domesday Book was compiled 20 years later. The Saxon Chronicle records that in 1085

at Gloucester at midwinter ... the King had deep speech with his counsellors ... and sent men all over England to each shire ... to find out ... what or how much each landholder held ... in land and livestock, and what it was worth ... The returns were brought to him.[1]

William was thorough. One of his Counsellors reports that he also sent a second set of Commissioners 'to shires they did not know, where they were themselves unknown, to check their predecessors' survey, and report culprits to the King.'[2]

The information was collected at Winchester, corrected, abridged, chiefly by omission of livestock and the 1066 population, and fair-copied by one writer into a single volume. Norfolk, Suffolk and Essex were copied, by several writers, into a second volume, unabridged, which states that 'the Survey was made in 1086'. The surveys of Durham and Northumberland, and of several towns, including London, were not transcribed, and most of Cumberland and Westmorland, not yet in England, was not surveyed. The whole undertaking was completed at speed, in less than 12 months, though the fair-copying of the main volume may have taken a little longer. Both volumes are now preserved at the Public Record Office. Some versions of regional returns also survive. One of them, from Ely Abbey,[3] copies out the Commissioners' brief. They were to ask

The name of the place. Who held it, before 1066, and now?
How many *hides*?[4] How many ploughs, both those in lordship and the men's?
How many villagers, cottagers and slaves, how many free men and Freemen?[5]
How much woodland, meadow and pasture? How many mills and fishponds?
How much has been added or taken away? What the total value was and is?
How much each free man or Freeman had or has? All threefold, before 1066,
    when King William gave it, and now; and if more can be had than at present?

The Ely volume also describes the procedure. The Commissioners took evidence on oath 'from the Sheriff; from all the barons and their Frenchmen; and from the whole Hundred, the priests, the reeves and six villagers from each village'. It also names four Frenchmen and four Englishmen from each Hundred, who were sworn to verify the detail.

The King wanted to know what he had, and who held it. The Commissioners therefore listed lands in dispute, for Domesday Book was not only a tax-assessment. To the King's grandson, Bishop Henry of Winchester, its purpose was that every 'man should know his right and not usurp another's'; and because it was the final authoritative register of rightful possession 'the natives called it Domesday Book, by analogy

---

[1] Before he left England for the last time, late in 1086.   [2] Robert Losinga, Bishop of Hereford 1079-1095 (see *E.H.R.* 22, 1907, 74).   [3] *Inquisitio Eliensis,* first paragraph.   [4] A land unit, reckoned as 120 acres.   [5] *Quot Sochemani.*

from the Day of Judgement'; that was why it was carefully arranged by Counties, and by landholders within Counties, 'numbered consecutively ... for easy reference'.[6]

Domesday Book describes Old English society under new management, in minute statistical detail. Foreign lords had taken over, but little else had yet changed. The chief landholders and those who held from them are named, and the rest of the population was counted. Most of them lived in villages, whose houses might be clustered together, or dispersed among their fields. Villages were grouped in administrative districts called Hundreds, which formed regions within Shires, or Counties, which survive today with minor boundary changes; the recent deformation of some ancient county identities is here disregarded, as are various short-lived modern changes. The local assemblies, though overshadowed by lords great and small, gave men a voice, which the Commissioners heeded. Very many holdings were described by the Norman term *manerium* (manor), greatly varied in size and structure, from tiny farmsteads to vast holdings; and many lords exercised their own jurisdiction and other rights, termed *soca*, whose meaning still eludes exact definition.

The Survey was unmatched in Europe for many centuries, the product of a sophisticated and experienced English administration, fully exploited by the Conqueror's commanding energy. But its unique assemblage of facts and figures has been hard to study, because the text has not been easily available, and abounds in technicalities. Investigation has therefore been chiefly confined to specialists; many questions cannot be tackled adequately without a cheap text and uniform translation available to a wider range of students, including local historians.

Previous Editions

The text has been printed once, in 1783, in an edition by Abraham Farley, probably of 1250 copies, at Government expense, said to have been £38,000; its preparation took 16 years. It was set in a specially designed type, here reproduced photographically, which was destroyed by fire in 1808. In 1811 and 1816 the Records Commissioners added an introduction, indices, and associated texts, edited by Sir Henry Ellis; and in 1861-1863 the Ordnance Survey issued zincograph facsimiles of the whole. Texts of individual counties have appeared since 1673, separate translations in the Victoria County Histories and elsewhere.

This Edition

Farley's text is used, because of its excellence, and because any worthy alternative would prove astronomically expensive. His text has been checked against the facsimile, and discrepancies observed have been verified against the manuscript, by the kindness of Miss Daphne Gifford of the Public Record Office. Farley's few errors are indicated in the notes.

[6] *Dialogus de Scaccario* 1,16.

The editor is responsible for the translation and lay-out. It aims at what the compiler would have written if his language had been modern English; though no translation can be exact, for even a simple word like 'free' nowadays means freedom from different restrictions. Bishop Henry emphasized that his grandfather preferred 'ordinary words'; the nearest ordinary modern English is therefore chosen whenever possible. Words that are now obsolete, or have changed their meaning, are avoided, but measurements have to be transliterated, since their extent is often unknown or arguable, and varied regionally. The terse inventory form of the original has been retained, as have the ambiguities of the Latin.

Modern English commands two main devices unknown to 11th century Latin, standardised punctuation and paragraphs; in the Latin, *ibi* ('there are') often does duty for a modern full stop, *et* ('and') for a comma or semi-colon. The entries normally answer the Commissioners' questions, arranged in five main groups, (i) the place and its holder, its hides, ploughs and lordship; (ii) people; (iii) resources; (iv) value; and (v) additional notes. The groups are usually given as separate paragraphs.

King William numbered chapters 'for easy reference', and sections within chapters are commonly marked, usually by initial capitals, often edged in red. They are here numbered. Maps, indices and an explanation of technical terms are also given. Later, it is hoped to publish analytical and explanatory volumes, and associated texts.

The editor is deeply indebted to the advice of many scholars, too numerous to name, and especially to the Public Record Office, and to the publisher's patience. The draft translations are the work of a team; they have been co-ordinated and corrected by the editor, and each has been checked by several people. It is therefore hoped that mistakes may be fewer than in versions published by single fallible individuals. But it would be Utopian to hope that the translation is altogether free from error; the editor would like to be informed of mistakes observed.

The map is the work of Jim Hardy.

The preparation of this volume has been greatly assisted by a generous grant from the Leverhulme Trust Fund.

Conventions

*   refers to a note to the Latin text.

[ ]   enclose words omitted in the MS.   ( )   enclose editorial explanations.

BEDEFORDSCIRE.

BEDEFORD . T.R.E . ꝑ dimidio hunꝺ se deſꝺeƀ.
7 m̃ facit . in expeditione 7 in nauibȝ . Terra
de hac uilla nunq̃ fuit hidata . nec m̃ eſt . p̃ter
unã hiꝺ quæ jacuit in æccta Ꞩ Pavli in elemoſina
T . R . E . 7 m̃ jacet recte . Sed Remigiꝰ eꝑs poſuit eã
extᵃ elemoſinã æcctæ Ꞩ Pauli injuſte ut h̄oēs dicuꝵ.
7 m̃ tenet . 7 quicqd ad eã ꝑtinet . Valet . c . ſolid.

BEDFORDSHIRE

B BEDFORD answered for a half Hundred before 1066, and does so now, in (military) expeditions, (by land) and in ships. The land of this town was never assessed in hides and is not now, except for 1 hide, which lay in (the lands of) St. Paul's Church before 1066, in alms, and now rightly so lies. But Bishop Remigius wrongfully placed it outside the alms (lands) of St. Paul's Church, as the men (of the Shire) state. He holds it now, and whatever belongs to it.
Value 100s.

.I.REX WILLELMVS
.II.Eps Baiocenfis.
.III. Eps Conftantienfis.
.IIII Eps Lincolienfis.
.V.Eps Dunelmfis.
.VI.Abb de S Edmundo.
.VII.Abb de Burg.
.VIII Abb de Ramefy.
.IX.Abb de Weftmon.
.X.Abb de Torny.
.XI.Abbatiffa de Berching.
.XII Canonici de Lundon.
.XIII Canonici de Bedeford.
.XII.Ernuinus pbr.
.XV.Euftachius comes.
.XVI.Walterius gifard.
.XVII.Wills de Warenna.
.XVI.Wills de Ouu.
.XIX.Milo crifpinus.
.XX.Ernulf de Hefding.
.XXI.Eudo dapifer
.XXII.Wills peurel
.XXIII.Hugo de belcap.
.XXII.Nigell de albingi.
.XXV Wills Spech.
.XXVI Robt de Todeni.
.XXVI.Giflebt de gand.
.XXVI Robt de olgi
.XXIX.Rannulf fr Ilgerij.
.XXX.Robt Fafiton.
.XXXI.Aluered de Lincolia.
.XXXII.Walter Flandrenfis.
.XXXI.Walter fr Seiherij.
.XXXII.Hugo Flandrensis.

XXXV.Hugo pincerna.
XXXVI.Sigarus de Cioches.
XXXVII.Gunfrid de Cioches.
XXXVIII Ricard fili Gislebti comitis.
.XXXIX.Ricardus pungiant.
.XL.Wills camerarius.
XLI.Wills Louet.
.XLII.Wills
.XLIII.Henricus filius Azor.
XLIIII.Osbn filius Ricardi.
.XLV.Osbn filius Walterii.
XLVI.Osbn pifcator.
.XLVII.Turftin camerarius.
.XLVIII.Giflebt fili Salom.
.XLIX.Albt Lotharienfis.
.L.Dauid de Argentom.
.LI.Radulf de infula.
.LII.Gozelin biito
.LIII.Judita comitiffa
.LIIII.Adeliz fem.H.de grent.
.LV.Azelina fem.R.talgeb.
.LVI.Burgenfes de bedeford.
.LVI.Pfecti regis 7 bedelli
7 elemofinarii.

[LIST OF LANDHOLDERS IN BEDFORDSHIRE]

1 King William
2 The Bishop of Bayeux
3 The Bishop of Coutances
4 The Bishop of Lincoln
5 The Bishop of Durham
6 The Abbot of St. Edmund's
7 The Abbot of Peterborough
8 The Abbot of Ramsey
9 The Abbot of Westminster
10 The Abbot of Thorney
11 The Abbess of Barking
12 The Canons of London
13 The Canons of Bedford
14 Ernwin the Priest
15 Count Eustace
16 Walter Giffard
17 William of Warenne
18 William of Eu
19 Miles Crispin
20 Arnulf of Hesdin
21 Eudo the Steward
22 William Peverel
23 Hugh of Beauchamp
24 Nigel of Aubigny
25 William Speke
26 Robert of Tosny
27 Gilbert of Ghent
28 Robert d'Oilly
29 Ranulf brother of Ilger
30 Robert [son of] Fafiton
31 Alfred of Lincoln
32 Walter of Flanders
33 Walter brother of Sihere
34 Hugh of Flanders

35 Hugh Butler
36 Sigar of Chocques
37 Gunfrid of Chocques
38 Richard son of Count Gilbert
39 Richard Poynant
40 William the Chamberlain
41 William Lovett
42 William
43 Henry son of Azor
44 Osbern son of Richard
45 Osbern son of Walter
46 Osbern Fisher
47 Thurstan the Chamberlain
48 Gilbert son of Solomon
49 Albert of Lorraine
50 David of Argenton
51 Ralph de L'Isle
52 Jocelyn the Breton
53 Countess Judith
54 Adelaide wife of Hugh of Grandmesnil
55 Azelina wife of Ralph Tallboys
56 The Burgesses of Bedford
[57] The King's Reeves and Beadles and Almsmen

TERRA REGIS.

ᛘ *LISTONE* dn̄icū Maneriū Regis
p.XLVII.hid ſe deſd modo.T.R.E. n̄ eraỿ niſi.xxx.hid.
De his.XLVII.hid ſuỿ in manu regis.XL.III.hid.
Tra.ē ad.LII.car̄.In dn̄io ſunt.VI.car̄.7 uiĩli hn̄t
XLVI.car̄.Ibi ſunt q̄ter x̄x̄ 7 II.uiĩli.7 xxx.bord.
7 II.ſerui.7 II.molini de.xxx.ſot.P̄tū.XL.car̄.Silua
c.porc.Theloneū de mercato redd.VII.lib.Int
totū redd p annū.XXII.lib ad penſū.7 dimid dīe
ad firmā regis.in fruīto 7 melle 7 aliis reb₃ ad firmā
ptinentib₃.Ad op̄ reginæ.II.uncias auri.7 p.I.ſūmario
7 c̄ſuetud cān.LXX.ſot.7 c.ſot ad penſū.7 XL.ſot de
albo argento.Hoc miſit de creīto Iuo talliebosc.
7 I.unc auri ad op̄ uicecomitis p annū.
De huj̄ ᛘ tra tenuit Weneſi camerari.x.hid de
rege Edw.quas Radulf̄ talliebosc appoſuit in Leſtone
ubi n̄ adjacebant.T.R.E.Et iterū iſd Radulf̄ appo
ſuit alias VII.hid huic Manerio quæ ibi n̄ eraỿ.T.R.E.
Has.VII.hid tenuit Starcher teign.R.E.
Æcclam huj̄ ᛘ ten̄ Rem ep̄s.cū.IIII.hid quæ ad eā
ptinent.7 Hæ.IIII.cōputant in.XLVII.hid manerii.
Tra.ē ad.III.car̄.In dn̄io.ē.I.car̄.7 uiĩli.I.car̄.7 alia
poſſet fieri.Ibi.VI.uiĩli 7 VI.bord p̄tū.III.car̄.H̄ tra
cū æccta uat 7 ualuit.IIII.lib.Wluui ep̄s ten̄.T.R.E.

ᛘ *LOITONE* dn̄icū ᛘ Regis p.xxx.hid ſe deſd.Tra.ē
ad q̄t x̄x̄ 7 II.car̄.In dn̄io.IIII.car̄.Viĩli q̄t xx.car̄.
II.min.Ibi.q̄t x̄x̄.uiĩli 7 XLVII.bord.7 VI.molini
redd.c.ſot.p̄tū.IIII.car̄.Silua.II.miliū porc.7 de
c̄ſuetud.x.ſot 7 VIII.den.De theloneo 7 mercato.c.ſot.

[In STANBRIDGE Hundred]

1a M. LEIGHTON (Buzzard), a household manor of the King's, now answers
for 47 hides; before 1066 there were only 30 hides. Of these 47
hides, 43 hides are in the King's hands. Land for 52 ploughs.
In lordship 6 ploughs. The villagers have 46 ploughs.
   82 villagers, 30 smallholders and 2 slaves.
   2 mills at 30s; meadow for 40 ploughs; woodland, 100 pigs;
      market tolls pay £7.
In total, it pays £22 by weight a year and half a day('s provisions)
to the King's revenue, in wheat, honey and other things which
belong to the revenue; for the Queen's work 2 ounces of gold;
for 1 pack-horse and for customary dog dues 70s, and 100s by
weight and 40s in white silver; Ivo Tallboys put this on from
the increase; 1 ounce of gold a year for the Sheriff's work.

b   Wynsi the Chamberlain held 10 hides of this manor's land from
King Edward. Ralph Tallboys placed them in Leighton, where
they were not attached before 1066; again, Ralph also placed
another 7 hides in this manor, which were not there before 1066.
Starker, a thane of King Edward's, held these 7 hides.

c   Bishop Remigius holds the church of this manor, with 4 hides
which belong to it. These 4 are accounted for in the 47 hides
of the manor. Land for 3 ploughs. In lordship 1 plough;
the villagers, 1 plough; another possible.
   6 villagers and 6 smallholders.
   Meadow for 3 ploughs.
The value of this land, with the church, is and was £4.
Bishop Wulfwy held it before 1066.

[In MANSHEAD Hundred]

a M. LUTON, a household manor of the King's, answers for 30 hides.
Land for 82 ploughs. In lordship 4 ploughs. The villagers, 80
ploughs less 2.
   80 villagers and 47 smallholders.
   6 mills which pay 100s; meadow for 4 ploughs;
      woodland, 2000 pigs; customary dues, 10s 8d; from tolls
      and the market, 100s.

Int́ tot́ redd́ p̄ annū . xxx . liƀ ad pensū . 7 dimid diē ·

in frum̄to 7 melle 7 aliis c̄fuetud ad firmā regis ptinent́.

Reginæ . IIII . unc auri . 7 de sūmario 7 aliis c̄fuetudinibȝ

minutis . LXX . fot́ . 7 de c̄fuetud canū . VI . liƀ 7 x . fot́ .

7 de crem̄to qd́ mifit Iuo tallebofc . VII . liƀ ad pensū .

7 XL . fot́ albi argenti . 7 unā unciā auri uicecomiti.

Ǽcctam huj́ m̄ teń Witt́s camerari de rege . cū . v .

hid́ træ quæ ad eā ptinent́ . Hǽ . v . hid́ fuꝗ de xxx . hid́ m̄.

Tra . ē . VI . caŕ in dn̄io . I . caŕ . 7 uitt́i hn̄t . v . caŕ . Ibi xi .

uitt́i 7 IIII . bord́ . 7 III . ferui . 7 I . molin̄ . x . fot́ . Ǽccła . xx . fot́

p̄ annū redd́ . Silua . L . porc . Int́ totū uat́ 7 ualuit

LX . fot́ . Hanc æcctam cū tra tenuit Morcaŕ pƀr . T.R.E.

m̄ HEVSTONE dn̄icū m̄ Regis . ꝓ x . hid́ fe defd́ . Tra . ē

★ . XXIꟾꟾ caŕ . In dn̄io . II . caŕ . 7 uitt́i . XXII . caŕ . Ibi xxx

7 VIII . uitt́i 7 XII . bord́ . I̊ ꝑtū . XII . caŕ . Silua . c . porć .

Int́ totū redd́ p̄ ann̄ . x . liƀ ad pensū . 7 dimid́ diē

de frum̄to 7 melle 7 aliis rebȝ ad firmā regis ptinentiƀ.

De minutis c̄fuetudiniƀ 7 de . I . sūmario . LXV . fot́ .

De c̄fuetud canū . LXV . fot́ . 7 Reginæ . II . unć auri .

De crem̄to qd́ mifit Iuo tallebofc . III . liƀ ad pensū . 7 xx₄

fot́ de albo argento . 7 I . unć auri uicecomiti.

Ǽcctam huj́ m̄ teń Witt́s camerari cū diḿ hida.

quæ ad eā ptiń . 7 de . x . hid́ Manerij . ē . Tŕa . ē dim̄ caŕ .

7 ibi eft́ . Valet . XII . fot́ . p̄ annū.

SEWELLE ꝓ . III . hid́ fe defd́ T.R.E. Tra . ē . II . caŕ . Ibi eft́

. I . caŕ 7 dim̄ . 7 adhuc dim̄ pot́ fieri . ꝑtū . IIII . boū.

Ibi . I . uitt́s 7 IIII . bord́ . Ħ tra uat́ 7 ualuit . xx . fot́ . Hanc

tenuit Walraue hō Eddid reginæ . 7 potuit dare cui

uoluit . In Odecroft hund jacuit . T.R.E. Radulf́ ū

taillebofc in m̄ houftone appofuit c̄cedente . W . rege

p̄ crem̄tū qd́ ei dedit . Hoc dn̄t hoēs ejd́ Rad . fcd́m

In total, it pays £30 a year by weight and half a day('s provisions) in wheat, honey and other customary dues which belong to the King's revenue; to the Queen 4 ounces of gold; for a pack-horse and other petty customary dues 70s; for customary dog dues, £6 10s; from the increase which Ivo Tallboys put on £7 by weight and 40s of white silver; 1 ounce of gold to the Sheriff.

2b William the King's Chamberlain holds the church of this manor, with 5 hides of land which belong to it. These 5 hides are of the 30 hides of the manor. Land for 6 ploughs. In lordship 1 plough. The villagers have 5 ploughs.
    11 villagers, 4 smallholders and 3 slaves.
    1 mill, 10s; the church pays 20s a year; woodland, 50 pigs.
In total, the value is and was 60s.
    Morcar the priest held this church with the land before 1066.

3 M. HOUGHTON (Regis), a household manor of the King's, answers   209 c
for 10 hides. Land for 24 ploughs. In lordship 2 ploughs.
The villagers, 22 ploughs.
    38 villagers and 12 smallholders.
    Meadow for 12 ploughs; woodland, 100 pigs.
In total, it pays £10 a year by weight and half a day('s provisions) in wheat, honey and other things which belong to the King's revenue; from petty customary dues and from 1 pack-horse 65s; from customary dog dues 65s; to the Queen 2 ounces of gold; from the increase which Ivo Tallboys put on £3 by weight and 20s in white silver; 1 ounce of gold to the Sheriff.
    William the Chamberlain holds the church of this manor, with ½ hide which belongs to it. It is of the 10 hides of the manor. Land for ½ plough; it is there. Value 12s a year.

4 SEWELL answered for 3 hides before 1066. Land for 2 ploughs. 1½ there; a further ½ possible.
    Meadow for 4 oxen.
    1 villager and 4 smallholders.
The value of this land is and was 20s.
    Walraven, Queen Edith's man, held it; he could grant to whom he would. It lay in 'Woodcroft' Hundred before 1066, but Ralph Tallboys placed it in the manor of Houghton with King William's assent through the increase it gave him. This is what Ralph's men

Bissopescote . p v . hiđ ſe defđ . T.R.E. Tra . ē . v . cař.
Ibi . ii . cař in dñio . 7 x . uiłłi hñt . iii . cař . Ibi . iii . ſerui.
7 p̄tū . iii . cař . In totis ualent ual xl . ſoł . Q̄do Radulf ^taillebofc 9
tenebat: ſimił . T.R.E. lx . ſoł . Hoc ꝏ tenuit Eduuin⁹
hō Aſgari ſtalri . 7 potuit inde facere qđ uoluit . Hanc
appoſuit Radulf⁹ talliebofc . ~~appoſuit~~ in Loitone ꝏ
regis . p crem̄tū qđ ei dedit . 7 foris miſit de hund ubi ſe
defendeƀ . T.R.E. Econt ū ſūpſit alias . v . hiđ de alio hunđ.
7 poſuit in Flictham hunđ.

.II. **ꝏ** E̅ps Baiocensis In dimidio hunđ de *STANBVRGE*
teñ *EITONE* . p xii . hiđ 7 i . uirḡ ſe defđ . Tra . ē xx.
cař . In dñio . ii . hidæ . 7 ibi ſunt . iiii . cař . 7 ii . adhuc
poſſunt fieri . Viłłi hñt . viii . cař . 7 adhuc . vi . poſ̄s . ēe.
Ibi xx uiłłi . 7 xiii . borđ . 7 ii . ſerui . p̄tū . vi . cař . Silua
ccc . porc . 7 xii . deñ inde . In totis ualent ual . xvi . lib.
Q̄do recep̄: xx . lib . T.R.E: ſimilit . Hoc ꝏ tenuit Alſi
hō regine Eddid . 7 dare 7 uendē potuit.

In *HVND* de Maneſheue teñ Anſgot de Roueceſtre
ii . hiđ in Eureſhot . de fedo epī Baioc . Tra . ē . ii . cař . Ibi
eſt una 7 alia poteſt fieri . Ibi ſunt . iiii . uiłłi . 7 i . borđ.
P̄tū . i . cař . Silua . l . porc . Int t̄otū ual . xx . ſoł . Q̄do
recep̄: xxx . ſoł . T.R.E: xl . ſoł . Hanc tr̄a T.R.E . iiii . teini
tenueř . 7 dare 7 uendē potueř.

Iſdem Anſgot teñ de eođ epo in Mildentone . iiii . hiđ.
Tra . iiii . cař . In dñio . i . cař . 7 altera pot fieri . Viłłi . ii.
cař . Ibi . iiii . uiłłi . 7 iii . borđ . 7 viii . ſerui . p̄tū . iiii . cař.
Silua . xxx . porc . Int totū ual 7 ualuit qdo recep̄.
iiii . lib . T.R.E. xl . ſoł . Hanc tram tenueř . vii . ſochi.
7 dare 7 uendē potueř T.R.E.

state, according to what they heard him say.

5 BISCOT answered for 5 hides before 1066. Land for 5 ploughs.
In lordship 2 ploughs.
   10 villagers have 3 ploughs.
   3 slaves; meadow for 3 ploughs.
Total value 40s; when Ralph Tallboys held it, the same;
before 1066, 60s.
   Edwin, Asgar the Constable's man, held this manor; he could
do what he would with it. Ralph Tallboys placed it in the King's
manor of Luton through the increase it gave him, and put it
outside the Hundred where it answered before 1066; against it
he took another 5 hides from another Hundred and placed
them in Flitt Hundred.

2   LAND OF THE BISHOP OF BAYEUX

In the Half-Hundred of STANBRIDGE
1 M. The Bishop of Bayeux holds EATON (Bray). It answers for 12
hides and 1 virgate. Land for 20 ploughs. In lordship 2 hides;
4 ploughs; a further 2 possible. The villagers have 8 ploughs;
a further 6 possible.
   20 villagers, 13 smallholders and 2 slaves.
   Meadow for 6 ploughs; woodland, 300 pigs and 12d therefrom.
Total value £16; when acquired £20; before 1066 the same.
   Alfsi, Queen Edith's man, held this manor; he could grant
and sell.

In the Hundred of MANSHEAD
2 Ansgot of Rochester holds 2 hides in EVERSHOLT from the
Bishop of Bayeux's Holding. Land for 2 ploughs; 1 there;
another possible.
   4 villagers and 1 smallholder.
   Meadow for 1 plough; woodland, 50 pigs.
In total, value 20s; when acquired 30s; before 1066, 40s.
   4 thanes held this land before 1066; they could grant and sell.

3 Ansgot also holds 4 hides in MILTON (Bryan) from the Bishop.
Land for 4 ploughs. In lordship 1 plough; a second possible.
The villagers, 2 ploughs.
   4 villagers, 3 smallholders and 8 slaves.
   Meadow for 4 ploughs; woodland, 30 pigs.
In total, the value is, and was when acquired, £4; before 1066, 40s.
   Before 1066, 7 Freemen held this land; they could grant and sell. 209 d

In Hund de Stodene . teñ Toui pͩr dim hid de ep̄o
in Boleheſtre . Tra . ē . I . caͬ . 7 ibi eſt . 7 I . uiɫɫs 7 I . borͩ
P̊tū dim caͬ . Silua ; xxx . porc . Inͭ totū uaɫ x . ſoɫ .
7 tantͩ qͩo receͫp . T.R.E.′ xii . ſoɫ . Hanc trͣ tenuit Azor
hͦ Bored . 7 uendͤ potuit cui uellet .

Iᴮɪᴅ tenent . ii . ſocͪi de ep̄o dim hid . Tra . ē . I . caͬ .
7 ibi . ē . cū . ii . borͩ . Silua . iiii . porc . Inͭ totū uaɫ . x . ſoɫ
7 tntͩ qͩo receͫp . T.Ꞃ . xii . ſoɫ . Idem ipſi qͩ tenent
tenueͬ T.R.E. 7 uendͤ 7 dare potueͬ .

In dimid hund de Boch . . ai . teñ Herbͭ filiͨ Iuonis de ep̄o
iii . hid 7 iii . uirg in Stach . . . e . Tra . ē . iiii . caͬ . Ibi ſuᴺ
nͨ . iii . caͬ 7 dim . 7 dim p . . fieri . Ibi xii . uiɫɫi 7 viᴵ
borͩ . p̊tū . I . caͬ . Silua . xl . porc . Inͭ toͭ uaɫ
vii . liᵬ . Qͩo receͫp ′ ix . liᵬ . T.R.E. ′ xii . liᵬ . Hanc trͣ
xii . ſocͪi tenueͬ hͦͤs regis . E . fueͬ . 7 uendͤ potueͬ

In Hund de Wilga ten . ii . ſocͪi in Carlentone
i . hid 7 I . uirg . de Herbͭo filio iuonis . 7 ipſe de ep̄o
Tra . ē . I . caͬ 7 dim . 7 ibi ſunt . P̊tū . I . caͬ . Inͭ totū uaɫ
xxvi . ſoɫ 7 viii . den . Qͩo receͫp . 7 T.R.E. ′ xxx . ſoɫ . Hanc
trͣ idͤ ipſi qui nͨ teneᴺ tenueͬ 7 dare 7 uendͤ potueͬ

In Torueie teñ Wimund de Herbͭo . 7 ipſe de ep̄o
i . hid . Tra . I . caͬ . 7 ibi . ē . p̊tū dim caͬ . Inͭ totū
uaɫ . xx . ſoɫ . Qͩo receͫp . 7 T.R.E. ′ xl . ſoɫ . Hanc trͣ
tenuit uñ hͦ Aluuoldi de Stiuetone . 7 uendͤ potuit .

ℳ In Hund de Bereforde . Herbͭ de ep̄o 7 hugo nepos ejͥ
de eo teñ v . hid in Wildene . Tra . ē xvi . caͬ In dͦnio
nulla . ē m̊ . 7 iii . poſſunt fieri Viɫɫi hͭn . x . caͬ . 7 adhuc
iii . poſͤ fieri . Ibi . xx . ſocͪi . 7 xii . borͩ . 7 I . ſeruus .
p̊tū . vi . caͬ . Silua . vi . porc . Inͭ totū uaɫ . ix . liᵬ .
Qͩo receͫp ′ xii . liᵬ . T.R.E. ′ xx . liᵬ . Hoc ℳ tenueͬ
xxiiii . ſocͪi . 7 potueͬ dare 7 uendͤ trͣ ſuͣ cui uolueͬ

In the Hundred of STODDEN

4 Tovi the priest holds ½ hide in BOLNHURST from the Bishop.
Land for 1 plough; it is there.
1 villager and 1 smallholder.
Meadow for ½ plough; woodland, 30 pigs.
In total, value 10s; when acquired as much; before 1066, 12s.
Azor, Burgred's man, held this land; he could sell to whom
he would.

5 There 2 Freemen also hold ½ hide from the Bishop.
Land for 1 plough; it is there, with
2 smallholders.
Woodland, 4 pigs.
In total, value 10s; when acquired as much; before 1066, 12s.
The present holders held it before 1066; they could sell and grant.

In the Half-Hundred of BUCKLOW

6 Herbert son of Ivo holds 3 hides and 3 virgates in STAGSDEN from
the Bishop. Land for 4 ploughs; 3½ ploughs there now; ½ possible.
12 villagers and 7 smallholders.
Meadow for 1 plough; woodland, 40 pigs.
In total, value £7; when acquired £9; before 1066 £12.
12 Freemen held this land; they were King Edward's men;
they could sell.

In the Hundred of WILLEY

7 2 Freemen hold 1 hide and 1 virgate in CARLTON from Herbert son of
Ivo; he holds from the Bishop. Land for 1½ ploughs; they are there.
Meadow for 1 plough.
In total, value 26s 8d; when acquired and before 1066, 30s.
The present holders held this land; they could grant and sell.

8 Wimund holds 1 hide in TURVEY from Herbert; he holds from
the Bishop. Land for 1 plough; it is there.
Meadow for ½ plough.
In total, value 20s; when acquired and before 1066, 40s.
A man of Alfwold of Stevington's held this land; he could sell.

In the Hundred of BARFORD

9 M. Herbert holds 5 hides in WILDEN from the Bishop and his nephew
Hugh from him. Land for 16 ploughs. In lordship now none; 3
possible. The villagers have 10 ploughs; a further 3 possible.
20 Freemen, 12 smallholders and 1 slave.
Meadow for 6 ploughs; woodland, 6 pigs.
In total, value £9; when acquired £12; before 1066 £20.
24 Freemen held this manor; they could grant and sell their
land to whom they would.

ⓂＥTERRA EP̄I CONSTANTIENS̄ *IN STODEN HVND*

Ⓜ Ēp̄s constantiensis ten̄ *CHENOTINGA*

p̄ v. hid̄ ſe defd̄. Tra . ē . v . car̄. In dn̄io . iii . hid̄

7 ii . car̄ ſunt ibi . Viłłi hn̄t . iii . car̄ . Ibi . viii . uiłłi

7 v . bord̄. 7 iiii . ſerui . P̄tū . ii . car̄ . Silua . cccc . porc̄.

Valet . iiii . lib̄ . Q̄do recep̄ꞏiii . lib̄ . 7 tntd̄ T.R.E. Hoc Ⓜ

tenuit Burret . T.R.E.

Ⓜ Ipſe ep̄s ten̄ *MELCEBVRNE*. p̄ x . hid̄ ſe defd̄. T̄ra

ē . x . car̄. In dn̄io . iii . hidæ 7 iii . car̄. Viłłi hn̄t . vii . car̄.

Ibi . xiii . uiłłi 7 xv . bord̄. 7 iii . ſerui . P̄tū   car̄.

Silua . c . porc̄. Valet . viii . lib̄ . Q̄do recep̄ꞏc . ſoł . T.R.E.ꞏ

vi . lib̄ . Hoc Ⓜ tenuit Burret . 7 ibi fuer̄ . vi . ſoc̄hi.

7 potuer̄ dare 7 uend̄e tr̄a ſuā abſq̄ lictia

★ Ⓜ Ipſe ep̄s ten̄ in *DENA* . iiii . hid̄ . Tra . ē   7 ibi ſuꞁ.

Ibi . vi . ſoc̄hi . 7 vi . bord̄. 7 ii . ſerui . Valet . lx . ſoł . Q̄do

recep̄ꞏſimił . T.R.E.ꞏxl . ſoł . Hoc Ⓜ tenuer̄ . vi . ſoc̄hi.

210 a

hōꞏs Borret fuer̄ . Dꞏ ſoca regꞏs . iii . hid̄ 7 dim̄ potuer̄

dare 7 uend̄e 7 ad alterū dn̄m reced̄e ſine lictia Borred.

Dim̄ ū hid̄ ſin̄e ej licentia ej dare ł uend̄e n̄ potuer̄.

Ⓜ GoisfrId̄ de Traillgi ten̄ de ep̄o c̄ſtantienſi *GIVELDENE*.

p̄ x . hid̄ ſe defd̄. Tra . ē . xv . car̄. In dn̄io ſunt . iiii . car̄. 7

uiłłi hn̄t . xi . car̄. Ibi xvii . uiłłi . 7 un̄ miles . 7 xii . bord̄.

7 i . ſeruus . P̄tū . iiii . car̄ . Silua . xx . porc̄ . In totis ualent̄

uał . ix . lib̄ . Q̄do recep̄ꞏc . ſoł . . . R.E.ꞏviii . lib̄ . Hoc Ⓜ

★ tenuit Borred. 7 in eo fuer̄ . v . . . chi q̄ tenuer̄ de hac tra

v . hid̄. 7 cui uoluer̄ dare ł uend̄e potuer̄.

Ⓜ De ipſo ep̄o ten̄ Wiłłs d . . . fer ej *ESELTONE* . p̄ . v . hid̄

ſe defd̄ . Tra . ē . vi . car̄ . In dn̄io . ii . car̄. 7 uiłłi hn̄t . iiii.

3   LAND OF THE BISHOP OF COUTANCES

In STODDEN Hundred

1 M. The Bishop of Coutances holds KNOTTING. It answers for 5 hides.
Land for 5 ploughs. In lordship 3 hides; 2 ploughs.
The villagers have 3 ploughs.
    8 villagers, 5 smallholders and 4 slaves.
    Meadow for 2 ploughs; woodland, 400 pigs.
Value £4, when acquired £3; the same before 1066.
Burgred held this manor before 1066.

2 M. The Bishop also holds MELCHBOURNE. It answers for 10 hides.
Land for 10 ploughs. In lordship 3 hides; 3 ploughs.
The villagers have 7 ploughs.
    13 villagers, 15 smallholders and 3 slaves.
    Meadow for ... ploughs; woodland, 100 pigs.
Value £8; when acquired 100s; before 1066 £6.
    Burgred held this manor. There were 6 Freemen there; they
could grant and sell their land without permission.

3 M. The Bishop also holds 4 hides in DEAN. Land for [5? ploughs];
they are there.
    6 Freemen, 6 smallholders and 2 slaves.
Value 60s; when acquired the same; before 1066, 40s.
    6 Freemen held this manor; they were Burgred's men.
They could grant or sell 3½ hides, of the King's jurisdiction,   210 a
or withdraw to another lord without Burgred's permission. But
½ hide they could not grant or sell without his permission.

4 M. Geoffrey of Trelly holds YELDEN from the Bishop of Coutances.
It answers for 10 hides. Land for 15 ploughs. In lordship 4
ploughs. The villagers have 11 ploughs.
    17 villagers, 1 man-at-arms, 12 smallholders and 1 slave.
    Meadow for 4 ploughs; woodland, 20 pigs.
In total, value £9; when acquired 100s; before 1066 £8.
    Burgred held this manor. In it were 5 Freemen who held 5
hides of land; they could grant or sell to whom they would.

5 M. William, his Steward, holds SHELTON from the Bishop.
It answers for 5 hides. Land for 6 ploughs. In lordship 2 ploughs.
The villagers have 4.

Ibi.xIIII.7 v.borđ.7 III.ſerui.7 I.moliñ.III.ſoliđ.P̃tu.
.I.car̃.Silua.IIII.porc̃.Valet.c.ſoł.Q̃do recep̃.LX.ſoł.
T.R.E.'IIII.liƀ.Hoc ᴍ tenuit Vlueua.ſub Borret.
ñ potuit dare nec uendē ſine ej licentia.

In Eſtone teneȵ.IIII.ſochi de epo c̃ſtant.III.uirg̃ træ.
T̃ra.I.car̃.7 ibi.ē.H̃ tra uał 7 ualuit x.ſoł.T.R.E.'v.ſoł.
Idē ipſi ꝗ teneȵ tenuer̃.hões Burred fuer̃.7 cui uoluer̃
dare potuer̃.In his.III.uirg̃ reclamat ep̃s ſuꝓ Sigarđ
de ciockes.xx.ac̃s ſiluæ.quæ ibi iacuer̃ T.R.E.7 hoc
hões de Hunđ atteſtant.

ᴍ In Riſelai tenent de epo.II.francig̃.7 ſex VI.angli.VI.hiđ.
T̃ra.ē.VII.car̃.7 ibi ſunt.Ibi.VI.uiłłi 7 VII.borđ.
7 un ſeruus.P̃tu..III.car̃.Silua.cc.porc̃.Valet
LXXII.ſoł.Q̃do recep̃.'ſimilit̃.T.R.E.'c.ſoł.De hac
tra tenuit Burred.II.hiđ in dñio.7 VI.ſochi hões ej
tenuer̃.IIII.hiđ.quas ubi uoluer̃ dare 7 uendē potuer̃.

In Buleheſtre ten iſdē ep̃s.III.uirg̃ tre.ꝓ excābio
de Bledone.T̃ra.ē.I.car̃ 7 dim̃.7 ibi ſunt.Vñ uiłłs
7 IIII.borđ.P̃tu.I.car̃.Silua.xx.porc̃.Vał.xv.ſoł.
Q̃do recep̃.'ſimilit̃.T.R.E.'xx.ſoł.Hanc t̃ra tenuit
Gudmunt hõ regis.E.uendē potuit cui uoluit.

In Neuuentone ten de epo Wiłłs dapifer ej.I.uirg̃.
Vał 7 ualuit.XII.deñ.T.R.E.'xvi.deñ.Hanc t̃ra
tenuit Aluuin hõ Borred.ñ potuit dare ł uendē ſine ej
ᴍ In Hunđ de Wilga ten Goisfriđ de tralgi ℔ licentia.
IIII.hiđ de epo.T̃ra.ē.v.car̃.In dñio ſunt.II.car̃.
7 uiłłi hñt.III.car̃.Ibi.xIIII.uiłłi.7 v.borđ.7 IIII.ſerui.
p̃tu.IIII.car̃.Vał 7 ualuit.c.ſoł.Hoc ᴍ tenuit
Turbt hõ regis.E.7 uendē potuit.Hanc t̃ra ten ep̃s
ꝓ Excābio de Bledone.ut hões ej dicunt.

14 [villagers], 5 smallholders and 3 slaves.
1 mill, 3s; meadow for 1 plough; woodland, 4 pigs.
Value 100s; when acquired 60s; before 1066 £4.

Wulfeva held this manor under Burgred; she could not grant
or sell without his permission.

6   In EASTON 4 Freemen hold 3 virgates of land from the Bishop
of Coutances. Land for 1 plough; it is there.
The value of this land is and was 10s; before 1066, 5s.

The present holders held it; they were Burgred's men; they
could grant to whom they would.

In these 3 virgates the Bishop claims against Sigar of
Chocques 20 acres of woodland which lay there before 1066;
this the men of the Hundred confirm.

7 M. In RISELEY   2 Frenchmen and 6 Englishmen hold 6 hides from
the Bishop. Land for 7 ploughs; they are there.
6 villagers, 7 smallholders and 1 slave.
Meadow for 3 ploughs; woodland, 200 pigs.
Value 72s; when acquired the same; before 1066, 100s.

Burgred held 2 hides of this land in lordship. 6 Freemen, his
men, held 4 hides which they could grant and sell where they would.

8   In BOLNHURST the Bishop also holds 3 virgates of land in
exchange for Bleadon. Land for 1½ ploughs; they are there.
1 villager and 4 smallholders.
Meadow for 1 plough; woodland, 20 pigs.
Value 15s; when acquired the same; before 1066, 20s.

Godmund, King Edward's man, held this land; he could
sell to whom he would.

9   In NEWTON (Bromshold) William, his Steward, holds 1 virgate
from the Bishop.
The value is and was 12d; before 1066, 16d.

Alwin, Burgred's man, held this land; he could not grant
or sell without his permission.

In the Hundred of WILLEY

10 M. Geoffrey of Trelly holds 4 hides from the Bishop. Land for 5
ploughs. In lordship 2 ploughs. The villagers have 3 ploughs.
14 villagers, 5 smallholders and 4 slaves.
Meadow for 4 ploughs.
The value is and was 100s.

Thorbert, King Edward's man, held this manor; he could
sell. The Bishop holds this land in exchange for Bleadon, as
his men state.

Ⓜ In *TORNAI* teñ iſd eƥs.iiii.hid̃.Tra.e.vi.caɼ.In dñio
ſunt.ii.hidæ.⁊ iii.caɼ.Ibi.iii.uiłłi hñt.iii.caɼ.⁊ viiii
bord̃.⁊ i.ſeruus.⁊ i.moliñ.xx.ſoł.Ƿ̃tũ.ii.caɼ.Silua
.xl.porc̃.Valet.vi.lib̃.Q̃do receƥ.xl.ſoł.T.R.E.
vi.lib̃.Hoc Ⓜ tenueɼ.iii.ſochi hoẽs regis.E.⁊ uendẽ
⁊ dare potueɼ.Hanc trã hĩ eƥs ƥ Excãbio de Bledone.
ut hoẽs ej dicunt.

In Hencuuic teñ Turſtiñ de eƥo.i.hid̃ ⁊ dim̃.Tra.e
ii.caɼ.In dñio eſt una.⁊ iii.uiłłi hñt.i.caɼ.⁊ i.bord̃.
Vał.xx.ſoł.

210 b

In Sernebroc teñ q̃dã Anglic̃ Turgiſus de eƥo dim̃
hid̃.Tra.e.i.caɼ.⁊ ibi eſt.⁊ uñ uiłłs.Ƿ̃tũ.i.caɼ.
Vał.vi.ſoł.Q̃do receƥ.iii.ſoł.T.R.E.xv.ſoł.Hanc
trã tenuit Aluuiñ hõ Borret.⁊ potuit dare cui uoluit.
In ead̃ uilla teneᵹ.vii.ſochi de eƥo.iii.hid̃.Trᴀ.iii.
caɼ.⁊ ibi ſunt.Silua.xxiiii.porc̃.Vał.xxiiii.ſoł.
Q̃do receƥ.ſimił.T.R.E.lx.ſoł.Idẽ ipſi tenueɼ.T.R.E.
hoẽs Borred fueɼ.⁊ dare ⁊ uendẽ ſine ej lictia potueɼ.
In ead̃ teñ Hunfrid de eƥo dim̃ hid̃.Tra.e.i.caɼ.
⁊ ibi eſt.⁊ ii.bord̃.Silua.xxx.porc̃.Vał.vi.ſoł.Q̃do
receƥ.x.ſoł.T.R.E.xx.ſoł.Hanc trã tenuit Aluric
hõ Borred.⁊ potuit dare ⁊ uendẽ cui uoluit.
In ead̃ teñ eƥs dim̃ hid̃.Tra.e.vi.boƀȝ.Ibi ſuᵹ.iiii.
bord̃.Vał.iii.ſoł.⁊ tntd̃ q̃do receƥ.T.R.E.v.ſolid̃.
Hanc trã tenuit Borred teigñ regis.E.⁊ pot face q̃d̃ uoł.
In Riſedene teñ Aluuold de eƥo dim̃ hid̃.Tra.vi.
boƀ.Ibi.e dim̃ caɼ.Ƿ̃tũ.vi.boũ.Vał.v.ſoł.⁊ tntd̃
q̃do receƥ.T.R.E.x.ſoł.Hanc trã tenuit Aluric
hõ Borred fuit.⁊ uendẽ potuit cui uoluit.

11 **M. In TURVEY** the Bishop also holds 4 hides. Land for 6 ploughs.
In lordship 2 hides; 3 ploughs there.
   3 villagers have 3 ploughs; 8 smallholders and 1 slave.
   1 mill, 20s; meadow for 2 ploughs; woodland, 40 pigs.
Value £6; when acquired 40s; before 1066 £6.
   3 Freemen, King Edward's men, held this manor; they could
sell and grant. The Bishop has this land in exchange for
Bleadon, as his men state.

12 In **HINWICK** Thurstan holds 1½ hides from the Bishop.
Land for 2 ploughs. In lordship 1.
   3 villagers have 1 plough; 1 smallholder.
Value 20s.

13 In **SHARNBROOK** an Englishman, Thorgils, holds ½ hide from   210 b
the Bishop. Land for 1 plough; it is there.
   1 villager.
   Meadow for 1 plough.
Value 6s; when acquired 3s; before 1066, 15s.
   Alwin, Burgred's man, held this land; he could grant to whom
he would.

14 In the same village 7 Freemen hold 3 hides from the Bishop.
Land for 3 ploughs; they are there.
   Woodland, 24 pigs.
Value 24s, when acquired the same; before 1066, 60s.
   The present holders held it before 1066; they were Burgred's
men; they could grant and sell without his permission.

15 In the same [village] Humphrey holds ½ hide from the Bishop.
Land for 1 plough; it is there.
   2 smallholders.
   Woodland, 30 pigs.
Value 6s; when acquired 10s; before 1066, 20s.
   Aelfric, Burgred's man, held this land; he could grant and sell
to whom he would.

16 In the same [village] the Bishop holds ½ hide. Land for 6 oxen.
   4 smallholders.
Value 3s; when acquired the same; before 1066, 5s.
   Burgred, a thane of King Edward's, held this land; he could
do what he would (with it).

17 In **RUSHDEN** Alfwold holds ½ hide from the Bishop.
Land for 6 oxen; ½ plough there.
   Meadow for 6 oxen.
Value 5s; as much when acquired; before 1066, 10s.
   Aelfric, Burgred's man, held this land; he could sell to
whom he would.

R TERRA EPI LINCOLIENS. *IN STODENE HVND.*

EMIGIVS eps ten in *DENE* . II . hid 7 dim uirg.

7 Godefrid de eo. Tra . e̅ . III . car 7 dim. In dn̅io suɣ

II . car. 7 uitti hn̅t . I . car 7 dim. Ibi . VIII . bord. 7 II.

serui . p̅tu̅ . I . car . Valet . XL . sot. Q̶do recep̅. xxx . sot.

7 tn̅td . T.R.E. Hanc tr̅a tenuit Godric teign . R.E.

7 qd uoluit de tra sua facere potuit.

In Estone ten Witts de caron dim hid 7 dim uirg de

epo. Tra . e̅ . I . car. 7 ibi est. 7 un bord 7 III . serui . p̅tu̅ . I . car.

Silua . c . porc . Valet. xv . sot. Q̶do recep̅. x . sot. 7 tn̅td

T.R.E. Hanc tr̅a tenuit Aluuin deule̅ hō epi Lincoliensis.

7 q̶ uoluit de ea facere potuit. Soca tam̅ sep̅ epi fuit.

In hac tra episcopat reclamat Witts de caron . LX . acr

int planū 7 siluam sup Hugonē de Belcap̅ . unde

Radulf taillebosc desaisiuit patr̅e ejd Witti. q̶ ipsa̅

tr̅a tenebat. T.R.E. ut hōes de hund dn̅t.

In Riselai ten Godefrid . I . hid de epo . Tra . e̅ . I . car.

7 ibi . e̅. Ibi . I . uitt. 7 I . bord . p̅tu̅ dim car . Silua porc

xx . porc . Vat 7 ualuit . x . sot . T.R.E. xx . sot . Hanc tr̅a

tenuit Godric teign . R.E. 7 qd uoluit facere potuit.

In dimid hund de Buchelai . Ernuin p̅b̅r ten de epo

Remigio . I . hid 7 I . uirg in Bideha̅. Tra . e̅ . I . car . 7 ibi e̅.

Ibi . I . uitts 7 I . mot redd p annū xxv . sot. p̅tu̅ . I . car.

Valet 7 ualuit . XL . sot. Hanc tr̅a tenuit Leuric hō

epi Lincoliensis . sed n̅ potuit dare nec uende̅ sine lictia ej.

In Hund de Bereforde ten Iuo tallebosc de epo dim

hid in Goldentone. Tra . e̅ dim car. 7 ibi est . cū . II . uittis.

p̅tu̅ dim car . Valet 7 ualuit . v . sot. Aluuin fac tenuit

4 LAND OF THE BISHOP OF LINCOLN

In STODDEN Hundred

1 Bishop Remigius holds 2 hides and ½ virgate in DEAN and
Godfrey from him. Land for 3½ ploughs. In lordship 2 ploughs.
The villagers have 1½ ploughs.
  8 smallholders and 2 slaves.
  Meadow for 1 plough.
Value 40s; when acquired 30s; as much before 1066.
  Godric, a thane of King Edward's, held this land; he could
do what he would with his land.

2 In EASTON William of Cairon holds ½ hide and ½ virgate
from the Bishop. Land for 1 plough; it is there.
  1 smallholder and 3 slaves.
  Meadow for 1 plough; woodland, 100 pigs.
Value 15s; when acquired 10s; as much before 1066.
  Alwin Devil, the Bishop of Lincoln's man, held this land; he
could do what he would with it. However, the jurisdiction was
always the Bishop's.
  In this land of the Bishopric, William of Cairon claims 60 acres
of open land and woodland from Hugh of Beauchamp, of which
Ralph Tallboys dispossessed this William's father, who held the
land before 1066, as the men of the Hundred state.

3 In RISELY Godfrey holds 1 hide from the Bishop.
Land for 1 plough; it is there.
  1 villager and 1 smallholder.
  Meadow for ½ plough; woodland, 20 pigs.
The value is and was 10s; before 1066, 20s.
  Godric, a thane of King Edward's, held this land; he could
do what he would (with it).

In the Half-Hundred of BUCKLOW

4 Ernwin the priest holds 1 hide and 1 virgate in BIDDENHAM from
Bishop Remigius. Land for 1 plough; it is there.
  1 villager.
  1 mill which pays 25s a year; meadow for 1 plough.
The value was and is 40s.
  Leofric, the Bishop of Lincoln's man, held this land; he
could not grant or sell without his permission.

In the Hundred of BARFORD

5 Ivo Tallboys holds ½ hide from the Bishop in GOLDINGTON.
Land for ½ plough; it is there, with
  2 villagers.
  Meadow for ½ plough.
The value is and was 6s.

hō epi Lincol̃.7 potuit inde face q̄d uoluit.

In hund de Bicheleſuuorde Witł̃s de caron ten̄ de epo . R
in Tamiſeforde . i . hid̄ . 7 i . uirg̃ 7 iii . part uni uirg̃ . Tra . ē
ii . car̄ . 7 ibi . ē un uitł̃s . P̃tū . i . car̄ . 7 ii . molini de xl . ſol̃.
7 cxx . Anguitł̃ . Val̃ . lx . ſol̃ . Q̇do recep̃ xl . ſol̃ . T.R.E. c . ſol̃.
Aluuin tenui⸱ . hō regis fuit . 7 q̄d uoluit de ea face potuit.

210 c

In HVND de Cliſtone . Witł̃s de caron de epo . R . iii.
hid̄ 7 dim̄ uirg̃ in Cliſtone . Tra . ē . ii . car̄ . Ibi . ē una
car̄ . 7 alia poteſt fieri . Ibi . iii . uitł̃i . 7 ii . ſerui . p̃tū
ii . car̄ . Val̃ . xx . ſol̃ . 7 tntd̄ q̇do recep̃ T.R.E . iiii . lib̃.
Hanc trā tenuit Aluuin hō.R.E . 7 potuit dare q̇ uol̃.
In Chicheſane ten̄ iſd̄e Witł̃s de eod̄ epo dim̄ hid̄.
Tra . ē dim̄ car̄ . Val̃ 7 ualuit . xii . den̄ . T.R.E. ii . ſol̃.
Aluuin tenuit . 7 cui uoluit dare potuit.

Eccł̃a de Bedeford cū adjacentib̃ ſibi ualet . c . ſol̃.
Æccł̃a de Leſtone ual̃ . iiii . lib̃ . Has ten̄ Remigi eps̃.

TERRA EP̃I DVNELM̃SIS. *BICHELESWADE HVND.*

Eps̃ Dvnelmensis . ten̄ de rege in Melehou
iiii . hid̄ 7 dim̄ . Tra . ē . iiii . car̄ . In dñio . iii . hid̄
7 dim̄ . 7 ibi . ē . i . car̄ . 7 alia pot fieri . Vitł̃i hn̄t . ii.
car̄ . Ibi . iiii . uitł̃i . 7 un ſeru . Val̃ . xl . ſol̃ . 7 tntd̄
q̇do recep̃ . T.R.E. lx . ſol̃ . Hanc trā dedit rex Edw
æcclæ S CRVCIS de Walthā . ut hōes de hund teſtant̃.
In Hund de Cliſtone . ten̄ iſd̄ eps̃ . viii . hid̄ in Alriceſei.
7 ii . part . i . uirg̃ . Tra . ē . viii . car̄ . In dñio. ſunt iii . car̄.
7 viii . uitł̃i hn̄t . iiii . car̄ . 7 v . pot fieri . Ibi . v . bord̄.
7 ii . ſerui . 7 ii . molini . xxvi . ſolid̄ . 7 viii . den̄ . p̃tū . iii . car̄.
Valet 7 ualuit . vii . lib̃ . T.R.E. viii . lib̃ . Hoc ꝏ tenuer̄
canonici S crucis de Wathā in elemoſina . T.R.E.

Alwin Sack, the Bishop of Lincoln's man, held it;
he could do what he would with it.

In the Hundred of BIGGLESWADE

6 William of Cairon holds 1 hide and 1 virgate and 3 parts of 1
virgate in TEMPSFORD from Bishop Remigius.
Land for 2 ploughs.
1 villager.
Meadow for 1 plough; 2 mills at 40s and 120 eels.
Value 60s; when acquired 40s; before 1066, 100s.
Alwin Devil held it; he was the King's man; he could do
what he would with it.

In the Hundred of CLIFTON   210 c

7 William of Cairon holds 3 hides and ½ virgate in CLIFTON from Bishop
Remigius. Land for 2 ploughs; 1 plough there; another possible.
3 villagers and 2 slaves.
Meadow for 2 ploughs.
Value 20s; as much when acquired; before 1066 £4.
Alwin Devil, King Edward's man, held this land;
he could grant where he would.

8 In CHICKSANDS William also holds ½ hide from the Bishop.
Land for ½ plough.
The value is and was 12d; before 1066, 2s.
Alwin Devil held it; he could grant to whom he would.

9 Bedford church, with what is attached to it, value 100s.
Leighton (Buzzard) church, value £4; Bishop Remigius holds them.

5   LAND OF THE BISHOP OF DURHAM

BIGGLESWADE Hundred

1 In MILLOW the Bishop of Durham holds 4½ hides from the King.
Land for 4 ploughs. In lordship 3½ hides; 1 plough there;
another possible. The villagers have 2 ploughs.
4 villagers and 1 slave.
Value 40s; as much when acquired; before 1066, 60s.
King Edward gave this land to the Church of Holy
Cross of Waltham, as the men of the Hundred testify.

In the Hundred of CLIFTON

2 The Bishop also holds 8 hides and 2 parts of 1 virgate in ARLESEY.
Land for 8 ploughs. In lordship 3 ploughs.
8 villagers have 4 ploughs; a fifth possible. 5 smallholders; 2 slaves.
2 mills, 26s 8d; meadow for 3 ploughs.
The value was and is £7; before 1066 £8.
Before 1066 the Canons of Holy Cross of Waltham held this
manor in alms.

ABBAS Balduin S̃ EDMVNDI h̃ in Bidenhā dim̄
hid.7 Ordui de Bedeford ten̄ ſub eo. Tra.ē dim̄ car̄.
7 ibi.ē.7 II.ſerui. p̃tū. dimid car̄. Val 7 ualuit. VI. ſot.
Hanc trā tenuit Vlmar p̃r regis. E. potuit dare
cui uoluit. ſed Ordui cū ēet p̃poſit burgi ei abſtulit.
ᵱ q̃dā forisfaĉtura.7 m̃ dicit ſe tenere de abbe S̃ Edm̄.
ſed hoēs de hund dūt q̃ā injuſte eā occupauit.

In Hund de Bicheleſuuade. ten̄ iſd abb S̃ Edmundi
Chenemondewiche. ᵱ. III. hid 7 III. uirg̃ ſe deſd.
Tra.ē. IIII. car̄. In dñio. I. hid 7 III. uirg.7 ibi ſunt
II. car̄.7 VI. uilli hñt. II. car̄.7 I. molin de. XIII. ſot.
7 IIII. den. p̃tū. I. car̄. Val. LX. ſot. Q̃do recep̃.′ XXX.
ſot. T.R.E.′ IIII. lib̄. Hanc trā tenuē. II. ſochi.7 cui
uoluē dare potuē. Hanc ded S̃ Edmundo Wallef^com'
7 uxor ej in elemoſina. T.R.Willi.

In Hund de Wich eſtaneſtou. ten̄ iſd abb. IIII. hid
7 I. uirg in Blunhā de rege. Tra.ē. IIII. car̄. In dñio
II. hid 7 III. uirg.7 ibi ſunt. II. car̄. Ibi. VIII. uilli
hñt. II. car̄.7 V. bord.7 I. ſeruus.7 I. molin. XX. ſot.
p̃tū. IIII. car̄. Valet. IIII. lib̄. Q̃do recep. LXX. ſot.
T.R.E.′ VI. lib̄. Hanc trā tenuē. IIII. ſochi.7 cui
uoluē dare t̃ uendere potuē. *IN STODENE HVND̄.*

Abb de BVRG ten̄ STANEWIGA. ᵱ II. hid 7 dim̄ ſe
deſd. Tra.ē. II. car̄.7 dim̄. Ibi.ē. I. car̄. Alia.7 dim̄ pot
fieri. Ibi ſuꝺ. II. uilli 7 II. bord. P̃tū. II. car̄. Val XXX. ſot.
Q̃do recep̃.′ L. ſot. T.R.E.′ XL. ſot. Hoc M̃ tenuit S̃ PETR
ſ̃ de burg. T.R.E.

6 LAND OF ST. EDMUND'S

In the Half-Hundred of BUCKLOW

1 Abbot Baldwin of St Edmund's has ½ hide in BIDDENHAM. Ordwy of Bedford holds it under him. Land for ½ plough; it is there.
2 slaves.
Meadow for ½ plough.
The value is and was 6s.
Wulfmer, a priest of King Edward's, held this land; he could grant to whom he would. But Ordwy took it from him when he was reeve of the borough, for a forfeiture; he now says that he holds it from the Abbot of St Edmund's, but the men of the Hundred state that he has appropriated it wrongfully.

In the Hundred of BIGGLESWADE

2 The Abbot of St Edmund's also holds 'KINWICK'.
It answers for 3 hides and 3 virgates. Land for 4 ploughs.
In lordship 1 hide and 3 virgates; 2 ploughs there.
6 villagers have 2 ploughs.
1 mill at 13s 4d; meadow for 1 plough.
Value 60s; when acquired 30s; before 1066 £4.
2 Freemen held this land; they could grant to whom they would. After 1066 Earl Waltheof and his wife gave it to St Edmund's in alms.

In the Hundred of WIXAMTREE

3 The Abbot also holds 4 hides and 1 virgate in BLUNHAM from the King. Land for 4 ploughs. In lordship 2 hides and 3 virgates; 2 ploughs there.
8 villagers have 2 ploughs. 5 smallholders and 1 slave.
1 mill, 20s; meadow for 4 ploughs.
Value £4; when acquired 70s; before 1066 £6.
4 Freemen held this land; they could grant or sell to whom they would.

7 LAND OF ST. PETER'S OF PETERBOROUGH

In STODDEN Hundred

1 The Abbot of Peterborough holds STANWICK. It answers for 2½ hides. Land for 2½ ploughs; 1 plough there; another 1½ possible.
2 villagers and 2 smallholders.
Meadow for 2 ploughs.
Value 30s; when acquired 50s; before 1066, 40s.
St Peter's of Peterborough held this manor before 1066.

.VIII. TERRA S̄ BENED̄ DE RAMESẎ. *IN RADEBVRNESOCA* ꜰʜᴠɴᴅ·

ℳ Abbas Sc̄ı Benedicti de Ramesẏ ten̄ *CRAN*
FELLE. ꝓ x . hid̄ ſe defd̄. Tra. ē . xıı . car̄. In dn̄io . ıı.

hidæ.7 ıı . car̄ ſunt ibi . Ibi xvııı . uiłłi hn̄t . x . car̄.

Ibi . ıı . bord̄ 7 v . ſerui . p̄tū . ıı . car̄. Silua mille porc̄.

7 ferrū car̄. Int̄ totū ual̄ . ıx . lib̄. Q̣do recep̄ ſimilit̄.

T.R.E. xıı . lib̄. Hoc ℳ̄ iacuit 7 iacet in æccła S̄ Bened̄.

ℳ Iſdē abb̄ ten̄ *BERTONE.*　　　 *In FLICTHĀ HVND.*

ꝓ xı . hid̄ ſe dcfd̄. Tra . ē . xıı . car̄. In dn̄io . ııı . hidæ.

7 ibi ſunt . ıı . car̄.7 tcia pot̄ fieri .7 xx . uiłłi hn̄t . ıx . car̄.

Ibi . vıı . bord̄.7 vı . ſerui .7 ı . molin̄ . ıı . ſoł . p̄tū . vı . car̄.

Silua . cc . porc̄. Int̄ totū ual̄ . x . lib̄.7 tn̄td̄ qdo

recep̄. T.R.E. xıı . lib̄. Hoc ℳ̄ iacuit ſēp in eccła Sc̄ı

Benedicti . Cū iſto ℳ̄ reclam̄ abb̄ . xıı . ac p̄ti . ſuꝑ

Nigellū albin̄ 7 Walter̄ flamenſ . quæ ibi iacuer̄ . T.R.E.

ſed Joħs de roches eū iniuſte deſaiſiuit.7 ħ hund̄ teſtat̄.

ℳ Ipſe abb̄ ten̄ *PECHESDONE* . ꝓ x . hid̄ ſe defd̄ . Tra

ē . xıııı . car̄. In dn̄io . ıı . hidæ.7 ibi ſuℲ . ıı . car̄.7 tcia

poteſt . ēe.7 xxxvıı . uiłłi hn̄t . xı . car̄. Ibi . vıı . bord̄.

7 v . ſerui .7 ıı . molini de xxvıı . ſoł 7 vııı . den̄. P̆tum

ııı . car̄. Silua . lx . porc̄. Valet x . lib̄.7 tn̄td̄ qdo

recep̄. T.R.E. xıı . lib̄. Hoc ℳ̄ iacuit 7 iacet in dn̄io æccłæ

S̄ Benedicti.　　　 *In BEREFORD HVND.*

In Wiboldeſtone ten̄ Eudo dapifer . ı . uirg 7 dim̄

ſub abb̄e de Rameſẏ. Vaſtata . ē . tam̄ . xvı . den̄ ual̄.

Ħ terra fuit in æccła S̄ Benedicti . T.R.E.

ℳ In Bereforde ten̄ Eudo dapif *IN BICHELESWADE HD̄*

v . hid̄ de feudo abb̄is.7 Osb̄n de eo . Tra . ē . v . car̄. In

dn̄io . ı . car̄.7 ıx . uiłłi hn̄t . ıııı . car̄. Ibi . ıııı . bord̄.

7 ııı . ſerui .7 ı . molin̄ . xıı . ſoł.7 cxxv . anguiłł . p̄tū.

In REDBORNSTOKE Hundred

1 M. The Abbot of St Benedict's of Ramsey holds CRANFIELD. It
answers for 10 hides. Land for 12 ploughs. In lordship 2 hides;
2 ploughs there.
   18 villagers have 10 ploughs. 2 smallholders and 5 slaves.
   Meadow for 2 ploughs; woodland, 1000 pigs and plough iron.
In total, value £9; when acquired the same; before 1066 £12.
   This manor lay and lies in (the lands of) St Benedict's church.

In FLITT Hundred

2 M. The Abbot also holds BARTON(-in-the-Clay). It answers for 11
hides. Land for 12 ploughs. In lordship 3 hides; 2 ploughs there;
a third possible.
   20 villagers have 9 ploughs. 7 smallholders and 6 slaves.
   1 mill, 2s; meadow for 6 ploughs; woodland, 200 pigs.
In total, value £10; the same when acquired; before 1066 £12.
   This manor always lay in (the lands of) St Benedict's Church.
With this manor the Abbot claims against Nigel of Aubigny and
Walter the Fleming 12 acres of meadow which lay there before
1066, but John of Les Roches dispossessed him wrongfully, and
this the Hundred testifies.

3 M. The Abbot also holds PEGSDON. It answers for 10 hides. Land for 14
ploughs. In lordship 2 hides; 2 ploughs there; a third possible.
   37 villagers have 11 ploughs. 7 smallholders and 5 slaves.
   2 mills at 27s 8d; meadow for 3 ploughs; woodland, 60 pigs.
Value £10; as much when acquired; before 1066 £12.
   This manor lay and lies in the lordship of St Benedict's Church.

In BARFORD Hundred

4 In WYBOSTON Eudo the Steward holds 1½ virgates under the
Abbot of Ramsey. It has been laid waste; value however 16d.
This land was in (the lands of) St. Benedict's Church before 1066.

In BIGGLESWADE Hundred

5 M. In (Little) BARFORD Eudo the Steward holds 5 hides from the
Abbot's Holding and Osbern from him. Land for 5 ploughs.
In lordship 1 plough.
   9 villagers have 4 ploughs. 4 smallholders and 3 slaves.
   1 mill, 12s and 125 eels; meadow for 2 ploughs.

II . caŕ . Val . IIII . liɓ . Q̨do recep̃.̃ III . liɓ . T.R.E.̃ IIII . liɓ.

Hoc ꝏ̃ teñ aɓɓ S̃ Benedicti .7 ibi in elemofina fuit . T.R.E.

In Cliftone teñ Leuuiñ . I . hiđ *IN CLISTONE HVND.*

fub aɓɓe . Tra . ē dim caŕ . 7 ibi . ē . Ptũ dim caŕ . Val

7 ualuit . x . fol . T.R.E.̃ xx . fol . Iftemet tc̃ tenuit . fed

ab æccła feparare ñ potuit.

ꝏ̃ Ipfe idē aɓɓ teñ *SETHLINDONE* . p̱ x . hiđ fe defđ.

Tra . ē . XIIII . caŕ . In dñio . II . hidæ . 7 ibi funt . II . caŕ.

7 xxvII . uiłłi hñt . XII . caŕ . Ibi . v . borđ . 7 IIII . ferui.

7 fract molin q̃ nichil redđ . p̃tũ . vI . caŕ . Silua . c.

porc . Val . XII . liɓ . 7 tntđ fēp̱ ualuit . Hoc ꝏ̃ iacuit

in dñio æccłæ S̃ Benedicti . T.R.E.

ꝏ̃ Ipfe aɓɓ teñ *HOLEWELLE* . p̱ . III . hiđ 7 dim . Tra . ē . IIII . caŕ.

In dñio . I . hiđ . 7 ibi . ē . I . caŕ . 7 vIII . uiłłi hñt . III . caŕ.

7 I . borđ . 7 II . ferui . Ptũ . I . caŕ . Val . IIII . liɓ . 7 tntđ fēp̱

ualuit . Hoc ꝏ̃ iacuit 7 iacet in dñio æccłæ S̃ Benedicti.

In Standone teñ ifđē aɓɓ dim hiđ . Tra . ē dim̃ caŕ.

7 ibi . ē . H̃ tra iacet 7 iacuit in dñio æccłæ S̃ Benedicti.

* Val . xv . fol.

211 a

.IX. TERRA S̃ PETRI WESTMON̄. *IN CLISTONE HVND*.

ꝏ̃ Abbas de WESTmonaſt . teñ vI . hiđ 7 dim in *IIO*

LEWELLA . Tra . ē . vI . caŕ . In dñio . III . hidæ 7 dim̃ uirg̃.

7 ibi funt . II . caŕ . 7 xI . uiłłi hñt . IIII . caŕ . Ibi . IIII.

borđ . 7 III . ferui . 7 II . molini . xx . fol . Ptũ . I . caŕ.

Valet 7 ualuit . c . fol . Hoc ꝏ̃ iacuit 7 iacet in dñio æccłæ

.X. TERRA SC̃Æ MARIÆ DE TORNỲG. ⌠S̃ PEŔI.

ꝏ̃ Abbas de Tornỳ teñ . II . hiđ 7 I . uirg̃ træ in Boleheftre.

extra.II.hidas.7 uirg̃.

Tra . ē . v . caŕ . In dñio . ē . I . carucata træ . 7 ibi . ē . I . caŕ.

Value £4; when acquired £3; before 1066, £4.
The Abbot of St. Benedict's holds this manor.
It was there, in alms, before 1066.

In CLIFTON Hundred

6   In CLIFTON Leofwin holds 1 hide under the Abbot. Land for ½
plough; it is there.
    Meadow for ½ plough.
    The value is and was 10s; before 1066, 20s.
    He held it himself then, but could not separate it from the Church.

7 M. The Abbot also holds SHILLINGTON. It answers for 10 hides.
    Land for 14 ploughs. In lordship 2 hides; 2 ploughs there.
    27 villagers have 12 ploughs. 5 smallholders and 4 slaves.
    1 broken mill which pays nothing; meadow for 6 ploughs;
      woodland, 100 pigs.
    The value is £12 and always was as much.
    This manor lay in the lordship of St. Benedict's Church
before 1066.

8 M. The Abbot also holds HOLWELL, for 3½ hides.
    Land for 4 ploughs. In lordship 1 hide; 1 plough there.
    8 villagers have 3 ploughs. 1 smallholder and 2 slaves.
    Meadow for 1 plough.
    The value is £4 and always was as much.
    This manor lay and lies in the lordship of St. Benedict's Church.

9   In STONDON the Abbot also holds ½ hide. Land for ½ plough;
it is there. This land lies and lay in the lordship of St Benedict's
Church.
    Value 15s.

9   **LAND OF ST. PETER'S OF WESTMINSTER**   211 a

In CLIFTON Hundred

1 M. The Abbot of Westminster holds 6½ hides in HOLWELL.
    Land for 6 ploughs. In lordship 3 hides and ½ virgate; 2
ploughs there.
    11 villagers have 4 ploughs. 4 smallholders and 3 slaves.
    2 mills, 20s; meadow for 1 plough.
    The value is and was 100s.
    This manor lay and lies in the lordship of St. Peter's Church.

10   **LAND OF ST. MARY'S OF THORNEY**

[In STODDEN Hundred]

1 M. The Abbot of Thorney holds 2 hides and 1 virgate of land in
    BOLNHURST. Land for 5 ploughs. In lordship 1 carucate
of land, as well as the 2 hides and the virgate; 1 plough there.

7 ıx . uilli hñt . v . cař . Ibi . v . borđ . p̃tu . ı . cař . Silua

c 7 vı . porc̃ . Val . lx . fot . Q̃do recep̃ . xl . fot . T . R . E.

. vı . lib̃ . Hoc ᛘ tenuit Ælfleda de rege . E . potuit dare

cui uoluit . In monafterio de Torni iacuit . die quo rex

Edw uiuus 7 mortuus fuit . Hoc hões de hund teftant .

.XI. TERRA ÆCCLÆ BERCHINGES. *IN RADBERNESTOCH HĐ*

ABBATISSA de Berchinges ten *LITINCLETONE* .

p̃ x . hiđ fe defđ . Tra . ē . xı . cař . In dñio . ıı . hidæ .

7 ibi funt . ıı . cař . tcia pot fieri . 7 xxııı . uilli hñt

vııı . cař . Ibi . xvı . borđ . 7 vıı . ferui . p̃tu . vııı . cař .

Silua . cccc . porc̃ . Val . vııı . lib̃ . 7 tntđ q̃do recep̃ .

T . R . E. xıı . lib̃ . Hoc ᛘ iacuit 7 iacet in dñio æcclæ

S̃ MARIE de Berchinges .

.XII. TERRA SC̃I PAVLI LVNDON. *IN FLICTHÁ HVND.*

ᛘ CANONICI S̃ PAVLI Lundon tc̃n *CADENDONE* .

p̃ v . hiđ fe defđ . Tra . ē . vı . cař . In dñio . ıı . hidæ .

7 ibi funt . ıı . cař . 7 adhuc . ıııı . pofs . eē . Ibi . ı . uilts

7 ıııı . borđ . 7 ıı . ferui . Silua . cc . porc̃ . Val . xl . fot .

Q̃do recep̃ . x . fot . T . R . E. c . fot . Hoc ᛘ tenuit

Leuuin . T . R . E . Canonici hñt breuē regis . in quo

habet qđ ipfe hoc ᛘ dedit æcclæ S̃ Pauli .

.XIII CSC̃I PAVLI de BEDEFORD *IN DIMIDIO HVND DE BVCHELAI.*

CANONICUS ofmund S̃ Pauli de Bedeford ten in Bidehã

de rege . ııı . uirg . Tra . ē . ı . cař . 7 ibi . ē . 7 ı . uilts

7 ı . borđ . P̃tu . ı . cař . Val 7 ualuit . x . fot . Hanc

trã tenuit Leuiet pb̃r in elemofina de rege . E .

7 poftea de rege . W . Qui pb̃r mories c̃ceffit æcclæ

S̃ Pauli . ı . uirg de hac trã . Radulf u tallgebofc

alias duas uirg addidit eiđ æcclæ in elemofina .

9 villagers have 5 ploughs. 5 smallholders.
Meadow for 1 plough; woodland, 106 pigs.
Value 60s; when acquired 40s; before 1066 £6.

Aelfled held this manor from King Edward; she could grant to whom she would. It lay in (the lands of) the monastery of Thorney in 1066. This the men of the Hundred testify.

1   **LAND OF BARKING CHURCH**

In REDBORNSTOKE Hundred

1   The Abbess of Barking holds LIDLINGTON. It answers for 10 hides. Land for 11 ploughs. In lordship 2 hides; 2 ploughs there; a third possible.

23 villagers have 8 ploughs. 16 smallholders and 7 slaves.
Meadow for 8 ploughs; woodland, 400 pigs.
Value £8; as much when acquired; before 1066 £12.

This manor lay and lies in the lordship of St. Mary's Church of Barking.

2   **LAND OF ST. PAUL'S OF LONDON**

In FLITT Hundred

1 M. The Canons of St. Paul's of London hold CADDINGTON. It answers for 5 hides. Land for 6 ploughs. In lordship 2 hides; 2 ploughs there; a further 4 possible.

1 villager, 4 smallholders and 2 slaves.
Woodland, 200 pigs.
Value 40s, when acquired 10s; before 1066, 100s.

Young Leofwin held this manor before 1066. The Canons have the King's writ in which is recorded that he gave this manor himself to St. Paul's Church.

3   **[LAND] OF ST PAUL'S OF BEDFORD**

In the Half-Hundred of BUCKLOW

1   Canon Osmund of St. Paul's of Bedford holds 3 virgates from the King in BIDDENHAM. Land for 1 plough; it is there.

1 villager and 1 smallholder.
Meadow for 1 plough.
The value is and was 10s.

Leofgeat the priest held this land in alms from King Edward and later from King William. When he was dying this priest assigned 1 virgate of this land to St. Paul's Church, but Ralph Tallboys added the other 2 virgates to this Church, in alms.

In ead̃ teñ Ansfrid canonic̃ . i . uirg̃ . Tra . ē . ii . bob̃.

7 ibi funt . P̊tū . ii . bob̃ . Val 7 ualuit . iii . fol̃ . Hanc

trã tenuit Maruuen. cui uoluit uend̃e potuit.

Hanc appofuit Rad̃ tallebofc in elem æcclæ S̃ Pauli.

E̲RNVI PR̃BI TERRA *IN WICHESTANESTOV HD̃.*

E̲RNVIN p̃br teñ . i . hid̃ in *HERGHETONE* . Tra . ē . i . car̃.

7 ibi . ē dim̃ car̃ . p̃tū dim̃ car̃ . Silua . iiii . porc̃.

Valet . x . fol̃ . Q̃do recep̃ . v . fol̃ . T.R.E. x . fol̃.

Hanc trã tenuit pat̃ huj p̃dicti hõis . hõ regis . E.

fuit. De hac tra non ht̃ ifte liberatorẽ . nec breuẽ.

fed occupauit fup̃ regẽ . ut hund̃ teftatur.

211 b

XV. E̲TERRA COMIT̃ EVSTACH *IN DIM̃ HD̃ DE BOCHELAI.*

E̲VSTACHIVS comes teñ in Brunehã . i . hid̃ 7 dim̃.

Ernulf de Arde teñ de eo . Tra . ē . i . car̃ 7 dim̃.

Ibi . ē dimid̃ car̃ . 7 i . car̃ poteft fieri . P̊tū . i . car̃ . 7 dim̃.

Val . x . fol̃ . Q̃do recep̃ . xx . fol̃ . 7 tntd̃ . T.R.E. Hanc

trã tenuit Aluuold̃ 7 Leuric hões regis . E. 7 cui uoluer̃

dare potuer̃ . 7 uendere.

M̃ In Stiuentone teñ ifd̃e Ernulf de ipfo comite

iii . hid̃ . Tra . ē xxiiii . car̃ . In dñio . ē . i . car̃ . 7 iii . car̃

poffunt fieri . 7 x . ujl̃ti hñt . v . car̃ . 7 adhuc xv . pof̃s . ee.

Ibi . xi . bord̃ . 7 ii . ferui . P̊tū . iiii . car̃ . Silua . xx . porc̃.

In totis ualent . ual xiiii . lib̃ . Q̃do recep̃ . xx . lib̃ . T.R.E.

xxx . lib̃ . Hoc M̃ tenuit Adelold̃ teign . R.E. 7 cui uoluit

uend̃e potuit.

In Stachedene teñ uñ Anglic̃ Goduui . i . uirg̃ de comite

Euft . Tra . ē dim̃ car̃ . 7 uñ bos ibi arat . H̃ tra ual . ii . fol̃.

Q̃do recep̃ . v . fol̃ . T.R.E. x . fol̃.

2   In the same (village) Canon Ansfrid holds 1 virgate.
Land for 2 oxen; they are there.
   Meadow for 2 oxen.
The value is and was 3s.
   Merwen held this land; she could sell to whom she would.
Ralph Tallboys placed it in the alms (lands) of St. Paul's Church.

14]   ## ERNWIN THE PRIEST'S LAND

In WIXHAMTREE Hundred

1   Ernwin the priest holds 1 hide in HARROWDEN.
Land for 1 plough; ½ plough there.
   Meadow for ½ plough; woodland, 4 pigs.
Value 10s; when acquired 5s; before 1066, 10s.
   The said man's father held this land; he was King Edward's man.
He does not have a deliverer or a writ for this land, but has
appropriated it in the King's despite, as the Hundred testifies.

15   ## LAND OF COUNT EUSTACE   211 b

In the Half-Hundred of BUCKLOW

1   Count Eustace holds 1½ hides in BROMHAM. Arnulf of Ardres
holds from him. Land for 1½ ploughs; ½ plough there; 1
plough possible.
   Meadow for 1½ ploughs.
Value 10s; when acquired 20s; as much before 1066.
   Alfwold and Leofric, King Edward's men, held this land; they
could grant or sell to whom they would.

2   M. In STEVINGTON Arnulf holds 3 hides from the Count. Land
for 24 ploughs. In lordship 1 plough; 3 possible.
   10 villagers have 5 ploughs; a further 15 possible.
      11 smallholders and 2 slaves.
   Meadow for 4 ploughs; woodland, 20 pigs.
Total value £14; when acquired £20;
before 1066 £30.
   Alfwold, a thane of King Edward's, held this manor;
he could sell to whom he would.

3   In STAGSDEN an Englishman, Godwy, holds 1 virgate from
Count Eustace. Land for ½ plough; 1 ox ploughs there.
Value of this land 2s; when acquired 5s; before 1066, 10s.

ⓂIn *PABENEHÁ* ten̄ Ernulf⁹ de Arde . ɪɪ . hid 7 dim.

Tra . ē . ɪɪɪ . car̄ . ſed n̄ ſunt ibi . jbi . ɪ . molin̄ . xx . ſol . 7 ɪɪ.

bord . p̄tū . ɪɪɪ . car̄ . Val . xxv . ſol . Qdo recep̄ . xʟ . ſol.

T.R.E. ɪɪɪɪ . lib̄ . Hoc Ⓜ tenuit Aluuold teign̄ regis . E.

In Wilge hund ten̄ Ernulf⁹ de arde in Torueie

. ɪ . hid . de comite Euſtachio . Tra . ē . ɪɪ . car̄ . In dn̄io eſt

una car̄ . 7 alia poteſt fieri . Ibi . ɪ . uiłłs 7 ɪ . bord . p̄tū

. ɪ . car̄ . Val . x . ſol . Qdo recep̄ . xx . ſol . 7 tntd T.R.E.

Hanc tr̄a tenuit Aluuold teign̄ . R.E. cui uoluit dare potuit.

In *WADELLE* ten̄ Ernulf⁹ de Arde . ɪɪɪɪ . hid 7 dim̄.

7 tcia part̄e . ɪ . uirg p̄ uno . Ⓜ . de comite euſtachio.

Ibi . ɪ . car̄ in dn̄io . 7 altera pot̄ fieri . 7 ɪɪɪ . uiłłi hn̄t

ɪɪ . car̄ . 7 tcia pot̄e fieri . Ibi . vɪɪ . bord . 7 ɪɪ . ſerui . p̄tū

. ɪɪɪ . car̄ . Silua . ʟ . porc . Val . ʟx . ſol . Qdo recep̄ . c . ſol.

T.R.E. vɪɪɪ . lib̄ . Hanc tr̄a tenuit Aluuold teign̄ . R.E.

7 cui uoluit uend̄e potuit.

In Serneburg ten̄ Rob̄t fili Rozelini de Euſt com̄

ɪɪ . hid . Tra . ē . ɪɪɪɪ . car̄ . In dn̄io . ɪɪ . car̄ . 7 ɪɪɪɪ . uiłłi

hn̄t . ɪɪ . car̄ . Ibi . ɪɪɪ . bord . 7 ɪɪɪɪ . ſerui . P̄tū . ɪɪ . car̄.

Silua . ʟx . porc . Val xʟ . ſol . 7 tntd qdo recep̄ . T.R.E.

ɪɪɪɪ . lib̄ . Hanc tr̄a tenuit Aluuold ho . R.E. 7 uend̄e pot̄.

.XVI. TERRA WALTERII GIFARD *IN MANESHEVE HVND*.

Ⓜ WALTERIVS Gifard ten̄ *WOBVRNE* . p̄ x . hid

ſe defd . Tra . ē . xxɪɪɪɪ . car̄ . Hugo de Bolebec

ten̄ de eo . Ibi in dn̄io . ɪɪ . car̄ . 7 aliæ duæ poſſunt . ee.

Ibi . vɪɪɪ . uiłłi hn̄t . vɪ . car̄ . 7 adhuc . xɪɪɪɪ . poſſ fieri.

Ibi . vɪɪ . bord 7 ɪɪɪɪ . ſerui . p̄tū . vɪ . car̄ . Silua . c . porc.

Val . c . ſol . Qdo recep̄ . xɪɪ . lib̄ . T.R.E. xv . lib̄.

Hoc Ⓜ tenuit Alric teign̄ . R.E. 7 in hoc Ⓜ fuer̄ vɪ.

ſochi . ɪɪ . hid de hac tra tenuer̄ . 7 qd uoluer̄ facere potuer̄.

4 M. In PAVENHAM Arnulf of Ardres holds 2½ hides.
Land for 3 ploughs, but they are not there.
1 mill, 20s; 2 smallholders; meadow for 3 ploughs.
Value 25s; when acquired 40s; before 1066 £4.
Alfwold, a thane of King Edward's, held this manor.

In WILLEY Hundred
5 Arnulf of Ardres holds 1 hide in TURVEY from Count Eustace.
Land for 2 ploughs. In lordship 1 plough; another possible.
1 villager and 1 smallholder.
Meadow for 1 plough.
Value 10s; when acquired 20s; as much before 1066.
Alfwold, a thane of King Edward's, held this land; he could
grant to whom he would.

6 In ODELL Arnulf of Ardres holds 4½ hides and the third part of 1
virgate as one manor from Count Eustace. 1 plough in lordship;
a second possible.
3 villagers have 2 ploughs; a third possible. 7 smallholders
and 2 slaves.
Meadow for 3 ploughs; woodland, 50 pigs.
Value 60s; when acquired 100s; before 1066 £8.
Alfwold, a thane of King Edward's, held this land;
he could sell to whom he would.

7 In SHARNBROOK Robert son of Rozelin holds 2 hides from
Count Eustace. Land for 4 ploughs. In lordship 2 ploughs.
4 villagers have 2 ploughs. 3 smallholders and 4 slaves.
Meadow for 2 ploughs; woodland, 60 pigs.
Value 40s; as much when acquired; before 1066 £4.
Alfwold, King Edward's man, held this land; he could sell.

16   **LAND OF WALTER GIFFARD**

In MANSHEAD Hundred
1 M. Walter Giffard holds WOBURN. It answers for 10 hides.
Land for 24 ploughs. Hugh of Bolbec holds from him.
In lordship 2 ploughs; another 2 possible.
8 villagers have 6 ploughs; a further 14 possible.
7 smallholders and 4 slaves.
Meadow for 6 ploughs; woodland, 100 pigs.
Value 100s; when acquired £12; before 1066 £15.
Alric, a thane of King Edward's, held this manor. In this
manor were 6 Freemen; they held 2 hides of the land; they
could do what they would (with them).

Ⓜ In *BADELESDONE* .teñ Ricard talebot .vIIII . hiđ
de Walť Gifard . Ťra . ē . vIII ; car̃ . In dñio|II . carucæ⁚

7 tcia poťeſt . ēē . Ibi . vII . uiłłi hñt . v . car̃ . Ibi . x . borđ
7 p̃tũ . vIII . car̃ . Vał . c . soł . 7 tñtđ qđo receꝑ . T.R.E⚆
vIII . liɓ . Hoc Ⓜ tenuer̃ . vII . ſochi . T.R.E . 7 qđ uoluer̃
de ťra ſua facere potuer̃ . *IN RADBORGESTOC HVND⚆*

In Mereſtone . teñ Hugo de Bolebec de Walterio Gifard
II . hiđ dim uirg min̄ . Ťra . ē . III . car̃ . In dñio . I . car̃ .
7 vI . uiłłi hñt . II . car̃ . Ibi . v . borđ . 7 p̃tũ . III . car̃ . Silua
ccc . porc̃ . Vał . L . ſoł . Qđo receꝑ⚆ xx . ſoł . T.R.E⚆ IIII . liɓ⚆
Hanc ťrã tenuer̃ . II . taigni . T.R.E . 7 cui uoluer̃ dare potuer⚆
Sup hanc ťrã reclamat Erfaſt hõ Nigelli Albinienſis .
dimiđ ſeꝑē . quæ jacebat ad Ⓜ Anteceſſoris Erfaſti ⚆ ut
hõēs de Hunđ teſtantur .

Ⓜ In Meldone teñ Hugo ⁀bolebec de eođ Walterio . III . hiđ . Ťra
ē . IIII . car̃ . In dñio ſunt . II . car̃ . 7 v . uiłłi hñt . II . car⚆
P̃tũ . IIII . car̃ . Silua . L . porc̃ . Valet L . ſoł . 7 tñtđ
qđo receꝑ . T.R.E⚆ IIII . liɓ . Hoc Ⓜ tenuit Aluuin fr̃
Wlui eꝑi . 7 cui uoluit dare potuit . *IN BICHELESWADE*
In Domtone teñ Radulf de Langetot   *Ƒ HVND⚆*
I . hiđ 7 III . uirg de Walterio Gifard . Ťra . ē . II . car̃ .
7 ibi ſunt . 7 IIII . uiłłi 7 . II . borđ . Valet xxxIII . ſoł .
7 IIII . den̄ . 7 ſēp tñtđ ualuit . Hanc ťrã . IIII . ſochi te
nuer̃ . 7 ťrã ſuã uende potuer̃ . Hõēs ⁀archieꝑi Stigandi fuer̃ .

Ⓜ In Melehou teñ ipſe Radulf de eođ Walterio . v .
hiđ . Ťra . ē . v . car̃ . 7 ibi ſunt . 7 vIII . uiłłi 7 IIII . borđ .
Vał 7 ualuit ſēp . c . ſolid . Hoc Ⓜ . x . ſochi tenuer̃ .
7 ťrã ſuã cui uoluer̃ dare ⱅ uende potuer̃ .

In Stratone teñ Fulcher pariſiac de Walť Gifardo
I . hiđ . 7 I . uirg 7 dim . Ťra . ē . II . car̃ . In dñio . I . car̃ .
7 un uiłłs 7 v . borđ cũ . I . car̃ . P̃tũ . II . car̃ . Vał . xxvIIIⱅ⚆

2 M. In **BATTLESDEN** Richard Talbot holds 9 hides from Walter Giffard.
   Land for 8 ploughs. In lordship 2 ploughs; a third possible.   211 c
       7 villagers have 5 ploughs. 10 smallholders.
       Meadow for 8 ploughs.
   Value 100s; as much when acquired; before 1066 £8.
       7 Freemen held this manor before 1066; they could do
   what they would with their land.

   In **REDBORNSTOKE** Hundred
3   In **MARSTON** (Moretaine) Hugh Bolbec holds 2 hides less ½ virgate
   from Walter Giffard. Land for 3 ploughs. In lordship 1 plough.
       6 villagers have 2 ploughs. 5 smallholders.
       Meadow for 3 ploughs; woodland, 300 pigs.
   Value 50s; when acquired 20s; before 1066 £4.
       2 thanes held this land before 1066; they could grant to
   whom they would. Herfast, Nigel of Aubigny's man, claims
   half an enclosure, which lay in the manor of Herfast's predecessor,
   as the men of the Hundred testify.

4 M. In **MAULDEN** Hugh of Bolbec also holds 3 hides from Walter.
   Land for 4 ploughs. In lordship 2 ploughs.
       5 villagers have 2 ploughs.
       Meadow for 4 ploughs; woodland, 50 pigs.
   Value 50s; as much when acquired; before 1066 £4.
       Alwin, Bishop Wulfwy's brother, held this manor;
   he could grant to whom he would.

   In **BIGGLESWADE** Hundred
5   In **DUNTON** Ralph of Lanquetot holds 1 hide and 3 virgates from
   Walter Giffard. Land for 2 ploughs; they are there.
       4 villagers and 2 smallholders.
   The value is 33s 4d and always was as much.
       4 Freemen held this land; they could sell their land;
   they were Archbishop Stigand's men.

6 M. In **MILLOW** Ralph holds 5 hides himself from Walter.
   Land for 5 ploughs; they are there.
       8 villagers and 4 smallholders.
   The value is and always was 100s.
       10 Freemen held this manor; they could grant or sell
   their land to whom they would.

7   In **STRATTON** Fulchere of Paris holds 1 hide and 1½ virgates from
   Walter Giffard. Land for 2 ploughs. In lordship 1 plough;
       1 villager and 5 smallholders with 1 plough.
       Meadow for 2 ploughs.

ſot.7 tntd q̄do recep̄.T.R.E.′xxx.ſot.Hanc t̄rā.iii.
ſochi tenuer̄.7 cui uoluer̄ dare t̄ uendē potuer̄.

ⓂIn Cudeſſane ten̄ Germund de Radulfo Langetot
iii.hid 7 dim̄.p uno Ⓜ.Tra.ē.iii.car̄.In dn̄io.ē
una car̄.7 i.uills 7 iii.bord cū.ii.car̄.7 un̄ ſeruus.
p̄tū.iii.car̄.Silua.xl.porc.Vat.xl.ſot.Q̄do
recep̄.′xx.ſot.T.R.E.′lx.ſot.7 i.molin̄ pot ibi fieri.
Hoc Ⓜ.iiii.ſochi tenuer̄.7 dare 7 uendē potuer̄.

ⓂIn Chābeltone ten̄ Rad de Langetot de Walt Gifard
iiii.hid 7 dim̄ 7 iiii.partē uni uirg.Tra.ē.iiii.car̄.
Ibi.i.car̄ in dn̄io.7 iiii.uilti hn̄t.iii.car̄.7 i.molinū
.iii.ſolid.7 iii.den̄.p̄tū.iiii.car̄.Silua.xl.porc.
Vat lx.ſot.Q̄do recep̄.′xx.ſot.T.R.E.′lxx.ſot.
hanc t̄rā.vi.ſochi tenuer̄.7 cui uoluer̄ dare potuer̄.

211 d

.XVII. TERRA WILLI DE WARENE. *IN STODENE HVND.*
WILLELM de Warenna ten̄ in *DENE*.ii.hid.
7 iii.ſochi de eo.Tra.ē.iii.car̄.7 ibi ſunt.Ibi.v.bord.
7 i.ſeru.Vat 7 ualuit ſēp.xxx.ſot.Hanc t̄rā tenuer̄
idē ipſi ſochi qui nc̄ tenent.Vn̄ eoᷣ n̄ potuit dare t̄ uen
dere t̄rā ſuā ſine licentia dn̄i ſui.Alij duo ū hoc face
potuer̄.
De dim̄ hid 7 dim̄ uirga huj t̄ræ fuit Wilts ſpec ſaiſit
p regē 7 ej libatorē.ſed W̄.de Warenna ſine breue
regis eū deſaiſiuit.7 ii.eqs ej hoibᷣ abſtulit.7 necdū
reddidit.Hoc hōes de hund atteſtant.

ⓂIpſe Wilts de War ten̄ Tilebroc.p.v.hid ſe defd̄.
Tra.ē.vi.car̄.7 ibi ſunt.7 xx.ſochi.7 iiii.bord.p̄tū
v.car̄.Vat.c.ſot.7 tntd q̄do recep̄.T.R.E.′iiii.lib.
Hoc Ⓜ idē ipſi ſochi qui teneᷧ tenuer̄.7 ita de ſoca 7 ſaca
regis fuer̄.qd̄ dare 7 uendē t̄rā ſuā cui noluiſſeᷧ po

Value 28s; as much when acquired; before 1066, 30s.
3 Freemen held this land; they could grant or sell
to whom they would.

[In CLIFTON Hundred]

8 M. In *CUDESSANE* Germund holds 3½ hides from Ralph Lanquetot
as one manor. Land for 3 ploughs. In lordship 1 plough;
1 villager and 3 smallholders with 2 ploughs; 1 slave.
Meadow for 3 ploughs; woodland, 40 pigs.
Value 40s; when acquired 20s; before 1066, 60s; 1 mill possible.
4 Freemen held this manor; they could grant and sell.

9 M. In CAMPTON Ralph of Lanquetot holds 4½ hides and the
fourth part of 1 virgate from Walter Giffard.
Land for 4 ploughs. 1 plough in lordship.
4 villagers have 3 ploughs.
1 mill, 3s 3d; meadow for 4 ploughs; woodland 40 pigs.
Value 60s; when acquired 20s; before 1066, 70s.
6 Freemen held this land; they could grant to whom they would.

17   LAND OF WILLIAM OF WARENNE   211 d

In STODDEN Hundred

1 William of Warenne holds 2 hides in DEAN and 3 Freemen
from him. Land for 3 ploughs; they are there.
5 smallholders and 1 slave.
The value is and always was 30s.
The same Freemen who now hold this land held it;
one of them could not grant or sell his land without
his lord's permission; but the other two could do this.
William Speke was put in possession of ½ hide and ½
virgate of this land through the King and his deliverer, but
William of Warenne dispossessed him without the King's writ
and took away two horses from his men and has not
yet given them back. This the men of the Hundred confirm.

2 M. William of Warenne also holds TILBROOK. It answers for 5 hides.
Land for 6 ploughs; they are there.
20 Freemen and 4 smallholders.
Meadow for 5 ploughs.
Value 100s; as much when acquired; before 1066 £4.
The same Freemen who hold this manor held it. They were so
far of the King's full jurisdiction that they could grant and sell

tuer̃.7 recede ad aliũ dñm fine lictia ej fub quo fuer̃.

Hanc tr̃a de Tilebroc r̃eclamat Hugo belcãp . fup . W.
7 hões de hund portañ inde teftim . qd̃ Rad tallebofc
Anteceffor ej de ea p rege faifit fuit.7 eã tenuit.

In Hanefelde ten . W . de Warenna . iii . uirg̃ tre . Tr̃a . ē
.i . car̃.7 ibi.ē . Val̃ 7 fẽp ualuit.x . fol̃ . H̃ tra jacuit
fẽp in Chenebaltone . f̧ Warrã ded̃ fẽp iufte in Bede

In Eftone ten . W . de War̃ . i . uirg . Tr̃a . ē . ii . car̃ ⌐ fordfcira.
7 ibi funt.7 i . uill̃s.7 ii . bord̃ . p̃tũ . i . car̃ . Silua . c . porc̃.
Val̃ . xx . fol̃ . Q̃do recep̃ . xl . fol̃ . T.R.E. xx . fol̃ . Hanc tr̃a
ten Auigi hõ Afchil antecefforis Hugon belcãp . potuit uende
cui uoluit . f̧ focã ipfe Afchil retinuit in Colmeborde m̃
fuo . Hanc tra reclamat Hugo fup . W . de War̃ . unde oms
q̃ iurauer̃ de uicecomitatu portañ teftim . qd̃ non p̃tiñ
ipfa tra ad Will̃m.

In ead uilla ten . W . de War̃ . i . hid 7 i . uirg̃ . Tr̃a . ē . i.
car̃.7 ibi . ē.7 ii . bord̃ . P̃tũ . i . car̃ . Val̃ . x . fol̃.7 tntd̃ q̃do
recep̃ . T.R.E. xv . fol̃ . Hanc tr̃a ten Avigi.7 potuit
dare cui uoluit . T.R.E.Hanc ei poftea . W . rex c̃ceffit.
7 p fuũ breuē Rad tallebofc c̃md̃auit . ut eũ feruaret
q̃diu uiueret . Hic die mortuus . ē dix fe . eē . hõem
.W . de War̃.7 id̃o . W . faifit . ē de hac terra.

In ead ten ift . W . i . uirg̃ tr̃æ . Tr̃a . ē . ii . bob̃.7 ibi fuñ
iiii . boues . Val̃ 7 ual̃ . ii . fol̃ . T.R.E. iii . fol̃ . Hanc tr̃a
ten Blach hõ Augi . pot̃ dare cui uoluit.

In ead ten Tedric de Will̃o . i . uirg 7 iiii . part̃ . i . uirg̃
Tr̃a . ē . i . car̃.7 ibi . ē . P̃tũ . i . car̃ . Silua . xx . iiii . porc̃.
Val̃ 7 ualuit . x . fol̃ . T.R.E. vi . fol̃ . Godric tenuit hõ
uicecomitis.7 cui uoluit dare potuit.

their land to whom they might wish. They could withdraw to
another lord without the permission of the one they were under.
Hugh Beauchamp claims this land of Tilbrook against William.
The men of the Hundred bear witness thereto, that Ralph
Tallboys his predecessor was put in possession of it through
the King and held it.

3   In *HANEFELDE* William of Warenne holds 3 virgates of land.
Land for 1 plough; it is there.
The value is and always was 10s.
    This land always lay in Kimbolton (lands) but it always rightfully
gave its defence obligations in Bedfordshire.

4   In EASTON William of Warenne holds 1 virgate.
Land for 2 ploughs; they are there.
    1 villager and 2 smallholders.
    Meadow for 1 plough; woodland, 100 pigs.
Value 20s; when acquired 40s; before 1066, 20s.
    Augi, a man of Askell, Hugh Beauchamp's predecessor, held this
land; he could sell to whom he would, but Askell kept the jurisdiction
himself in his manor in Colmworth. Hugh of Beauchamp claims this
land against William of Warenne, whereto all the sworn men of the
Sheriffdom bear witness, that this land does not belong to William.

5   In the same village William of Warenne holds 1 hide and 1 virgate.
Land for 1 plough; it is there.
    2 smallholders.
    Meadow for 1 plough.
Value 10s; as much when acquired; before 1066, 15s.
    Augi held this land; he could grant to whom he would before 1066.
Later on, King William assigned it to him, and commended him
through his writ to Ralph Tallboys that he should protect him as
long as he lived. On the day he died, he said he was William of
Warenne's man, and William therefore took possession of this land.

6   In the same (village) William also holds 1 virgate of land.
Land for 2 oxen; 4 oxen there.
The value is and was 2s; before 1066, 3s.
    Black, Augi's man, held this land; he could grant to
whom he would.

7   In the same village Theodoric holds 1 virgate and the fourth
part of 1 virgate from William. Land for 1 plough; it is there.
    Meadow for 1 plough; woodland, 24 pigs.
The value is and was 10s; before 1066, 6s.
    Godric, the Sheriff's man, held it; he could grant
to whom he would.

Ｗ TERRA WILLI DE . OW. *IN FLICTHA HVND.*

Ｗ́ILLELM de Ow . tenet *SONEDONE* . p x . hid ſe
defd . Tra . ē . xvi . car . In dño . iiii . hidæ . 7 ibi ſuꝫ . iiii . car.
Ibi . xx . uiłłi hñt xii . car . Ibi . xi . borđ . 7 xii . ſerui.
P̊tū . iiii . car . Silua . c . porc . In totis ualent uał . x . liƀ.
Q̣do recep̃ . viii . liƀ . T.R.E . xx . liƀ . Hoc ᷜ tenuit Aleſtan
de Boſcūbe . teign . R.E . In eađ uilla hī . i . miles . i . car.

212 a

Ịn Stradlei ten Walter de Wiłło de ow . i . hid . Tra . ē
. ii . car . In dño . i . car . 7 ii . uiłłi . i . car . hñt . 7 iii . borđ.
7 iii . ſerui . p̊tū . i . car . Silua . xx . porc . Vał . xxx . ſoł.
Q̣do recep̃ . xx . ſoł . T.R.E . xl . ſoł . Hanc tenuit Goduin
hō Aleſtan teigni regis . E . uende potuit cui uoluit.

Ịn Melehou ten Wiłłs de ow *IN BICHELESWADE HVND.*
dim hid . Tra . ē dim car . 7 ibi . ē . cū . i . borđ . Vał 7 ualuit
x . ſoł . Hanc trā tenuit Godmar hō Aleſtan . 7 uende
potuit cui uoluit.

ᷜ Ịn Edeuuorde teneꝫ . ii . milites de Wiłło de ow . vii . hid
7 iii . uirg 7 dim . Tra . ē . viii . car . In dño . iii . car.
7 viii . uiłłi hñt . v . car . Ibi . ii . borđ . 7 v . ſerui . P̊tū
ii . car . Vał . viii . liƀ . Q̣do recep̃ . x . liƀ . 7 tñtđ T.R.E.
Hoc ᷜ ten Aleſtan de Boſcūme . 7 ibi . ii . ſochi hōēs ej
fueꝛ . 7 i . hiđ 7 dim habueꝛ . 7 cui uolueꝛ uende potueꝛ.

Ịn Holme ten Vluric de Wiłło de ow . iii . uirg træ
Tra . ē . i . car . 7 ibi . ē . Vał . xvi . ſoł . Q̣do recep̃ . xii . ſoł.
T.R.E . xx . ſoł . Hanc trā tenuit Ǣlueua , hō Aſchil.
7 cui uoluit dare potuit .　　*IN CLISTONE HVND.*

Ịn Alriceſeie ten Burnard . v . hid 7 dim 7 ii . part
uni hidæ . Tra . ē . vi . car . In dño . i . car . 7 xiii . uiłłi
hñt . v . car . 7 x . borđ . 7 i . molenđ . x . ſolid . p̊tū . vi . car.
Mercatū . ē ibi de . x . ſoł . Vał 7 ualuit ſep̃ . vii . liƀ.
Hoc ᷜ tenuit Aleſtan de Boſcūme . 7 ibi . i . ſochs hō
ej fuit . ii . partes . i . hidæ habuit . 7 cui uoluit dare potuit.

LAND OF WILLIAM OF EU

In FLITT Hundred

1 M. William of Eu holds SUNDON. It answers for 10 hides.
Land for 16 ploughs. In lordship 4 hides; 4 ploughs there.
20 villagers have 12 ploughs. 11 smallholders; 12 slaves.
Meadow for 4 ploughs; woodland, 100 pigs.
Total value £10; when acquired £8; before 1066 £20.
Alstan of Boscombe, a thane of King Edward's, held this manor.
In the same village 1 man-at-arms has 1 plough.

2 In STREATLEY Walter holds 1 hide from William of Eu.   212 a
Land for 2 ploughs. In lordship 1 plough.
2 villagers have 1 plough; 3 smallholders and 3 slaves.
Meadow for 1 plough; woodland, 20 pigs.
Value 30s; when acquired 20s; before 1066, 40s.
Godwin, a man of Alstan, a thane of King Edward's, held this
land; he could sell to whom he would.

In BIGGLESWADE Hundred

3 In MILLOW William of Eu holds ½ hide. Land for ½ plough;
it is there, with
1 smallholder.
The value is and was 10s.
Godmer, Alstan's man, held this land; he could sell to whom
he would.

4 M. In EDWORTH 2 men-at-arms hold 7 hides and 3½ virgates from
William of Eu. Land for 8 ploughs. In lordship 3 ploughs.
8 villagers have 5 ploughs. 2 smallholders and 5 slaves.
Meadow for 2 ploughs.
Value £8; when acquired £10; before 1066 as much.
Alstan of Boscombe held this manor. 2 Freemen, his men, were
there; they had 1½ hides; they could sell to whom they would.

5 In HOLME Wulfric holds 3 virgates of land from William of Eu.
Land for 1 plough; it is there.
Value 16s; when acquired 12s; before 1066, 20s.
Aelfeva, Askell's man, held this land; she could grant to whom
she would.

In CLIFTON Hundred

6 In ARLESEY Bernard holds 5½ hides and 2 parts of 1 hide.
Land for 6 ploughs. In lordship 1 plough.
13 villagers have 5 ploughs; 10 smallholders.
1 mill, 10s; meadow for 6 ploughs. A market, at 10s.
The value is and always was £7.
Alstan of Boscombe held this manor. 1 Freeman, his man, was
there; he had 2 parts of 1 hide; he could grant to whom he would.

In Chābeltone teń Fulbt dim̄ hid de. Witło de ow.

Tra. ē dim̄ car̄.7 ibi. ē. cū. ī. uiłło. H tra ual 7 ualuit

sēp. v. soł. Hanc trā tenuit Aluuin̄ hō Aleſtan.7 potuit

.XIX. TERRA MILONIS CRISPIN. ſdare cui uoluit.

MILO criſpin teń *CLOPEHA* IN STODEN HVND.

p v. hid.ſe defd. Tra. ē. xxx. car̄. Pter has. v.

hidas ſunt in dñio. x. carucate træ.7 ibi ſuʒ. viii.

car̄.7 adhuc. ii. poſſ. ēē. Ibi. xviii. uiłłi hn̄t. xx. car̄.

7 xv. bord.7 iiii. ſerui. Ptū. vi. car̄.7 i. molin̄. xl.

ſolid. Silua. cc. porc.7 vi. deń. In totis ualeńt ual

xxiiii. lib.7 tntd qdo recep. T.R.E. xii. lib. Hoc ḿ tenuit

Bricxtric teign̄. R.E. de abbe de Rameſy. Abb 7 mona

chi reclamaʒ hoc ḿ.qm eſt 7 fuit T.R.E. de uictu eoʒ.

7 totū hund portat de hoc teſtimoniū.

In Middeltone habuer. ii. ſocħi. xvi. acs træ.7 ſuā

Warrā in ead Middeltone deder. ſʒ tra jcui uoluer

dare ł uende potuer. Hos ſocħos Robt de Olgi in

Clopehā appoſuit injuſte ut hōes de hund dicuńt.

qa nunq ibi. T.R.E. jacuer. IN WILGA HVND.

In *LALEGA* teń Leuric de Milone. i. uirg træ. Tra. ē

.i. car̄.7 ibi. ē. Val 7 ualuit sēp. x. soł. Ide ipſe. T.R.E.

tenuit. hō Brixtrici fuit.7 uende 7 dare eā potuit.

.XX. TERRA ERNVLFI de HESDING IN MANESHEVE HVND.

ERNVLFVS de Heſding teń *DODINTONE* de rege.

p xv. hid 7 dim̄ ſe defd. Tra. ē. xxx. car̄. Ibi. x.

carucatæ træ in dñio.7 ibi ſunt. vii. car̄.7 adhuc. iii.

poſſunt. ēē. pter. xv. hid 7 dim̄. Ibi. xlii. uiłłi hn̄t. xx. car̄.

212 b

Ibi. xix. bord.7 xix. ſerui. Ptū. xxx. car̄. Silua. cco

porc. In totis ualent ual. xxv. lib.7 tntd qdo recep.

T.R.E. xxx. lib. Hoc ḿ tenuit Wluuard leuet. T.R.E.

7   In CAMPTON Fulbert holds ½ hide from William of Eu.
Land for ½ plough; it is there, with
1 villager.
The value of this land is and always was 5s.
Alwin, Alstan's man, held this land; he could grant to whom
he would.

19   LAND OF MILES CRISPIN

In STODDEN Hundred

1   M. Miles Crispin holds CLAPHAM. It answers for 5 hides. Land for 30
ploughs. Besides these 5 hides there are 10 carucates of land in
lordship; 8 ploughs there; a further 2 possible.
18 villagers have 20 ploughs; 15 smallholders and 4 slaves.
Meadow for 6 ploughs; 1 mill, 40s; woodland, 200 pigs and 6d too.
Total value £24; as much when acquired; before 1066 £12.
Brictric, a thane of King Edward's, held this manor from Ramsey
Abbey. The Abbot and the monks claim this manor, since it is, and
was before 1066, for their supplies; the whole Hundred bears
witness to this.

2   In MILTON (Ernest) 2 Freemen had 16 acres of land. They also gave
their defence obligations in Milton, but they could grant or sell
their land to whom they would. Robert d'Oilly placed these Freemen
in Clapham, wrongfully, as the men of the Hundred state,
because they never lay there before 1066.

In WILLEY Hundred

3   In THURLEIGH Leofric holds 1 virgate of land from Miles.
Land for 1 plough; it is there.
The value is and always was 10s.
He also held it himself before 1066; he was Brictric's man; he
could sell and grant it.

20   LAND OF ARNULF OF HESDIN

In MANSHEAD Hundred

1   Arnulf of Hesdin holds TODDINGTON from the King. It answers for
15½ hides. Land for 30 ploughs. In lordship 10 carucates of land,
7 ploughs there; a further 3 possible; besides the 15½ hides.
42 villagers have 20 ploughs. 19 smallholders and 19 slaves.   212 b
Meadow for 30 ploughs; woodland, 300 pigs.
Total value £25; as much when acquired; before 1066 £30.
Wulfward [son of?] Leofed held this manor before 1066.

In Celgraue ten Ernulf tcia parte uni uirg træ.

Val 7 ualuit sep.ii.fol.Hanc tra tenuit Eduuard.T.R.E.

.XXI. TERRA EVDONIS FILIJ HVBERTI.

Evdo Dapifer ten ETONE.p xx.hid fe defd.Tra.e
xvi.car.In dnio.vii.hid 7 dim.7 ibi funt.iiii.car.

Ibi.xxxviii.uilli.hnt.xii.car.Ibi.vii.bord.7 viii.ferui.

7 ii.fochi.qui n poteran tra fua dare t uende.Ibi.ii.

molini de xxxvi.fol.7 vi.den.7 c.anguill.Ptu.xii.

car.Silua.cccc.porc.7 ii.acs uineæ.Int totu ual.xv.lib.

Qdo recep.viii.lib.T.R.E.x.lib.Hoc M tenuit Vlmar
de Etone.teign.R.E.7 in hoc M fuer.ii.fochi q tram
fua uende potuer 7 dare.De hac tra reclamat Tedbald
ho juditæ comitiffæ.i.hid.de qua eu Eudo defaifiuit
pqua ad hoc M uenit.

In WIBOLDESTONE ten Eudo.vi.hid 7 iii.uirg.Tra.e.v.car.

In dnio.iiii.hidæ 7 dim.7 ibi funt.ii.car.7 viii.uilli hnt
iiii.car.Ibi.viii.bord 7 iii.ferui.Ptu.ii.car.Int totu
ual iii.lib.Qdo recep.xx.fol.T.R.E.x.lib.Hanc tra
.iiii.teigni R.E.tenuer.7 cui uoluer uende potuer.

In Chaueleftorne ten Eudo.i.hid 7 i.uirg.Tra.e.i.car.

7 ibi.e.Ibi.iiii.uilli.7 ptu.i.car.Val 7 ualuit.x.fol.

T.R.E.xx.fol.Hanc tra.ii.hoes R.E.tenuer.7 ea dare pot

In Tamiseforde ten Eudo ten.i.hid. IN BICHELESWADA HD.

7 i.uirg træ.Tra.e.ii.car.In dnio.i.hida.7 ibi.e.i.car.

7 i.uilts cu.i.car.7 ii.bord 7 i.feru.7 i.molin x.fol.

7 ptu.ii.car.Val 7 ualuit.xl.fol.T.R.E.xlv.fol.Hanc
tra.ii.fochi tenuer.7 cui uoluer dare potuer.

In ead uilla ten Witts de carun iiii.hid 7 i.uirg de Eudone
Tra.e.iiii.car.In dnio.ii.car.7 viii.uilli hnt.ii.car.

7 vi.ferui.7 i.molin.xii.fol.Ptu.iiii.car.Val.lx.fol.

Qdo recep.xl.fol.T.R.E.lx.fol.Hanc tra tenuer

2 In CHALGRAVE Arnulf holds the third part of 1 virgate of land.
The value is and always was 2s.
Edward White held this land before 1066.

21 # LAND OF EUDO SON OF HUBERT

[In BARFORD Hundred]
1 M. Eudo the Steward holds EATON (Socon). It answers for 20 hides.
Land for 16 ploughs. In lordship 7½ hides; 4 ploughs there.
38 villagers have 12 ploughs. 7 smallholders and 8 slaves;
2 Freemen who could not grant or sell their land.
2 mills at 36s 6d and 100 eels; meadow for 12 ploughs;
woodland, 400 pigs; vineyard, 2 acres.
In total, value £15; when acquired £8; before 1066 £10.
Wulfmer of Eaton, a thane of King Edward's, held this manor.
In this manor were 2 Freemen who could sell and grant their land.
Theodbald, Countess Judith's man, claims 1 hide of this land,
of which Eudo dispossessed him after he came to this manor.

2 In WYBOSTON Eudo holds 6 hides and 3 virgates. Land for 5
ploughs. In lordship 4½ hides; 2 ploughs there.
8 villagers have 4 ploughs. 8 smallholders and 3 slaves.
Meadow for 2 ploughs.
In total, value £3; when acquired 20s; before 1066 £10.
4 thanes of King Edward's held this land; they could sell
to whom they would.

3 In CHAWSTON Eudo holds 1 hide and 1 virgate.
Land for 1 plough; it is there.
4 villagers.
Meadow for 1 plough.
The value is and was 10s; before 1066, 20s.
2 of King Edward's men held this land; they could grant and sell.

In BIGGLESWADE Hundred
4 In TEMPSFORD Eudo holds 1 hide and 1 virgate of land.
Land for 2 ploughs. In lordship 1 hide; 1 plough there.
1 villager with 1 plough; 2 smallholders and 1 slave.
1 mill, 10s; meadow for 2 ploughs.
The value is and was 40s; before 1066, 45s.
2 Freemen held this land; they could grant to whom they would.

5 In the same village William of Cairon holds 4 hides and 1 virgate
from Eudo the Steward. Land for 4 ploughs. In lordship
2 ploughs.
8 villagers have 2 ploughs; 6 slaves.
1 mill, 12s; meadow for 4 ploughs.
Value 60s; when acquired 40s; before 1066, 60s.

.III. ſochi hōēs Vlmari de Etone. Vñ eoꝝ trā ſuā dare

ñ potuit fine lictia dñi ſui. alij . II . qđ uolueꝛ facere potueꝛ.

ⓂSANDEIA teñ Eudo dapifer. IN DIM HVND DE WENESLAI.

,p XVI. hiđ ſe defđ.7 una uirg. Tra.ē.XVI.car. In dñio

VIII. hiđ 7 I. uirg.7 ibi ſunt. III. caꝛ.7 XXIIII. uilti hñt

VIII. caꝛ.7 adhuc. V. poſs fieri. Ibi. VI. borđ.7 II.ſerui.

7 II. molini. de. L. ſot.p̄tu. XVI. car. Paſta ad peꝯuñ uillæ.

Int totū uat. XII. lib. Q̇do recēp: VIII. lib. T.R.E: x. lib.

Hoc Ⓜ tenuit Vlmar de Etone teign. R.E. Hic reclamat

Eudo. III. ac ſiluæ ſup Hug belcāp. q̇s Vlmar tenuit.

f̡ Rađ q̇do erat uicecom eū deſaiſiuit. idōꝗ Eudo noluit

dare Warras de eađ ſilua. Hoc iđē hōēs de hund atteſtant.

In Suttone teñ Aluuin de Eudone. III. uirg træ. Tra.ē

VI. bobꝝ.7 ibi ſunt.7 I. uilts. p̄tu bobꝝ. Vat. VI. ſot. Q̇do

recēp: III. ſot. T.R.E: x. ſot. Hanc trā. II. ſochi tenueꝛ.

7 potueꝛ uende cui uolueꝛ. IN WICHESTAVESTOV HVND.

In Sudgiuele teñ Wilts de caron dim uirg de

Eudone. Tra.ē. II. bobꝝ.7 ibi ſunt. P̊tu. II. bobꝝ. Vat. III.ſot.

T.R.E: IIII. ſot. Hanc trā tenuit Alric 7 cui uoluit dare potuit

212 c

In Stanford teñ Wilts de caron. IIII. hiđ de Eudone

Tra.ē. IIII. caꝛ. In dñio. II. caꝛ.7 III. uilti hñt. II. caꝛ.

7 II. ſerui.7 II. molini de. XXIX. ſot.7 L. anguilt. P̊tu

IIII. caꝛ. Silua. LX. porc.7 II. ſot. Int totū uat. IIII.

lib. Q̇do recēp: XL. ſot. T.R: IIII. lib. Hanc trā tenuit

Vlmar de Etone. teign. R.E. In hac tra fuit. I. ſochs

hō huj Vlmari. dim hiđ habuit.7 uende potuit.

In eađ ſunt VII. ſochi. teneñtes VII. acras træ. hōēs

Vlmari fueꝛ.7 trā ſuā dare potueꝛ. Modo Hugo

de belcāp tenet eā.

In Blunehā teñ Domnic. I. uirg tre de Eudone.

Tra.ē. II. bob.7 ibi ſunt. p̄tu. II. bobꝝ. Vat. II. ſot. Q̇do

3 Freemen, Wulfmer of Eaton's men, held this land. One
of them could not grant his land without his lord's permission;
the other two could do what they would.

In the Half-Hundred of WENSLOW

6 M. Eudo the Steward holds SANDY. It answers for 16 hides
and 1 virgate. Land for 16 ploughs. In lordship 8 hides
and 1 virgate; 3 ploughs there.
 24 villagers have 8 ploughs; a further 5 possible.
  6· smallholders and 2 slaves.
 2 mills at 50s; meadow for 16 ploughs; pasture for the
 village livestock.
In total, value £12; when acquired £8; before 1066 £10.
 Wulfmer of Eaton, a thane of King Edward's, held this manor.
Here Eudo claims 3 acres of woodland against Hugh Beauchamp,
which Wulfmer held; but Ralph dispossessed him when he was
Sheriff. Therefore Eudo refused to give the defence obligations
from this woodland. This the men of the Hundred also confirm.

7 In SUTTON Alwin holds 3 virgates of land from Eudo.
Land for 6 oxen; they are there.
 1 villager.
Meadow for the oxen.
Value 6s; when acquired 3s; before 1066, 10s.
 2 Freemen held this land; they could sell to whom they would.

In WIXAMTREE Hundred

8 In SOUTHILL William of Cairon holds ½ virgate from Eudo.
Land for 2 oxen; they are there.
 Meadow for 2 oxen.
Value 3s; before 1066, 4s.
 Alric held this land; he could grant to whom he would.

9 In STANFORD William of Cairon holds 4 hides from Eudo. 212 c
Land for 4 ploughs. In lordship 2 ploughs.
 3 villagers have 2 ploughs. 2 slaves.
 2 mills at 29s and 50 eels; meadow for 4 ploughs;
 woodland, 60 pigs and 2s too.
In total, value £4; when acquired 40s; before 1066 £4.
 Wulfmer of Eaton, a thane of King Edward's, held this land.
 On this land was 1 Freeman, Wulfmer's man; he had ½
hide; he could sell.

10 In the same (village) are 7 Freemen who hold 7 acres of land;
they were Wulfmer's men; they could grant their land.
Now Hugh of Beauchamp holds it.

11 In BLUNHAM Domnic holds 1 virgate of land from Eudo.
Land for 2 oxen; they are there.
 Meadow, 2 oxen.

recep̄. iii . ſol . T.R.E. v . ſol . Hanc t̄ra . iiii . ſocħi tenuer̄.
7 uende 7 dare potuer̄.

In BISTONE teñ Rolland de Eudone . iii . hiđ . T̄ra . ē
iii . car̄ . 7 ibi ſunt . In dñio . ii . car̄ . 7 iiii . uitti hñt . i .
car̄ . Ibi . ii . borđ . 7 i . ſeru . P̄tū . iii . car̄ . Val xxx . ſol .
Q̇do recep̄. xx . ſol . T.R.E. xl . ſol .

In ead teñ Normann de Eudone . iiii . hiđ . T̄ra . ē
iiii . car̄ . In dñio . i . car̄ . 7 iiii . uitti hñt . iii . car̄ .
Ibi . ii . ſerui . 7 i . moliñ . xx . ſol . P̄tū . iiii . car̄ . Valet
xl . ſol . 7 tntđ q̇do recep̄ . T.R.E. l . ſol . Has . iiii . hiđ
7 iii . ſupiores tenuit iſte Normann T.R.E . 7 T.R. Witti .
Nc̄ ħt Eudo de rege ut hōes ej dñt . ſ̧ ñ eſt de feudo

In ead teñ Pirot de Eudone . i . hiđ .   Liſois.
T̄ra . ē . i . car̄ . 7 ibi . ē . cū . i . borđ . p̄tū . i . car̄ . Valet
x . ſol . Q̇do recep̄. v . ſol . T.R.E. xx . ſol . Hanc t̄ra
tenuit Rauan hō Vlmari . 7 cui uoluit dare potuit. *de Etone*

In Nortgiue teñ Pirot de Eud . i . hiđ 7 dim . T̄ra . ē . i . car̄
7 dim . Ibi . ē . i . car̄ . 7 dim pot fieri . 7 iii . uitti ſuɴ 7 i . borđ .
P̄tū . i . car̄ 7 dim . 7 i . moliñ . xiiii . ſol . Val xx . ſol . Q̇do
recep̄. x . ſol . T.R.E. xxv . ſol . Hanc t̄ra tenuit Rauan
hō Vlmari de Etone . 7 uende potuit.

In ead teñ Rađ . i . hiđ 7 dim de Eudone . T̄ra . ē . ii . car̄ .
7 ibi ſunt . 7 v . borđ 7 iii . ſerui . P̄tū . ii . car̄ . Silua . c .
porc . Val . iii . lib . Q̇do recep̄. xl . ſol . T.R.E. lx . ſol .
Hanc t̄ra tenuer̄ . ii . ſocħi . 7 dare 7 uende potuer̄.

(M) In CLISTONE teñ Witts de caron IN CLISTON HVNĐ .
de Eudone . vi . hiđ 7 dim . T̄ra . ē . iiii . car̄ 7 dim . In dñio
. ii . car̄ . 7 ix . uitti hñt . ii . car̄ 7 dim . Ibi . i . borđ 7 iii . ſerui .
7 ii . molini de . xl . ſol . 7 cl . anguitt . P̄tū . iiii . car̄ 7 dim .
Int totū ual . c . ſol . Q̇do recep̄. iiii . lib . T.R.E. vi . lib .
Hoc (M) tenuit Vlmar de Etone . 7 ibi fuer̄ . iii . ſocħi .
. i . hiđ 7 dim uirg habuer̄ . 7 cui uoluer̄ uende potuer̄.

Value 2s; when acquired 3s; before 1066, 5s.

4 Freemen held this land; they could sell and grant.

12   In BEESTON Roland holds 3 hides from Eudo. Land for 3 ploughs; they are there. In lordship 2 ploughs.

4 villagers have 1 plough. 2 smallholders and 1 slave.

Meadow for 3 ploughs.

Value 30s; when acquired 20s; before 1066, 40s.

13   In the same (village) Norman holds 4 hides from Eudo. Land for 4 ploughs. In lordship 1 plough.

4 villagers have 3 ploughs. 2 slaves.

1 mill, 20s; meadow for 4 ploughs.

Value 40s; as much when acquired; before 1066, 50s.

This Norman held these 4 hides and the 3 above before and after 1066. Now Eudo has it from the King, as his men state; but it is not of Lisois' Holding.

14   In the same (village) Pirot holds 1 hide from Eudo. Land for 1 plough; it is there, with

1 smallholder.

Meadow for 1 plough.

Value 10s; when acquired 5s; before 1066, 20s.

Raven, Wulfmer of Eaton's man, held this land; he could grant to whom he would.

15   In NORTHILL Pirot holds 1½ hides from Eudo. Land for 1½ ploughs. 1 plough there; ½ possible.

3 villagers and 1 smallholder.

Meadow for 1½ ploughs; 1 mill, 14s.

Value 20s; when acquired 10s; before 1066, 25s.

Raven, Wulfmer of Eaton's man, held this land; he could sell.

16   In the same (village) Ralph holds 1½ hides from Eudo. Land for 2 ploughs; they are there.

5 smallholders and 3 slaves.

Meadow for 2 ploughs; woodland, 100 pigs.

Value £3; when acquired 40s; before 1066, 60s.

2 Freemen held this land; they could grant and sell.

In CLIFTON Hundred

17 M. In CLIFTON William of Cairon holds 6½ hides from Eudo. Land for 4½ ploughs. In lordship 2 ploughs.

9 villagers have 2½ ploughs. 1 smallholder and 3 slaves.

2 mills at 40s and 150 eels; meadow for 4½ ploughs.

In total, value 100s; when acquired £4; before 1066 £6.

Wulfmer of Eaton held this manor. There were 3 Freemen there; they had 1 hide and ½ virgate; they could sell to whom they would.

.XXII. **TERRA WILLI PEVREL.** *IN STANBVRGE HVND.*

Wills peurel ten de rege PILEWORDE.7 Ambrosi de eo.

p x. hid se defd. Tra. ē. viii. car. In dnio. i. car. 7 alia

poteſt fieri. 7 x. uilti hnt. vi. car. Ibi. vi. bord 7 iii. ſerui.

Ptū. vi. car. Silua. c. porc. Hanc ſiluā Oſuui abſtulit.

7 hund dicit qa in hoc ꝏ jacuit. T.R.E. Int totū

uat. vi. lib. Qdo recep. iiii. lib. T.R.E. x. lib. Hoc ꝏ

tenuit Leuric fili Oſmundi teign regis. E. *IN WILGA* ᴴⱽᴺᴰ·

In Riſedene ten Malet de Willo peurel. i. uirg træ

212 d

Tra. ē. ii. bob. 7 ibi ſunt. Vat 7 ualuit. xvi. den. T.R.E.

ii. ſot. Hanc trā tenuit Samar hō Godæ comitiſſæ. 7 cui

uoluit dare potuit.

.XXII. **TERRA HVGON DE BELCAMP.** *IN STODENE IIVND.*

Hvgo de belcāp ten CHAISOT. p. v. hid ſe defd.

. i. uirg min. Tra. ē. v. car. 7 ibi ſunt. 7 ix. uilti. 7 vi.

bord. 7 un ſeruus. 7 i. molin. ii. ſot. Ptū. iiii. car.

Silua. cc. porc. In totis ualent uat. c. ſot. Qdo recep.

iiii. lib. T.R.E. c. ſot. Hanc trā tenuit Aſchil teign

regis. E. 7 ibi fuer. xii. ſochi. q habuer iii. hid 7 dimid.

7 cui uoluer uende 7 dare potuer.

In Riſelai ten Hugo. i. hid. 7 ē Bereuuich de Caiſot.

Tra. ē. ii. car. 7 ibi ſunt. Hanc tenuit Aſchil anteceſſor ej.

ꝏ Ipſe Hugo ten PVTENEHOV. *IN BVCHELAI DIMID HVND.*

p iiii. hid ſe defd. Tra. ē. v. car. In dnio. ii. hid. 7 ibi

ſunt. ii. car. 7 vi. uilti hnt. iii. car. Ibi. iiii. bord. 7 ii.

ſerui. 7 i. molin. xxx. ſot. 7 c. anguill. Silua. c. porc.

Vat. iiii. lib. Qdo recep. xl. ſot. 7 tntd T.R.E. Hoc ꝏ

tenuit Aſchil teign regis. E.

LAND OF WILLIAM PEVEREL

In STANBRIDGE Hundred

1 M. William Peverel holds TILSWORTH from the King and Ambrose from him. It answers for 10 hides. Land for 8 ploughs. In lordship 1 plough; another possible.
>   10 villagers have 6 ploughs. 6 smallholders and 3 slaves.
>   Meadow for 6 ploughs; woodland, 100 pigs.
>   Oswy took away this woodland; the Hundred states that
>   it lay in this manor before 1066.
> In total, value £6; when acquired £4; before 1066 £10.
>   Leofric son of Osmund, a thane of King Edward's, held
> this manor.

In WILLEY Hundred

2 In RUSHDEN Malet holds 1 virgate of land from William Peverel. Land for 2 oxen; they are there.   212 d
The value is and was 16d; before 1066, 2s.
>   Saemer the priest, Countess Gytha's man, held this land;
> he could grant to whom he would.

LAND OF HUGH OF BEAUCHAMP

In STODDEN Hundred

1 M. Hugh of Beauchamp holds KEYSOE. It answers for 5 hides.
>   less 1 virgate. Land for 5 ploughs; they are there.
>   9 villagers, 6 smallholders and 1 slave.
>   1 mill, 2s; meadow for 4 ploughs; woodland, 200 pigs.
> Total value 100s; when acquired £4; before 1066, 100s.
>   Askell, a thane of King Edward's, held this land. There
> were 12 Freemen who had 3½ hides; they could sell and
> grant to whom they would.

2 In RISELEY Hugh holds 1 hide. It is an outlier of Keysoe.
Land for 2 ploughs; they are there.
>   Askell his predecessor held it.

In BUCKLOW Half-Hundred

3 M. Hugh holds PUTNOE himself. It answers for 4 hides.
>   Land for 5 ploughs. In lordship 2 hides. 2 ploughs there.
>   6 villagers have 3 ploughs. 4 smallholders and 2 slaves.
>   1 mill, 30s and 100 eels; woodland, 100 pigs.
> Value £4; when acquired 40s; as much before 1066.
>   Askell, a thane of King Edward's, held this manor.

ᴍ Ipſe Hugo teñ STACHEDENE . ꝑ v . hiđ ſe defđ . Ťra . ē . v.

cař . In dñio . ii . hidæ . 7 ibi ſunt . ii . cař . 7 xii . uiłłi hñt

iii . cař . Ibi . viii . borđ 7 ii . ſerui . ꝑˉtū . i . cař . Silua

. c . porc . ※ Hoc ᴍ tenueř . ii . hoˉes regis . E . 7 uñ hōˉ Heraldiˌ comitis

7 uñ qˊſq̗ cui uoluit ťra ſuāˉ dare potuit.

ᴍ Ipſe Hugo teñ CHAINHALLE . ꝑ . v . hiđ ſe defđ . Ťra . ē

v . cař . In dñio . ii . hidæ . 7 ibi ſunt . ii . cař . 7 xii . uiłłi hñt

iii . cař . Ibi . ix . borđ 7 v . ſerui . ꝑˉtū . iii . cař . 7 i . moliñ

xl . ſoł . 7 c . anguiłł . Silua . c . porc . In totis ualentijs

uał . viii . liƀ . Qˊdo receꝑˊ . c . ſoł . T . R . E . ˊ vii . liƀ . Hoc ᴍ

tenuit Aſchil teigñ regis . E.

In eađ teñ Hugo dimiđ hiđ quæ jacet in putènehou

Ťra . ē . i . cař . 7 iiii . boues ſuɴˊ ibi . 7 ii . borđ . Vał 7 ualuit

ii . ſoł . Hanc ťra tenuit Anſchil teigñ regis . E.

In Goldentone teñ Hugo . iii . hiđ . 7 i . uirg quæ jacet

in Putenehou . Ťra . ē . iii . cař . 7 ibi ſunt . 7 vii . uiłłi 7 i.

borđ . ꝑˉtū . i . cař . 7 i . moliñ . xxx . ſoliđ 7 c . anguiłł . Int

totūˉ uał . lx . ſoł . 7 tñtđ qˊdo receꝑ . T . R . E . ˊ iiii . liƀ.

De hac ťra habuit Radulfˊ tallgeboſc . ii . hiđ 7 iii . uirg.

ꝑ excābio de Warres . Hanc ťra tenueř . ix . ſochi . ꝼ HĐ.

7 cui uolueř dare ł uendè potueř . IN WICHESTANESTOV

In Sudgible teñ Hugo . ii . hiđ 7 i . uirg . Ťra . ē . iii.

cař . 7 ibi ſunt . Ptū . iii . cař . Silua . c . porc . Vał 7 ualuit

xl . ſoł . T . R . E . ˊ l . ſoł . Hanc ťra . viii . ſochi tenueř . 7 qđ

uolueř inde facere potueř.

In Stanford teñ Hugo . i . hiđ 7 dimˉ uirg træ . Ťra . ē

. i . cař 7 dimiđ . 7 ˉibi ſunt . 7 iiii . uiłłi 7 i . borđ . ꝑˉtū . i . cař

7 dimˉ . Vał 7 ualuit ſēp . xx . ſoł . Hanc ťra tenueř . iiii.

ſochi . quoꝛ . iii . liberi fueř . iiii . ů unāˉ hiđ habuit . ſed

nec dare nec uendè potuit.

4   M. Hugh holds STAGSDEN himself. It answers for 5 hides.
Land for 5 ploughs. In lordship 2 hides; 2 ploughs there.
12 villagers have 3 ploughs. 8 smallholders and 2 slaves.
Meadow for 1 plough; woodland, 100 pigs.
*(Words omitted are entered at the foot of the column, in 23,10 below,
with transposition signs).*
2 of King Edward's men and a man of Earl Harold's held
this manor; each could grant his land to whom he would.

5   M. Hugh holds *CHAINHALLE* himself. It answers for 5 hides.
Land for 5 ploughs. In lordship 2 hides; 2 ploughs there.
12 villagers have 3 ploughs. 9 smallholders and 5 slaves.
Meadow for 3 ploughs; 1 mill, 40s and 100 eels;
woodland, 100 pigs.
Total value £8; when acquired 100s; before 1066 £7.
Askell, a thane of King Edward's, held this manor.

6   In the same (village) Hugh holds ½ hide which lies in Putnoe
(lands). Land for 1 plough; 4 oxen there.
2 smallholders.
The value is and was 2s.
Askell, a thane of King Edward's, held this land.

7   In GOLDINGTON (Highfields) Hugh holds 3 hides and 1 virgate
which lies in Putnoe (lands). Land for 3 ploughs; they are there.
7 villagers and 1 smallholder.
Meadow for 1 plough; 1 mill, 30s and 100 eels.
In total, value 60s; as much when acquired; before 1066 £4.
Ralph Tallboys had 2 hides and 3 virgates of this land in
exchange for Ware.
9 Freemen held this land; they could grant or sell to whom
they would.

In WIXAMTREE Hundred

8   In SOUTHILL Hugh holds 2 hides and 1 virgate. Land for 3 ploughs;
they are there.
Meadow for 3 ploughs; woodland, 100 pigs.
The value is and was 40s; before 1066, 50s.
8 Freemen held this land; they could do what they would
with it.

9   In STANFORD Hugh holds 1 hide and ½ virgate of land.
Land for 1½ ploughs; they are there.
4 villagers and 1 smallholder.
Meadow for 1½ ploughs.
The value is and always was 20s.
4 Freemen held this land; 3 of them were free; the fourth
had 1 hide but could neither grant nor sell.

ⱳ **I**n Chernetone ten̄ Hugo.vi.hiđ 7 dim̄ 7 ii.part.i.uirg
Tra.ē.viii.cař.In dn̄io.ii.hiđ 7 dim̄.7 i.car eſt ibi.
7 xii.uitti hn̄t.vii.cař.Ibi.vi,borđ.P̃tū.iii.cař.Silua ⌐ c.xx.porc.

※Ibi.ē parcħ ferarū ſiluatic.Int totū uat.c.ſot.

Q̧do recep̃.xl.ſot.T.R.E.c.ſot

213 a
7 i.molin̄.xl.ſot.7 c.anguitt.Int totū uat.vi.lib.

Q̧do recep̃.c.ſot.T.R.E.vi.lib.Hoc ⱳ.xiii.ſocħi
tenuer̄.7 quó uoluer̄ cū tra ſua recedere potuer̄.

ⱳ **I**pſe Hugo ten̄ *WELITONE*.p x.hiđ ſe defđ.Tra
eſt.ix.car.In dn̄io.v.hide.7 ibi ſunt.iii.cař.

7 iiii.poteſt fieri.7 xiii.uitti hn̄t.v.cař.Ibi.viii.
ſerui.7 i.molin̄.xii.ſoliđ 7 c.anguitt.P̃tū.v.car.

Silua.xl.porc.In totis ualent uat.vii.lib.

Q̧do recep̃.xl.ſot.T.R.E.vi.lib.Hoc ⱳ tenuit
Aſchil teign regis.E.7 ibi fuer̄.viii.ſocħi.q̧ cū tra
ſua quo uoluer̄ recede potuer̄.De hac tra.vii.hiđ.

ⱳ **I**pſe Hugo ten̄ *STOTFALT. IN GLIFTON HVND.* ⌐ habuer̄.
p xv.hiđ ſe defđ.Tra.ē.xv.cař.In dn̄io.v.hidæ.
7 ibi ſunt.iii.cař.7 xxi.uitti hn̄t.xii.cař.Ibi xiiii.
borđ 7 vi.ſerui.7 iiii.molini de.iiii.lib.7 cccc.anguit.
p̃tū.vii.car.In totis ualent uat.xxv.lib.Q̧do re
cep̃.xii.lib.T.R.E.xx.lib.Die quá Rađ tallebofc
obijt.p xxx.lib erat ad firm̄a.Hoc ⱳ tenuit Aſchil
teign regis.E.Ipſe habuit.ix.hiđ 7 dim̄.7 vii.ſocħi
reliquā trā tenuer̄.7 cui uoluer̄ uendere potuer̄.

De hac tra ptin.i.hida ad æcclam ⑁ Albani.7 ut hōes
de hunđ dn̄t ibi jacuit.T.R.E.⌐IN *RÆTBORGESTOV HD*.
In Meldone ten̄ Hugo dim̄ hiđ 7 dim̄ uirg.Tra.ē
.i.cař.7 ibi eſt.7 un̄ uitts 7 i.borđ.p̃tū.i.cař.Silua
xx.porc.Vat x.ſot.Q̧do recep̃.v.ſot.T.R.E.xii.
ſot.Hanc trā tenuit Goduin hō Aſchil.7 dare 7 uendĕ potuit.

10 M. In CARDINGTON Hugh holds 6½ hides and 2 parts of 1 virgate.
Land for 8 ploughs. In lordship 2½ hides; 1 plough there.
12 villagers have 7 ploughs. 6 smallholders.
Meadow for 3 ploughs; woodland, 120 pigs;

(23,4 Words omitted, directed to their proper place by transposition signs)

A park for woodland beasts.
In total, value 100s; when acquired 40s; before 1066, 100s.

(23,10 continued)

1 mill, 40s and 100 eels.   213 a
In total, value £6; when acquired 100s; before 1066 £6.
13 Freemen held this manor; they could withdraw where
they would with their land.

11 M. Hugh holds WILLINGTON himself. It answers for 10 hides.
Land for 9 ploughs. In lordship 5 hides; 3 ploughs there.
a fourth possible.
13 villagers have 5 ploughs. 8 slaves.
1 mill, 12s and 100 eels; meadow for 5 ploughs;
woodland 40 pigs.
Total value £7; when acquired 40s; before 1066 £6.
Askell, a thane of King Edward's, held this manor.
8 Freemen were there; they could withdraw with their land
where they would; they had 7 hides of this land.

In CLIFTON Hundred
12 M. Hugh holds STOTFOLD himself. It answers for 15 hides.
Land for 15 ploughs. In lordship 5 hides; 3 ploughs there.
21 villagers have 12 ploughs. 14 smallholders and 6 slaves.
4 mills at £4 and 400 eels; meadow for 7 ploughs.
Total value £25; when acquired £12; before 1066 £20. On the
day that Ralph Tallboys died it was at a revenue for £30.
Askell, a thane of King Edward's, held this manor. He
had 9½ hides himself. 7 Freemen held the rest of the land;
they could sell to whom they would. 1 hide of this land
belongs to St. Alban's Church; as the men of the Hundred
state, it lay there before 1066.

In REDBORNSTOKE Hundred
13 In MAULDEN Hugh holds ½ hide and ½ virgate.
Land for 1 plough; it is there.
1 villager and 1 smallholder.
Meadow for 1 plough; woodland, 20 pigs.
Value 10s; when acquired 5s; before 1066, 12s.
Godwin, Askell's man, held this land; he could grant and sell.

Ⓜ In *HOVSTONE* . teñ Hugo . v . hiđ . Tra̅ . e̅ . vi . ca̅r . 7 ibi
funt . 7 viii . uilli 7 vi . borđ 7 ii . ferui . P̊tu̅ . vi . ca̅r .
Silua . cc . porc̃ . Val 7 ualuit . c . fol . T.R.E. vii . liƀ .
Hoc Ⓜ . vii . fochi tenue̅r . 7 cui uolue̅r dare potue̅r .

Ⓜ Ipfe Hugo teñ *HAGENES* . ᵱ . v . hiđ *IN FLICTHÁ HVND*.
fe defđ . Tra̅ . e̅ . viii . ca̅r . In dñio . ii . hidæ 7 dimiđ . 7 ibi
funt . iii . ca̅r . 7 xiiii . uilli hn̅t . v . ca̅r . Ibi . ix . borđ . 7 i .
feruus . p̊tu̅ . i . ca̅r . Silua q̅ngent porc̃ . In totis ualent
ual . x . liƀ . Q̨do recep̅. vii . liƀ . 7 tntđ . T.R.E . Hoc Ⓜ
tenuit Achi teign̅ regis . E. *IN BEREFORDE HVND*.

Ⓜ Ipfe Hugo teñ *SALCHOV* . ᵱ v . hiđ fe defđ . Tra̅ . e̅ . viii .
ca̅r . 7 ibi funt . Hanc tra̅ teneŭ xi . fochi . 7 idem ipfi
tenue̅r . T.R.E . 7 cui uolue̅r dare 7 uendere potue̅r .
p̊tu̅ . ii . ca̅r . Silua . l . porc̃ . Int totu̅ ual . c . fol . 7 tntđ
q̅do recep̅ . T.R.E. viii . liƀ . Hanc tra̅ habuit Rađ
tallgebofc ᵱ excābio de Wares ut dn̅t hões ej̅ . 7 q̅do
recep̅ . viii . liƀ ualebat . *IN MANESHEVE HVND*.

Ⓜ *ASPELEIA* ᵱ x . hiđ fe defđ . Acard de iuri teñ de
Hugone . Terra̅ . e̅ . xii . ca̅r . In dñio . ii . ca̅r . 7 tcia
poteft fieri . 7 xvi . uilli hn̅t . viii . ca̅r . 7 nona poteft
fieri . Ibi . iiii . borđ 7 v . ferui . 7 i . moliñ . x . folidoɀ .
P̊tu̅ . x . ca̅r . Silua . l . porc̃ . In totis ualent ual
viii . liƀ . Q̨do recep̅. c . fol . T.R.E. x . liƀ . Hoc Ⓜ tenuit
Leueua co̅mdata Wallef comitis . 7 quo uoluit
cu̅ terra fua recedere potuit .

Ⓜ *SALEFORD* ᵱ . v . hiđ fe defđ . Tra̅ . e̅ . v . ca̅r . In dñio
e̅ . i . ca̅r . 7 xii . uilli hn̅t . iiii . ca̅r . Ibi . i . borđ . 7 iiii . ⌠ ferui .
213 b
Ibi . i . moliñ . ix . fol . 7 iiii . den̅ . P̊tu̅ . v . ca̅r . Silua . cl .
porc̃ . 7 de alia c̅fuetudine . x . fol . In totis ualent ual
iiii . liƀ . Q̨do recep̅. lx . fol . T.R.E. c . fol . Hoc Ⓜ
tenuit Turchil teign̅ . R.E . 7 cui uoluit dare potuit .

14 M. In HOUGHTON (Conquest) Hugh holds 5 hides. Land for 6 ploughs; they are there.
   8 villagers, 6 smallholders and 2 slaves.
   Meadow for 6 ploughs; woodland, 200 pigs.
   The value is and was 100s; before 1066 £7.
   7 Freemen held this manor; they could grant to whom they would.

In FLITT Hundred

15 M. Hugh holds HAYNES himself. It answers for 5 hides.
   Land for 8 ploughs. In lordship 2½ hides; 3 ploughs there.
   14 villagers have 5 ploughs. 9 smallholders and 1 slave.
   Meadow for 1 plough; woodland, 500 pigs.
   Total value £10; when acquired £7; as much before 1066.
   Aki (Askell?), a thane of King Edward's, held this manor.

In BARFORD Hundred

16 M. Hugh holds SALPH himself. It answers for 5 hides.
   Land for 8 ploughs; they are there.
   11 Freemen hold this land; they also held it before 1066; they could grant and sell to whom they would.
   Meadow for 2 ploughs; woodland, 50 pigs.
   In total value 100s; as much when acquired; before 1066 £8.
   Ralph Tallboys had this land in exchange for Ware, as his men state; when he acquired it the value was £8.

In MANSHEAD Hundred

17 M. ASPLEY (Guise) answers for 10 hides. Acard of Ivry holds from Hugh. Land for 12 ploughs. In lordship 2 ploughs; a third possible.
   16 villagers have 8 ploughs; a ninth possible.
   4 smallholders and 5 slaves.
   1 mill, 10s; meadow for 10 ploughs; woodland, 50 pigs.
   Total value, £8; when acquired 100s; before 1066 £10.
   Leofeva, commended to Earl Waltheof, held this manor; she could withdraw where she would with her land.

18 M. SALFORD answers for 5 hides. Land for 5 ploughs.
   In lordship 1 plough.
   12 villagers have 4 ploughs. 1 smallholder and 4 slaves.
   1 mill, 9s 4d; meadow for 5 ploughs; woodland 150 pigs;   213 b
   from other customary dues 10s.
   Total value £4; when acquired 60s; before 1066, 100s.
   Thorkell, a thane of King Edward's, held this manor; he could grant to whom he would.

ⲙ̅ In Eureſhot ten̄ Radulf⁹ vii . hiđ 7 dim̄ de Hugone.

ꝑ uno ⲙ̅.Tra . ē . viii . car̄ . In dn̄io . ii . car̄ . 7 xv . uiⱡli

hn̄t . vi . car̄ . Ibi . iiii . ſerui . P̊tū . viii . car̄ . Silua . c .

porc̄ . Vaⱡ . c . ſoⱡ . Q̨do recep̄.́ iii . liƀ . 7 tn̄tđ T.R.E.

Hoc ⲙ̅ tenuit Turgis teign̄ R.E. 7 uende potuit.

ⲙ̅ In Middeltone ten̄ Wilⱡs froiſſart de Hugone

vi . hiđ . ꝑ uno ⲙ̅.Tra . ē . vi . car̄ . In dn̄io . iii . car̄ .

7 vi . uiⱡli hn̄t . iii . car̄ . Ibi . iii . borđ . 7 iiii . ſerui . P̊tū

vi . car̄ . Silua . xl . porc̄ . Vaⱡ . vi . liƀ . Q̨do recep̄⸍

iiii . liƀ . T.R.E.́ viii . liƀ . Hoc ⲙ̅ tenuit Auti huſcarle

comitis Algari . 7 qđ uoluit inde facere potuit.

ⲙ̅ Idem Wilⱡs ten̄ de Hugone Crauenheſt . ꝑ . iii . hiđ

7 dim̄ ſe defđ . Tra . ē . iiii . car̄ . In dn̄io . ii . car̄ . 7 iiii .

uiⱡli hn̄t . i . car̄ . 7 alia poteſt fieri . Ibi . iii . borđ .

7 iiii . ſerui . P̊tū . iiii . car̄ . Silua . c . porc̄ . Vaⱡ . lx . ſoⱡ .

7 tn̄tđ qdo recep̄ . T.R.E.́ c . ſoⱡ . Hoc ⲙ̅ tenuer̄

v . ſocħi . 7 cui uoluer̄ tr̄a ſuā dare 7 uende potuer̄.

ⲙ̅ In Straillei ten̄ Wilⱡs de Locels . iiii . hiđ 7 i . uirḡ

de Hugone . ꝑ uno ⲙ̅.Tra . ē . vi . car̄ . In dn̄io . i . car̄ .

7 alia poteſt fieri . 7 vii . uiⱡli hn̄t . iiii . car̄ . Ibi . v . borđ .

7 un⁹ ſeruus . Silua . xvi . porc̄ . Vaⱡ . iiii . liƀ . Q̨do

recep̄.́ xl . ſoⱡ . T.R.E.́ c . ſoⱡ . Hoc ⲙ̅ tenⱴit Aſchil

teign̄ . R.E. 7 ibi fuer̄ . i . ſocħs hō ej . hn̄s . i . hiđ . 7 cui

uoluit dare potuit.

ⲙ̅ Idem Wilⱡs ten̄ Echā de Hugone . ꝑ . viii . hiđ ſe defđ .

Tra . ē . xi . car̄ . In dn̄io . iiii . car̄ . 7 xiiii . uiⱡli hn̄t

vii . car̄ . Ibi . ii . borđ . 7 v . ſerui . P̊tū . vi . car̄ . Silua

. c . porc̄ . Vaⱡ . viii . liƀ . 7 tn̄tđ qdo recep̄ . T.R.E.́ xii . liƀ .

Hoc ⲙ̅ tenuer̄ . v . ſocħi . 7 cui uoluer̄ tr̄a ſuā dare potuer̄.

In Eſtone ten̄ Wimund⁹ de Hugone dim̄ hiđ . Tra . ē . iii . *IN STODDEN*

car̄ . 7 ibi ſunt . Ibi . ii . uiⱡli 7 vi . borđ . Silua . xl . porc̄ . *HVND.*

19 M. In EVERSHOLT Ralph holds 7½ hides from Hugh as one manor. Land for 8 ploughs. In lordship 2 ploughs.
    15 villagers have 6 ploughs. 4 slaves.
    Meadow for 8 ploughs; woodland, 100 pigs.
Value 100s; when acquired £3; as much before 1066.
    Thorgils, a thane of King Edward's, held this manor; he could sell.

20 M. In MILTON (Bryan) William Froissart holds 6 hides from Hugh as one manor. Land for 6 ploughs. In lordship 3 ploughs.
    6 villagers have 3 ploughs. 3 smallholders and 4 slaves.
    Meadow for 6 ploughs; woodland, 40 pigs.
Value £6; when acquired £4; before 1066 £8.
    Auti, one of Earl Algar's Guards, held this manor; he could do what he would with it.

[In FLITT Hundred]

21 M. William also holds GRAVENHURST from Hugh. It answers for 3½ hides. Land for 4 ploughs. In lordship 2 ploughs.
    4 villagers have 1 plough; another possible.
      3 smallholders and 4 slaves.
    Meadow for 4 ploughs; woodland, 100 pigs.
Value 60s; as much when acquired; before 1066, 100s.
    5 Freemen held this manor; they could grant and sell their land to whom they would.

22 M. In STREATLEY William of Loucelles holds 4 hides and 1 virgate from Hugh as one manor. Land for 6 ploughs. In lordship 1 plough; another possible.
    7 villagers have 4 ploughs. 5 smallholders and 1 slave.
    Woodland, 16 pigs.
Value £4; when acquired 40s; before 1066, 100s.
    Askell, a thane of King Edward's, held this manor; there was 1 Freeman, his man, who had 1 hide; he could grant to whom he would.

23 M. William also holds HIGHAM (Gobion) from Hugh. It answers for 8 hides. Land for 11 ploughs. In lordship 4 ploughs.
    14 villagers have 7 ploughs. 2 smallholders and 5 slaves.
    Meadow for 6 ploughs; woodland, 100 pigs.
Value £8; as much when acquired; before 1066 £12.
    5 Freemen held this manor; they could grant their land to whom they would.

In STODDEN Hundred

24   In EASTON Wimund holds ½ hide from Hugh.
Land for 3 ploughs; they are there.
    2 villagers; 6 smallholders.
    Woodland, 40 pigs.

Val.xxx.ſol.Q̇do recep̃.7 T.R.E.′xx.ſol.Hanc tram
tenuit Ouiet hō Aſchil.7 dare 7 uendĕ potuit.ſʒ ſoca
ſēp jacuit in Culmeuuorde ⊙ Aſchil.

In Riſelai ten Aluric dim hiđ de Hugone.Ťra.ē dim
caŕ.7 ibi.ē.7 iiii.borđ.Val.v.ſol.Q̇do recep̃.′ſimil.
T.R.E.′viii.ſol.Hanc trā tenuit Vuenot hō Godrici
uicec.7 potuit dare cui uoluit.

In Middeltone teñ Wills baſſet de Hugone.ii.hiđ.
dim uirg̃ miñ.Ťra.ē.iii.caŕ.In dñio.ii.caŕ.7 uñ uills
hƀ.i.caŕ.Ibi.iiii.borđ.7 ii.ſerui.p̃tū.ii.caŕ.Silua
vi.porc̃.Val.xxx.ſol.7 tntđ q̇do recep̃.T.R.E.′xl.ſol.

⊙ In Blecheſhou teñ Osƀt IN DIMID HĐ DE BOCHELAI.
de broilg.ii.hiđ 7 dim de Hugone.Ťra.ē.iiii.caŕ.
In dñio.i.caŕ.7 vii.uilti hñt.iii.caŕ.Ibi.ii.borđ.
7 ii.ſerui.7 dim moliñ.x.ſoliđ.P̃tū.i.caŕ.Silua.c.
porc.Val 7 ual ſēp.lx.ſol.Hoc ⊙̄ tenuit Aſchil.

213 c

7 iii.ſochi habueŕ ibi.iii.uirg.7 cui uolueŕ uendĕ pot.
In Bidehā teñ Serlo de ros.i.hiđ de hugone.Ťra
ē.i.caŕ.7 ibi eſt.7 uñ borđ 7 i.ſeru.p̃tū.i.caŕ.Val
7 ualuit ſēp.x.ſol.Hanc trā tenuit Alſi de Brunehā.
hō Eddid regine.7 cui uoluit dare potuit.

⊙ In BRVNEllA.ten Serlo de ros.vi.hiđ de hugone.
Ťra.ē.vi.caŕ.In dñio.ii.caŕ.7 xvi.uilti hñt.iiii.caŕ.
Ibi.v.borđ 7 vi.ſerui.7 i.moliñ.xx.ſoliđ.7 cxxv.an
guilt.P̃tū.vi.caŕ.Silua.xl.porc.Int totū ualet
vii.liƀ.Q̇do recep̃.′c.ſol.T.R.E.′iiii.liƀ.Hanc tram
tenuit Alſi hō regine Eddid.7 uendĕ potuit. IN WILGA
In Toruei ten Warneri.i.hid de hugone. Ƒ HVND.
Ťra.ē.ii.caŕ.In dñio.i.caŕ.7 uñ uills.i.caŕ.Ibi.iiii.
borđ.Val.x.ſol.7 tntđ q̇do recep̃.T.R.E.′xx.ſoliđ.
Hanc trā.ii.ſochi tenueŕ.7 cui uolueŕ dare potueŕ.

Value 30s; when acquired and before 1066, 20s.

Wulfgeat, Askell's man, held this land; he could grant and sell; but the jurisdiction always lay in Colmworth, Askell's manor.

In RISELEY Alric the priest holds ½ hide from Hugh.
Land for ½ plough; it is there.
4 smallholders.
Value 5s; when acquired the same; before 1066, 8s.

Wulfnoth, Godric the Sheriff's man, held this land; he could grant to whom he would.

In MILTON (Ernest) William Basset holds 2 hides less ½ virgate from Hugh. Land for 3 ploughs. In lordship 2 ploughs.
1 villager has 1 plough. 4 smallholders and 2 slaves.
Meadow for 2 ploughs; woodland, 6 pigs.
Value 30s; as much when acquired; before 1066, 40s.

In the Half-Hundred of BUCKLOW
M. In BLETSOE Osbert of Breuil holds 2½ hides from Hugh.
Land for 4 ploughs. In lordship 1 plough.
7 villagers have 3 ploughs. 2 smallholders and 2 slaves.
½ mill, 10s; meadow for 1 plough; woodland, 100 pigs.
The value is and always was 60s.
Askell held this manor.
3 Freemen had 3 virgates; they could sell to whom they would.   213 c

In BIDDENHAM Serlo of Rots holds 1 hide from Hugh.
Land for 1 plough; it is there.
1 smallholder and 1 slave.
Meadow for 1 plough.
The value is and always was 10s.
Alfsi of Bromham, Queen Edith's man, held this land; he could grant to whom he would.

M. In BROMHAM Serlo of Rots holds 6 hides from Hugh. Land for 6 ploughs. In lordship 2 ploughs.
16 villagers have 4 ploughs. 5 smallholders and 6 slaves.
1 mill, 20s and 125 eels; meadow for 6 ploughs; woodland, 40 pigs.
In total, value £7; when acquired 100s; before 1066 £4.
Alfsi, Queen Edith's man, held this land; he could sell.

In WILLEY Hundred
In TURVEY Warner holds 1 hide from Hugh. Land for 2 ploughs.
In lordship 1 plough.
1 villager, 1 plough. 4 smallholders.
Value 10s; as much when acquired; before 1066, 20s.
2 Freemen held this land; they could grant to whom they would.

In Sernebroc teñ Osbñ de Broilg . i . uirg 7 dim̄ de
hugone . Tra . ē . iii . boū . Val 7 ualuit sēp . ii . fol . Hanc
trā tenuer̄ . iii . fochi . 7 dare 7 uendē potuer̄.
In Lalega teñ Leuiet dim̄ hid . Tra . ē . ii . car̄ . 7 ibi fuᴎ.
Ibi . iiii . bord̄ . 7 i . feru . Silua . xxx . porc̄ . Val . xxx . fol.
Q̄do recep̄ : xv . fol . T . R . E : xxx . fol . Hanc trā tenuit
Moding . hō reginæ Eddid . 7 uendē potuit . IN BEREFORD
In Wiboldeftone teñ Wimund dim̄ uirg.   𝔏 HVND.
de Hugone . 7 ual 7 ualuit sēp . ii . fol . Hanc trā tenuit
Afchil teign . R . E.
In Calneftorne teñ Riuualo : iiii . uirg de hugone.
Tra . ē . ii . boū . Ibi . ii . bord̄ . 7 p̄tū . ii . boū . Silua . lx . porc̄.
Val . x . fol . Q̄do recep̄ : xv . fol . T . R . E : xx . fol . Hanc trā
ii . fochi tenuer̄ . 7 cui uoluer̄ dare potuer̄.
In Rocheftone . teñ Rualon . i . hid 7 i . virg . de hugone.
Tra . ē . i . car̄ . P̄tū . i . car̄ . Silua . iiii . porc̄ . Ibi . ii . bord̄.
7 i . feruus . Val x . fol . Q̄do recep̄ : 7 T . R . E : xx . fol.
Hanc trā . iiii . fochi tenuer̄ . hōes . R . E . 7 uendē potuer̄.
In Bereforde teñ Rualon de Hugone . iii . car̄ . Tra . ē
iiii . car̄ . In dñio . iii . car̄ . 7 iii . uilli hn̄t . i . car̄ . Ibi . v . bord̄.
7 iii . ferui . 7 i . moliñ . xxii . folid . 7 q̄t xx . Anguill . P̄tū.
ii . car̄ . Val . iii . lib . Q̄do recep̄ : xxx . fol . T . R . E : iii . lib.
Hanc trā tenuer̄ . iii . fochi hōes regis . E . 7 uendē potuer̄.
In ead̄ teñ Wimund de Taiffel de Hugone . v . hidas
7 ii . part . uni hidæ . Tra . ē . xi . car̄ . In dñio . v . car̄ . 7 xvi.
uilli . hn̄t . vi . car̄ . Ibi . vi . bord̄ . 7 i . feruus . P̄tū . i . car̄.
Val . x . lib . Q̄do recep̄ : xx . fol . T . R . E : lx . fol . Hoc 𝔐
. iii . fochi tenuer̄ . 7 dare 7 uendē potuer̄.

31 In SHARNBROOK Osbert of Breuil holds 1½ virgates from Hugh.
Land for 3 oxen.
The value is and always was 2s.
3 Freemen held this land; they could grant and sell.

32 In THURLEIGH Leofgeat holds ½ hide. Land for 2 ploughs; they are there.
4 smallholders and 1 slave.
Woodland, 30 pigs.
Value 30s; when acquired 15s; before 1066, 30s.
Moding, Queen Edith's man, held this land; he could sell.

In BARFORD Hundred
33 In WYBOSTON Wimund holds ½ virgate from Hugh.
The value is and always was 2s.
Askell, a thane of King Edward's, held this land.

34 In CHAWSTON Rhiwallon holds 4 virgates from Hugh. Land for 2 oxen.
2 smallholders.
Meadow for 2 oxen; woodland, 60 pigs.
Value 10s; when acquired 15s; before 1066, 20s.
2 Freemen held this land; they could grant to whom they would.

35 In ROXTON Rhiwallon holds 1 hide and 1 virgate from Hugh.
Land for 1 plough.
Meadow for 1 plough; woodland, 4 pigs.
2 smallholders and 1 slave.
Value 10s; when acquired and before 1066, 20s.
4 Freemen, King Edward's men, held this land; they could sell.

36 In (Great) BARFORD Rhiwallon holds 3 hides from Hugh. Land
for 4 ploughs. In lordship 3 ploughs.
3 villagers have 1 plough. 5 smallholders and 3 slaves.
1 mill, 22s and 80 eels; meadow for 2 ploughs.
Value £3; when acquired 30s; before 1066 £3.
3 Freemen, King Edward's men, held this land; they could sell.

37 In the same (village) Wimund of Tessel holds 5 hides and 2 parts
of 1 hide from Hugh. Land for 11 ploughs. In lordship 5 ploughs.
16 villagers have 6 ploughs. 6 smallholders and 1 slave.
Meadow for 1 plough.
Value £10; when acquired 20s; before 1066, 60s.
3 Freemen held this manor; they could grant and sell.

Ꝭ Ipſe Wimund teñ *COLMEWORDE*. de hugone . ꝑ v . hiđ

ſe defđ . Tra . ē . x . caꝛ . In dñio . ii . caꝛ . 7 xii . uiłłi hñt . viii.

caꝛ . Ibi . xiii . borđ . 7 i . ſeruus . Silua . cc . porc . Vał 7 ualuit

c . ſoł . T.R.Eꞏiiii . liƀ . Hoc Ꝭ teñ Achi teign . R.E . 7 ibi . viii.

ſocħi fueꝛ . q̇ dare 7 uende tꝛa ſuā potueꝛ cui uolueꝛ.

In Bereforde teñ Anſchetil pƀr . i . hiđ 7 dim de Hugone.

Tra . ē . ii . caꝛ . In dñio . i . caꝛ . 7 un uiłłs . i . caꝛ . Ibi . vi . borđ

7 iii . ſerui . 7 i . moł . vii . ſoł . p̃tū . i . caꝛ . Vał 7 ualuit sēp.

xl . ſoł . Hanc tꝛa . ii . ſocħi tenueꝛ . 7 uende potueꝛ.

In eađ teñ Tetbaud de Hugone . i . hiđ 7 iii . uirg 7 tcia

part uni uirg . Tra . ē . iii . caꝛ . In dñio . ii . 7 un uiłłs hī . i.

caꝛ . Ibi . viii . borđ . 7 i . ſeruus . p̃tū . i . caꝛ . Vał . xl . ſoł.

Qdo recep̃ꞏxx . ſoł . T.R.Eꞏlx . ſoł . Hoc Ꝭ . iii . ſocħi te

nueꝛ . 7 dare 7 uende potueꝛ.

In Goldentone teñ Roger fili Teodrici . ii . hiđ . de hugone.

Tra . ē . iii . caꝛ . In dñio . ii . caꝛ . 7 iii . uiłłi hñt . i . caꝛ.

Ibi . ii . borđ . p̃tū . i . caꝛ . Vał xxx . ſoł . Qdo recep̃ꞏ

xx . ſoł . T.R.Eꞏxl . ſoł . Has . ii . hiđ tenuit Radulf tałłƀ

ꝑ excābio de Wares . Hanc tꝛa tenueꝛ . iii . ſocħi . q̇ dare

potueꝛ tꝛa ſua cui uolueꝛ.

In eađ teñ Ricard . iii . hiđ de Hugone . ꝑ uno Ꝭ . Tra . ē

iii . caꝛ . In dñio . ii . caꝛ . 7 v . uiłłi hñt . i . caꝛ . Ibi un ſeru

P̃tū . ii . caꝛ . Vał xl . ſoł . Qdo recep̃ꞏx . ſoł . T.R.Eꞏlx . ſoł.

Has . iii . hiđ tenuit Rad tallgebofc ꝑ excābio de Wares.

Hoc Ꝭ tenuit Almær hō Afchil . 7 uende potuit.

In eađ teñ Walter . i . hiđ de Hugone . Tra . ē . i . caꝛ.

7 ibi . ē . P̃tū dim caꝛ . 7 ibi . ii . ſerui . Vał . xv . ſoł . Qdo

recep̃ꞏx . ſoł . T.R.Eꞏxv . ſoł . Ħ tꝛa . ē efcābiū de Wares.

Hanc tꝛa tenueꝛ hōes uiłłæ cōmunit . 7 uende potueꝛ.

8 M. Wimund holds COLMWORTH himself from Hugh. It answers for
5 hides. Land for 10 ploughs. In lordship 2 ploughs.
    12 villagers have 8 ploughs. 13 smallholders and 1 slave.
    Woodland, 200 pigs.
The value is and was 100s; before 1066 £4.
    Aki (Askell?), a thane of King Edward's, held this manor.
8 Freemen were there; they could grant and sell their land
to whom they would.

9 In (Great) BARFORD Ansketel the priest holds 1½ hides from Hugh.
Land for 2 ploughs. In lordship 1 plough.
    1 villager (has) 1 plough. 6 smallholders and 3 slaves.
    1 mill, 7s; meadow for 1 plough.
The value is and always was 40s.
    2 Freemen held this land; they could sell.

0 In the same (village) Theodbald holds 1 hide, 3 virgates and the third
part of 1 virgate from Hugh. Land for 3 ploughs. In lordship 2.
    1 villager has 1 plough. 8 smallholders and 1 slave.
    Meadow for 1 plough.
Value 40s; when acquired 20s; before 1066, 60s.   213 d
    3 Freemen held this manor; they could grant and sell

1 In GOLDINGTON Roger son of Theodoric holds 2 hides from Hugh.
Land for 3 ploughs. In lordship 2 ploughs.
    3 villagers have 1 plough. 2 smallholders.
    Meadow for 1 plough.
Value 30s; when acquired 20s; before 1066, 40s.
    Ralph Tallboys held these 2 hides in exchange for Ware. 3
Freemen held this land; they could grant their land to whom they
would.

2 In the same (village) Richard holds 3 hides from Hugh as one manor.
Land for 3 ploughs. In lordship 2 ploughs.
    5 villagers have 1 plough. 1 slave.
    Meadow for 2 ploughs.
Value 40s; when acquired 10s; before 1066, 60s.
    Ralph Tallboys held these 3 hides in exchange for Ware.
Aelmer, Askell's man, held this manor; he could sell.

43 In the same (village) Walter holds 1 hide from Hugh.
Land for 1 plough; it is there.
    Meadow for ½ plough.
    2 slaves.
Value 15s; when acquired 10s; before 1066, 15s.
    This land is in exchange for Ware. The men of the village held
this land in common; they could sell.

In Holma ten Mortuing In BICHELESWADE HVND.

de Hugone.I.uirg.Tra.III.bob.7 ibi funt.Val.III.fol.

T.R.E.'v.fol.Hanc trā tenuit.I.fochs fub Afchillo.

7 uende 7 dare potuit.

In Eftuuiche ten Bernard de Hug.I.hid 7 I.uirg.

Tra.ē.II.car 7 dim.In dnio.I.car.7 II.uilli hnt.II.

car 7 dim.Ibi.III.bord.7 ptū.IIII.bou.Val xx.fol.

Qdo recep.7 T.R.E.'x.fol.Hoc M tenuer.VI.fochi.

7 uende potuer.

In ead ten Wenelinc dim hid de Hugone.Tra.ē.I.car.

7 ibi.ē.Ibi.III.bord.Val.x.fol.Qdo recep:'v.fol.T.R.E.'

xx.fol.7 uende potuer.

In ead ten Ledmar dim hid.Tra.ē dim car.7 ibi eft.

Ibi.III.bord.7 I.molin de.IX.fol.7 IIII.den.Val 7 ualuit

sep xx.fol.Ifdem q̃ ten tenuit T.R.E.hō comitis Tofti.

7 cui uoluit uende potuit. IN WICHESTANESTOV HVND.

In Stanforde ten Roger de Hugone.I.hid.Tra.ē

.I.car.7 dim.7 ibi funt.7 IIII.uilli 7 I.bord.Ptū.I.car

7 dim.Silua.XVI.porc.7 dim molin de.v.fol.Int

totū ual.xv.fol.Qdo recep:'v.fol.T.R.E.'x.fol.Hanc

trā tenuit Æilmar de Ouu.7 potuit uende cui uoluit.

In Cochepol ten Robt de Hug.IIII.hid.p uno.M.

Tra.ē.IIII.car.In dnio.II.car.7 VI.uilli hnt.II.car.

Ibi un bord 7 un feru.ptū.I.car.Silua.ē fup totā

Chochepol.c.porc.Val.LX.fol.Qdo recep:'xx.fol.T.R.E.'

LX.fol.Hanc trā.III.fochi tenuer.7 uende potuer.

In ead ten Raynald de Hug.I.hid 7 I.uirg.Tra.ē.I.car.

7 ibi.ē.7 II.bord.7 ptū.IIII.bob.Val.x.fol.Qdo recep:'

v.fol.T.R.E.'x.fol.Hanc trā.II.fochi tenuer.7 cui

uoluer uende potuer.

In BIGGLESWADE Hundred

44 In HOLME Mordwing holds 1 virgate from Hugh. Land for 3 oxen; they are there.
Value 3s; before 1066, 5s.
1 Freeman held this land under Askell; he could sell and grant.

45 In ASTWICK Bernard holds 1 hide and 1 virgate from Hugh.
Land for 2½ ploughs. In lordship 1 plough.
2 villagers have 2½ ploughs. 3 smallholders.
Meadow for 4 oxen.
Value 20s; when acquired and before 1066, 10s.
6 Freemen held this manor; they could sell.

46 In the same (village) Weneling holds ½ hide from Hugh.
Land for 1 plough; it is there.
3 smallholders.
Value 10s; when acquired 5s; before 1066, 20s.
[...and...held it;] they could sell.

47 In the same (village) Ledmer holds ½ hide. Land for ½ plough; it is there.
3 smallholders.
1 mill at 9s 4d.
The value is and always was 20s.
The same holder, Earl Tosti's man, held it before 1066; he could sell to whom he would.

In WIXAMTREE Hundred

48 In STANFORD Roger holds 1 hide from Hugh. Land for 1½ ploughs; they are there.
4 villagers and 1 smallholder.
Meadow for 1½ ploughs; woodland, 16 pigs; ½ mill at 5s.
In total, value 15s; when acquired 5s; before 1066, 10s.
Aelmer of Hoo held this land; he could sell to whom he would.

49 In COPLE Robert holds 4 hides from Hugh as one manor.
Land for 4 ploughs. In lordship 2 ploughs.
6 villagers have 2 ploughs. 1 smallholder and 1 slave.
Meadow for 1 plough; woodland in the whole of Cople, 100 pigs.
Value 60s, when acquired 20s; before 1066, 60s.
3 Freemen held this land; they could sell.

In the same (village)
50 Reginald holds 1 hide and 1 virgate from Hugh. Land for 1 plough; it is there.
2 smallholders.
Meadow for 4 oxen.
Value 10s; when acquired 5s; before 1066, 10s.
2 Freemen held this land; they could sell to whom they would.

In ead ten Gonfrid .1. hid 7 dim uirg de Hugone.
Tra.ē.1.car.7 ibi eſt. Ibi un uilts 7 un ſeru.ptū.1111.
boū. Vat.x.ſot. Q̇do recep:́v . ſot.T.R.E:́x.ſot. Hanc
trā.11.ſochi tenuer. Hōes regis fuer.7 uende potuer:
In ead ten Norman.1.hid de Hug. Tra.ē.1.car.7 11.
boues ibi ſunt.Ptū.1111.boū. Vat.vi.ſot.Q̇do recep:́
ſimilit.T.R.E:́viii.ſot.De hac trā.111.uirg ten Aſchil

214 a

quiæ jacuer in Weltone ꝏ ej.7 Aleſtan tenuit.1.uirg
quā potuit uende cui uoluit.
In ead tenuit Brahting.1.hid.de Hugone.Tra.ē.1.car.
7 ibi.ē.Ptū.1111.boḃz. Vat 7 ualuit sēp.x.ſot.Hanc
trā.111.ſochi tenuer.7 cui uoluer uende potuer.
In ead ten Robt.111.uirg de hugone.Tra.ē.1.car.
7 ibi.ē.ptū.1111.bob. Vat 7 ualuit sēp.vii.ſot 7 dim.
Hanc trā.11.ſochi tenuer.7 uende potuer.
In ead ten Rogeri 7 Liboret dim hid 7 dim uirg.
Tra.ē.vi.bob.7 ibi ſunt.ptū.1111.boḃz. Vat 7 ual sēp
v.ſot.Hanc trā.111.ſochi tenuer.7 cui uoluer uende
potuer.De hoc ꝏ Chochepol.habuit Rad tallgeb
ix.hid ꝑ excābio de Wares ut dnt hōes ej.7 q̇do eas
recep:́1111.lib ualuer.
In Nortgible ten Walter dim hid de Hugone.Tra
ē dim car.7 ibi.ē.Ptū dim car. Vat.v.ſot.Q̇do re
cepit:́ſimit.T.R.E:́x.ſot. Hanc trā tenuit Oſiet hō
R.E.7 cui uoluit uende potuit. IN CLISTONE HVND.
In Cudeſſane ten.111.ſochi de Hugone.11.hid.Tra.ē
.1.car 7 dim.7 ibi ſunt.7 1.bord.ptū.1.car 7 dim.
Silua.1111.porc. Vat.xx.ſot.7 tntd q̇do recep.T.R.E:́
xxx.ſot.Hanc trā.1111.ſochi tenuer.7 cui uoluer
uende potuer.

51 Gunfrid holds 1 hide and ½ virgate from Hugh. Land for 1 plough;
it is there.
1 villager and 1 slave.
Meadow for 4 oxen.
Value 10s; when acquired 5s; before 1066, 10s.
2 Freemen held this land; they were the King's men; they could sell.

52 Norman holds 1 hide from Hugh. Land for 1 plough; 2 oxen there.
Meadow for 4 oxen.
Value 6s; when acquired the same; before 1066, 8s.
Askell held 3 virgates of this land which lay in (the lands of)   214 a
his manor, Willington. Alstan held 1 virgate which he could sell
to whom he would.

53 Branting held 1 hide from Hugh. Land for 1 plough; it is there.
Meadow for 4 oxen.
The value is and always was 10s.
3 Freemen held this land; they could sell to whom they would.

54 Robert holds 3 virgates from Hugh. Land for 1 plough; it is there.
Meadow for 4 oxen.
The value is and always was 7½s.
2 Freemen held this land; they could sell.

55 Roger the priest and Liboret hold ½ hide and ½ virgate.
Land for 6 oxen; they are there.
Meadow for 4 oxen.
The value is and always was 5s.
3 Freemen held this land; they could sell to whom they would. Ralph
Tallboys had 9 hides of this manor of Cople in exchange for Ware as
his men say; when he acquired them the value was £4.

56 In NORTHILL Walter holds ½ hide from Hugh. Land for ½ plough;
it is there.
Meadow for ½ plough.
Value 5s; when acquired the same; before 1066, 10s.
Osgeat, King Edward's man, held this land; he could sell to
whom he would.

In CLIFTON Hundred
57 In CUDESSANE 3 Freemen hold 2 hides from Hugh. Land for 1½ ploughs;
they are there.
1 smallholder.
Meadow for 1½ ploughs; woodland, 4 pigs.
Value 20s; as much when acquired; before 1066, 30s.
4 Freemen held this land; they could sell to whom they would.

TERRA NIGELLI DE ALBINGI. *IN MÆNESHEVE HVND.*

℥ In *CRAWELAI* ten̄ Turgiſus de Nigello Albinienſi.
v. hiđ. p. 1. man̄. Tra. ē. v. car̄. In dn̄io. 11. car̄. 7 111.
car̄ uilloʒ poſſ fieri. Ibi un̄ uilłs 7 v11. borđ. 7 1. ſeru.
p̄tū. v. car̄. Int totū ual. xxx. ſoł. Q̄do recep̄. xL. ſoł.
T.R.E. c. ſoł. Hoc m̄ tenuer̄. 1x. teigni. 7 cui uoluer̄
tr̄a ſuā dare 7 uende potuer̄.

In eođ Hunđ ten̄ Turgis de Nigello. 1. hiđ. Tra. ē. 1.
car̄. 7 ibi. ē. car̄. 7 11. ſerui. Silua. x. porc̄. H̄ tra
uał. xv. ſoł. Q̄do recep̄. x. ſoł. T.R.E. xx. ſoł.
Hanc tr̄a tenuit Suglo h̄o Alrici filij Godingi.
7 cui uoluit uende potuit.

℥ TINGREI ten̄ Turgis de Nigello. p. 11. hiđ 7 1. uirg.
Tra. ē. 111. car̄. In dn̄io. 1. car̄. 7 1111. uilłi hn̄t. 11. car̄.
Ibi. 11. borđ. p̄tū. 111. car̄. Silua. c.L. porc̄. Valet
xL. ſoł. Q̄do recep̄. xxx. ſoł. T.R.E. c. ſoł. Hoc m̄
11. teigni tenuer̄. 7 cui uoluer̄ uende potuer̄.

In Preſtelai ten̄ Turgis de Nigello. 1. hiđ 7 dim̄. Tra
ē. 11. car̄. 7 ibi ſuǸ. p̄tū. 11. car̄. Silua. xL. porc̄. Ibi
un̄ uilłs 7 1111. borđ. Vał. xx. ſoł. 7 tn̄tđ q̄do recep̄.
T.R.E. Lx. ſoł. Hanc tr̄a. v. teigni tenuer̄. 7 dare
7 uende potuer̄.

℥ NIGELLVS ten̄ *HERLINGDONE.* p. v. hiđ ſe defđ.
Tra. ē. x. car̄. In dn̄io. 111. car̄ 7 dim̄. 7 11. adhuc poſſ
fieri. Ibi. x11. uilłi hn̄t. v. car̄. Ibi. v1. borđ 7 x. ſerui.
p̄tū. 1111. car̄. Silua. cccc. porc̄. 7 1. aries. 7 1. ſūmā auenæ
de ſilua. Vał. v1. lib. Q̄do recep̄. 1111. lib. T.R.E. 1x. lib.
Hoc m̄. 1111. teigni tenuer̄. 7 cui uoluer̄ uende potuer̄.

In Eſſeltone tenet Erſaſtus *IN RATBORGESTOCHE HĐ.*
de Nigello. 1. hiđ. Tra. ē. 1. car̄. 7 ibi. ē car̄. p̄tū dim̄ car̄.
Silua. xL. porc̄. Ibi un̄ uilłs. 7 11. borđ. 7 1. ſeruus. Vał. xx. ſoł.

LAND OF NIGEL OF AUBIGNY

In MANSHEAD Hundred

1 M. In (Husborne) CRAWLEY Thorgils holds 5 hides from
Nigel of Aubigny as one manor. Land for 5 ploughs.
In lordship 2 ploughs. 3 villagers' ploughs possible.
1 villager, 7 smallholders and 1 slave.
Meadow for 5 ploughs.
In total value 30s; when acquired 40s; before 1066, 100s.
9 thanes held this manor; they could grant and sell their land
to whom they would.

2 In the same Hundred Thorgils holds 1 hide from Nigel.
Land for 1 plough; the plough is there.
2 slaves.
Woodland, 10 pigs.
Value of this land 15s; when acquired 10s; before 1066, 20s.
Fuglo, Alric son of Goding's man, held this land; he could sell
to whom he would.

3 M. Thorgils holds TINGRITH from Nigel. (It answers) for 2 hides and 1
virgate. Land for 3 ploughs. In lordship 1 plough.
4 villagers have 2 ploughs. 2 smallholders.
Meadow for 3 ploughs; woodland, 150 pigs.
Value 40s; when acquired 30s; before 1066, 100s.
2 thanes held this manor; they could sell to whom they would.

4 In PRIESTLEY Thorgils holds 1½ hides from Nigel. Land for 2
ploughs; they are there.
Meadow for 2 ploughs; woodland, 40 pigs.
1 villager and 4 smallholders.
Value 20s; as much when acquired; before 1066, 60s.
5 thanes held this land; they could grant and sell.

5 M. Nigel holds HARLINGTON. It answers for 5 hides. Land for 10
ploughs. In lordship 3½ ploughs; a further 2 possible.
12 villagers have 5 ploughs. 6 smallholders and 10 slaves.
Meadow for 4 ploughs; woodland, 400 pigs; 1 ram;
a pack-load of oats from the woodland.
Value £6; when acquired £4; before 1066 £9.
4 thanes held this manor; they could sell to whom they would.

In REDBORNSTOKE Hundred

6 In SHELTON Herfast holds 1 hide from Nigel. Land for 1 plough;
the plough is there.
Meadow for ½ plough; woodland, 40 pigs.
1 villager; 2 smallholders and 1 slave.

Q̃do recep̃.ꞌxv . ſot . T.R.E.ꞌxx . ſot . Hanc trā tenuit
Aluuard hō Alrici filij Godingi.7 cui uoluit dare potuit.
In ead̃ teñ Stefan de Nigello dim̃ hid̃ . Tra . ē dim̃ car̃.
7 ibi . ē . cū . ii . bord̃ . p̃tū . ii . bob . Silua . xii . porc̃.
Vat . vi . ſot . Q̃do recep̃.ꞌiii . ſot . T.R.E.ꞌx . ſot . Hanc trā
teñ Fuglo hō Alrici filij Godingi.7 uend̃e potuit.cui uoluit.
m̃) In Merſtone teñ Erfaſt de Nigello . viii . hid̃ 7 dim̃ uirg̃.
Tra . ē . x . car̃ . In dñio . iii . car̃.7 xiiii . uitti cū . viii . car̃.
Ibi . ii . bord̃.7 iiii . ſerui . p̃tū . viii . car̃ . Silua . ccc . porc̃.
Vat . vii . lib . Q̃do recep̃.ꞌc . ſot . T.R.E.ꞌxii . lib . Hoc m̃)
xxi . ſochi tenuer̃.q̃ uend̃e 7 dare potuer̃ tras ſuas cui
m̃) Nigellus de Waſt teñ de Nigello albinienſi ꝭ uoluer̃.
Melebroc . p̃ v . hid̃ ſe defd̃ . Tra . ē . vi . car̃ . In dñio . ii . car̃.
7 iiii . uitti cū . iiii . car̃ . Ibi . ii . bord̃.7 ii . molini de . vi . ſot.
P̃tū . ii . car̃ . Silua . c . porc̃ . Vat . iii . lib . Q̃do recep̃.ꞌ
xxx . ſot . T.R.E.ꞌc . ſot . Hoc m̃) teñ Goduin fili Leuuini.
qui om̃s potuer̃ dare t̃ uend̃e trā ſuā cui uolueruñ.
m̃) Ipſe Nigellus teñ de Nigello albñ AMMETELLE . p̃ . v . hid̃
ſe defd̃ . Tra . ē . viii . car̃ . In dñio . ii . car̃.7 vi . uitti hñt
iiii . car̃.7 adhuc.ii.car̃ poſ fieri.Ibi.ii.bord̃.7 i.ſeruus.
p̃tū.vi.car̃.Silua.ccc.porc̃.Vat.iiii.lib.Q̃do recep̃.ꞌ
xl.ſot.T.R.E.ꞌniii.lib.Hoc m̃) tenuer̃.vii.ſochi.7 cui
uoluer̃ trā ſuā uend̃e 7 dare potuer̃.

Id.Ni.ten de Ni. BRVME.
p̃.v.hid̃ ſe defd̃.Tra.ē.v.car̃.
7 tot iſ ibi cū.ix.uitiis 7 v.bord̃
Silua.xxx.porc̃.Vat.xl.ſot
Septē ſochi tenuer̃.7 dare
7 uende potuer̃.

Value 20s; when acquired 15s; before 1066, 20s.
   Alfward, Alric son of Goding's man, held this land; he could grant to whom he would.

7   In the same village Stephen holds ½ hide from Nigel.
Land for ½ plough; it is there, with
   2 smallholders.
   Meadow for 2 oxen; woodland, 12 pigs.
Value 6s; when acquired 3s; before 1066, 10s.
   Fuglo, Alric son of Goding's man, held this land; he could sell to whom he would.

8 M. In MARSTON (Moretaine) Herfast holds 8 hides and ½ virgate from Nigel. Land for 10 ploughs. In lordship 3 ploughs;
   14 villagers with 8 ploughs. 2 smallholders and 4 slaves.
   Meadow for 8 ploughs; woodland, 300 pigs.
Value £7; when acquired 100s; before 1066, £12.
   21 Freemen held this manor; they could sell and grant their lands to whom they would.

9 M. Nigel of Le Vast holds MILLBROOK from Nigel of Aubigny. It answers for 5 hides. Land for 6 ploughs. In lordship 2 ploughs;
   4 villagers with 4 ploughs. 2 smallholders.
   2 mills at 6s; meadow for 2 ploughs; woodland, 100 pigs.
Value £3; when acquired 30s; before 1066, 100s.
   Godwin son of Leofwin held this manor; . . . they could all grant or sell their land to whom they would.

10 M. Nigel of Le Vast holds AMPTHILL himself from Nigel of Aubigny.
   It answers for 5 hides. Land for 8 ploughs. In lordship 2 ploughs.
   6 villagers have 4 ploughs; a further 2 ploughs possible.
    2 smallholders and 1 slave.
   Meadow for 6 ploughs; woodland, 300 pigs.
Value £4; when acquired 40s; before 1066 £4.
   7 Freemen held this manor; they could sell and grant their land to whom they would.

   [In WIXAMTREE Hundred]
11   Nigel also holds BROOM from Nigel. It answers for 5 hides. Land for 5 ploughs; as many there, with
   9 villagers and 5 smallholders.
   Woodland, 30 pigs.
Value 40s.
   7 Freeman held it; they could grant and sell.

In Meldone Johes de Roches occupauit injuſte xxv . acs.
ſup hões qui uillā teneȷ̃ . ut hões de hund atteſtant.

7 m̃ h̃t Nigellus de albinie

ⓂNIGELL⁹ Albinienſis ten⁷ Weſcote . p . ɪɪɪ . hid una uirga min⁹
ſe defd . Tra . ē . vɪ . car⁷ . Ibi ſunt . v . 7 vɪᵗᵃ . poteſt fieri . Ibi
v . uilli 7 xɪ . bord . P̊tu . ɪɪ . car⁷ . Silua . c . porc⁷ . 7 ferrũ
car⁷ . Val . ʟx . ſol . Q̲do recep̃ ́ xʟ . ſol . T . R . ́ vɪ . lib . Hoc Ⓜ
tenuer⁷ . vɪɪ . ſochi . 7 cui uoluer⁷ trā ſuā dare 7 uende potuer⁷.

ⓂIpſe Nigell⁹ ten⁷ Clopelle . p . v . hid IN FLICTHĀ HVNẒ.
ſe defd . Tra . ē . vɪɪɪ . car⁷ . In dñio . ɪɪɪ . hidæ . 7 ibi ſuȷ̃ . ɪɪ . car⁷.
7 v . uilli hñt . vɪ . car⁷ . Ibi . v . bord . 7 un⁹ ſeruus . p̊tu.
ɪɪɪɪ . car⁷ . Silua . cc . porc⁷ . 7 xɪɪ . den . Val . ʟx . ſol . Q̲do
recep̃ ́ xxx . ſol . T . R . E . ́ vɪɪɪ . lib . Hoc Ⓜ . ɪɪ . teigni tenuer⁷.
Hões Toſti comitis . De his . v . hid clam Nigell ipſe . ɪ . uirg⁷
q̇ tenuit Anteceſſor ej⁹ T . R . E . Ipſe Nigell⁹ inde ſaiſit fuit
poſtq̇ ad honorē uenit . ſed Radulf⁹ tallgeboſc eũ deſaiſiuit.

 ⓂIpſe Nigell⁹ ten⁷ Chainehou . p ɪɪɪɪᵒʳ . hid ſe defd . Tra . ē . vɪ . car⁷.
Ibi . ɪɪ . hidæ 7 ɪɪɪ . uirg⁷ in dñio . 7 ɪɪ . car⁷ . 7 aliæ . ɪɪ . poſs fieri.
Ibi . ɪɪɪ . uilli hñt . ɪɪ . car . 7 ɪ . molin de . vɪ . ſol . p̊tu . vɪɪɪ . car.
Silua . c . porc⁷ . 7 ɪɪ . ſol . Ibi . ɪɪɪ . bord . 7 v . ſerui . Val . ʟx . ſol.
Q̲do recep̃ ́ xxx . ſol . T . R . E . ́ c . ſol . Hoc Ⓜ tenuit Aluric⁹
teign⁹ . R . E . 7 potuit dare 7 uende abſq̇ licentia ejus.

ⓂIn Siuuileſſou . ten⁷ quædā c̃cubina Nigelli . ɪɪ . hid . Tra . ē
ɪɪɪɪ . car⁷ . In dñio ; ɪ . car⁷ . 7 ɪɪ . uilli hñt . ɪɪ . car⁷ . 7 tcia poteſt fieri.
Ibi . ɪɪɪ . bord . 7 ɪ . ſeruus . p̊tu . ɪɪɪ . car⁷ . Silua . ʟ . porc⁷ . Valet
xxx . ſol . 7 tntd q̇do recep̃ . 7 tntd T . R . E . Hanc trā tenuit
Aluric⁹ paruus teign⁹ regis . E.

ⓂRoger 7 Ruallon ten⁷ Nigell de albin ten⁷ POLOCHESSELE.
p . x . hid ſe defd . Tra . ē . xɪɪɪ . car . In dñio . ɪɪ . car⁷ . 7 aliæ . ɪɪ.ᵉ

[In REDBORNSTOKE Hundred]

2   In MAULDEN John of Les Roches appropriated 25 acres wrongfully from the men who hold the village, as the men of the Hundred testify. Now Nigel of Aubigny has them.

13   M. Nigel of Aubigny holds 'WESTCOTTS'. It answers for 3 hides less 1 virgate. Land for 6 ploughs. 5 there; a sixth possible.
     5 villagers and 11 smallholders.
     Meadow for 2 ploughs; woodland, 100 pigs and plough iron.
     Value 60s; when acquired 40s; before 1066 £6.
     7 Freemen held this manor; they could grant and sell their land to whom they would.

In FLITT Hundred

14   M. Nigel holds CLOPHILL himself. It answers for 5 hides. Land for 8 ploughs. In lordship 3 hides. 2 ploughs there.
     5 villagers have 6 ploughs. 5 smallholders and 1 slave.
     Meadow for 4 ploughs; woodland, 200 pigs and 12d.
     Value 60s; when acquired 30s; before 1066 £8.
     2 thanes held this manor; they were Earl Tosti's men.
     Of these 5 hides, Nigel claims 1 virgate himself which his predecessor held before 1066. Nigel was put in possession himself after he came to the Honour, but Ralph Tallboys dispossessed him.

15   M. Nigel holds CAINHOE himself. It answers for 4 hides. Land for 6 ploughs. In lordship 2 hides and 3 virgates; 2 ploughs there; another 2 possible.
     3 villagers have 2 ploughs.
     1 mill at 6s; meadow for 8 ploughs; woodland, 100 pigs and 2s too.
     3 smallholders and 5 slaves.
     Value 60s; when acquired 30s; before 1066, 100s.
     Aelfric, a thane of King Edward's, held this manor; he could grant and sell without his permission.

16   M. In SILSOE a concubine of Nigel's holds 2 hides.
     Land for 4 ploughs. In lordship 1 plough.
     2 villagers have 2 ploughs; a third possible. 3 smallholders and 1 slave.
     Meadow for 3 ploughs; woodland, 50 pigs.
     Value 30s; as much when acquired; as much before 1066.
     Aelfric Small, a thane of King Edward's, held this land.

17   M. Roger and Rhiwallon hold PULLOXHILL from Nigel of Aubigny.
     It answers for 10 hides. Land for 13 ploughs. In lordship 2 ploughs; another 2 possible.

poſs fieri.7 xi . uitti hn̄t . ix . car̄ . Ibi . xiii . borđ .7 ii .ſerui.

p̄tū . vi . car̄ . Silua . c . porc̄ . Val . x . lib̄ . Q̄do recep̄: viii . lib̄,

214 c

T.R.E: xiii . lib̄ . Hoc M̄ tenuer̄ . viii . ſochi . 7 potuer̄

dare 7 uendē trā ſuā cui uoluer̄.

M̄ In Stradli . ten Pirot de Nigello . iiii . hiđ .7 tciā

parte uni hidæ . p uno M̄ . Tra . ē . vi . car̄ . In dn̄io

.ii . car̄ .7 iiii . uitti hn̄t . i . car̄ .7 adhuc . iii . poſs fieri,

Ibi . iiii . borđ 7 un ſeruus . P̄tū . iii . car̄ . Silua . xx .

porc̄ . Ibi q̄dā . i . car̄ h̄t . Val . iiii . lib̄ . Q̄do recep̄:

xl . ſot . T.R.E: vi . lib̄ . Hoc M̄ tenuit Leuuin .7 alij

tres teigni regis . E .7 cui uoluer̄ trā ſuā uendē potuer̄.

De iſta tra ten Pirot . iii . hiđ de maritagio ſuæ femi

næ .7 unā hiđ 7 tciā parte uni hiđ ten in feudū de

Nigello albinienſi.

In Mildentone ten Turgiſus de Nigello . iii . hiđ . una

uirg min . Tra . ē . iiii . car̄ , In dn̄io . i . car̄ .7 iiii . uitti

ii . car̄ 7 dim .7 dim car̄ uitt .7 iii . borđ . p̄tū . iii . car̄ .

Val xxx; ſot .7 tntđ q̄đo recep̄ . T.R.E: xl . ſot.

Hanc trā tenuer̄ . vi . ſochi .7 potuer̄ dare t̄ uendē

trā ſuā cui uoluer̄.   IN WILGE HVND.

In Carlentone ten Chetel de Nigello . i . hidā

7 tciā parte uni hiđ . Tra . ē . i . car̄ 7 dim .7 ibi ſunt.

7 iii . uitti .7 ii . borđ . P̄tū . i . car̄ 7 dim . Val xx .

ſot . Q̄do recep̄: x . ſot . T.R.E: xv . ſot . Hanc trā

tenuit Golderon h̄o Leuenot .7 pot dare cui uoluit.

In ead ten Bernard de Nigello . i . hiđ 7 dim uirg.

Tra . ē . i . car̄ 7 dim .7 ibi ſunt; 7 v . borđ . P̄tū . i . car̄ .

7 un molin xiii . ſolid .7 iiii . den . Val . xl . ſot . Q̄do

recep̄: xx . ſot . T.R.E: xxx . ſot . Hanc trā tenuer̄ . iii .

ſochi .7 cui uoluer̄ dare potuer̄.

214 b, c

11 villagers have 9 ploughs. 13 smallholders and 2 slaves.
Meadow for 6 ploughs; woodland, 100 pigs.
Value £10; when acquired £8; before 1066 £13.
8 Freemen held this manor; they could grant and sell their land
to whom they would.

18 M. In STREATLEY Pirot holds 4 hides and the third part of 1 hide from
Nigel of Aubigny, as one manor. Land for 6 ploughs. In lordship 2
ploughs.
4 villagers have 1 plough; a further 3 possible. 4 smallholders
   and 1 slave.
Meadow for 3 ploughs; woodland, 20 pigs.
Someone has 1 plough there.
Value £4; when acquired 40s; before 1066 £6.
Young Leofwin and 3 other thanes of King Edward's held this
manor; theycould sell their land to whom they would.
Pirot holds 3 hides of this land from his wife's marriage portion and
1 hide and the third part of 1 hide as a Holding from Nigel of Aubigny.

[In STODDEN Hundred]
19 In MILTON (Ernest) Thorgils holds 3 hides less 1 virgate from Nigel.
Land for 4 ploughs. In lordship 1 plough;
4 villagers, 2½ ploughs; ½ villagers' plough [possible];
   3 smallholders.
Meadow for 3 ploughs.
Value 30s; as much when acquired; before 1066, 40s.
6 Freemen held this land; they could grant or sell their land to
whom they would.

In WILLEY Hundred
20 In CARLTON Ketel holds 1 hide and the third part of 1 hide from Nigel.
Land for 1½ ploughs; they are there.
3 villagers and 2 smallholders.
Meadow for 1½ ploughs.
Value 20s; when acquired 10s; before 1066, 15s.
Golderon, Leofnoth's man, held this land; he could grant to whom
he would.

21 In the same (village) Bernard holds 1 hide and ½ virgate from Nigel.
Land for 1½ ploughs; they are there.
5 smallholders.
Meadow for 1 plough; 1 mill, 13s 4d.
Value 40s; when acquired 20s; before 1066, 30s.
3 Freemen held this land; they could grant to whom they would.

In Radeuuelle ten Nigell de Nigello . vii . hiđ . 7 unã

uirg 7 dim . Tra . ē . v . car . In dñio . i . 7 vi . uilti hñt

iiii . car . Ibi . vi . borđ . 7 iii . ſerui . 7 i . moliñ de . x . ſoł.

Ptũ . v . car . Vał . iiii . lib . 7 tñtđ qdo receƥ . T.R.E.

viii . lib . Hoc ᴔ tenueř . x . ſochi . 7 cui uolueř trã

ſuã dare potueř.

In Torneia ten Nigell de Nigello . i . hiđ 7 dim uirg.

Tra . ē . i . car 7 dim . 7 ibi ſunt . 7 v . borđ . Ptũ . i . car . Silua

xx . porc . Vał . xiii . ſoł . 7 tñtđ qdo receƥ . T.R.E. xxx . ſoł.

Hanc trã tenuit Aluuarđ hõ Wluui epi . 7 cui uoluit

dare potuit.   IN BEREFORDE HVNĐ.

In Wiboldeſtune ten Pirot . ix . hiđ 7 una uirg de rege.

de feudo Nigelli . Tra . ē . ix . car . In dñio . iiii . car . 7 xii.

uilti hñt . v . car . Ibi . vi . borđ . ptũ . ii . car . Vał . vi.

lib . Qdo receƥ . iiii . lib . T.R.E. x . lib . Hoc ᴔ . xii.

ſochi tenueř . 7 cui uolueř uende potueř.

Fulcherus pariſiacenſis IN BICHELESWADE HVNĐ.

ten dim hiđ de Nigello . Tra . ē . i . car . 7 ibi . ē . Ptũ . i . car.

7 un ſeru . Vał . lii . ſoł . Qdo receƥ . x . ſoł . T.R.E.

xxx . ſoł . Hanc trã ten Samar hõ Leuuini . 7 uende

In Holme ten ipſe Fulcher de Nigello ꝃ potuit.

unã hiđ 7 dim uirg . Tra . ē . ii . car . 7 ibi ſunt . 7 iii.

uilti . Ptũ . i . car . Vał . xx . ſoł . Qdo receƥ . x . ſoł . T.R.E.

xxx . ſoł . Hanc trã . vii . ſochi tenueř . 7 uende 7 dare potř.

In Herghetone ten Nigell IN WICHESTANESTOV HVNĐ.

vi . hiđ . Tra . ē . viii . car . In dñio . i . hiđ 7 dim . 7 dim

uirg . 7 ibi . ē . i . car . 7 xiiii . uilti hñt . vii . car . Ibi . x . borđ.

214 d

7 ii . ſerui . Ptũ . ii . car . Silua . l . porc . Int tot uał . c . ſoł.

Qdo receƥ . iiii . lib . T.R.E. c . ſoł . Hoc ᴔ . xiiii . ſochi

tenueř . 7 cui uolueř trã ſuã dare 7 uende potueř.

22 In RADWELL Nigel of Le Vast holds 7 hides and 1½ virgates from Nigel
of Aubigny. Land for 5 ploughs. In lordship 1.
6 villagers have 4 ploughs. 6 smallholders and 3 slaves.
1 mill at 10s; meadow for 5 ploughs.
Value £4; as much when acquired; before 1066 £8.
10 Freemen held this manor; they could grant their land to whom
they would.

23 In TURVEY Nigel of Le Vast holds 1 hide and ½ virgate from Nigel of
Aubigny. Land for 1½ ploughs; they are there.
5 smallholders.
Meadow for 1 plough; woodland, 20 pigs.
Value 13s; as much when acquired; before 1066, 30s.
Alfward, Bishop Wulfwy's man, held this land; he could grant to
to whom he would.

In BARFORD Hundred
24 In WYBOSTON Pirot holds 9 hides and 1 virgate from the King, from
Nigel's Holding. Land for 9 ploughs. In lordship 4 ploughs.
12 villagers have 5 ploughs. 6 smallholders.
Meadow for 2 ploughs.
Value £6; when acquired £4; before 1066 £10.
12 Freemen held this manor; they could sell to whom they would.

In BIGGLESWADE Hundred
25 Fulchere of Paris holds ½ hide from Nigel. Land for 1 plough;
it is there.
Meadow for 1 plough. 1 slave.
Value 52s; when acquired 10s; before 1066, 30s.
Saemer, Leofwin's man, held this land; he could sell.

26 In HOLME Fulchere holds 1 hide and ½ virgate himself from Nigel.
Land for 2 ploughs; they are there.
3 villagers.
Meadow for 1 plough.
Value 20s; when acquired 10s; before 1066, 30s.
7 Freemen held this land; they could sell and grant.

In WIXAMTREE Hundred
27 In HARROWDEN Nigel holds 6 hides. Land for 8 ploughs. In lordship 1½
hides and ½ virgate; 1 plough there.
14 villagers have 7 ploughs. 10 smallholders and 2 slaves.   214 d
Meadow for 2 ploughs; woodland, 50 pigs.
In total, value 100s; when acquired £4; before 1066, 100s.
14 Freemen held this manor; they could grant and sell their land to
whom they would.

In Cliſtone ten Wilłs de caron IN CLISTON HVND.

ii . hid de Nigello. Tra . e . i . car 7 dim . Ibi . e una car.

7 dim poteſt fieri. Ptu . i . car . Vał . xv . ſoł. Qdo recep:

x . ſoł. T.R.E: xx . ſoł. Hanc trā . iiii . ſochi tenuer.

7 dare 7 uende potuer.

In Haneſlau ten Erfaſt de Nigello . v . hid 7 dim.

Tra . e . v . car 7 dim . In dnīo . ii . car. 7 x . uiłłi hnt

iii . car 7 dim . Ibi . iii . ſerui. 7 i . molin de . v . ſoł. ptu

v . car . De paſtura . x . den. Int tot uał . c|.x . ſoł.

Qdo recep: iiii . lib. T.R.E: vii . lib. Hanc trā . ix . ſochi

tenuer. 7 cui uoluer dare 7 uende potuer.

De his . v . hid 7 dimida: tenet m̃ S Nicolai Ande

gauenſis. iii . uirg de Nigello in elemoſina.

In Alriceſeia . ten Erfaſt de Nigello . iii . uirg 7 tciā

parte uni uirg. Tra . e . i . car. 7 ibi . e . Ptu . i . car.

Vał . xvii . ſoł. 7 tntd qdo recep. T.R.E: xx . ſoł. Hanc

trā . ii . ſochi tenuer. 7 cui uoluer uende potuer.

.XXV.   TERRA WILLI SPECH. IN MANESHEVE HVND.

M̃ Wilłs SPECH ten in holecote. iiii . hid ꝑ uno M̃.

7 Radulf paſſaq de eo. Tra . e . iii . car . In dnīo . i.

car. 7 v . uiłłi hnt. ii . car. Ibi . viii . bord 7 un ſeru. 7 un

molin. v . ſolid 7 iiii . den . Silua . l . porc . Int tot uał

lx . ſoł. Qdo recep: xx . ſoł. T.R.E: xl . ſoł . Hoc M̃ tenuit

Aluuard belrap hō Alrici. 7 cui uoluit uende potuit.

H̃ tra e de excābio de Totingedone q excābiauit.

Wilłs fili Rainaldi tenet   IN RATBERNESTOCHE HVND.

de Wiłło ſpech Stepigelai. ꝑ . v . hid ſe defd . Tra . e

vii . car. In dnīo . i . car 7 dim. 7 xiiii . uiłłi hnt. v . car

7 dim. 7 ii . ſerui. Ptu . vii . car . Silua . c . porc. Int totu

In CLIFTON Hundred

8 In CLIFTON William of Cairon holds 2 hides from Nigel.
Land for 1½ ploughs. 1 plough there; ½ possible.
　Meadow for 1 plough.
Value 15s; when acquired 10s; before 1066, 20s.
　4 Freemen held this land; they could grant and sell.

9 In HENLOW Herfast holds 5½ hides from Nigel. Land for 5½ ploughs.
In lordship 2 ploughs.
　10 villagers have 3½ ploughs. 3 slaves;
　1 mill at 5s; meadow for 5 ploughs; from pasture 10d.
In total, value 110s; when acquired £4; before 1066 £7.
　9 Freemen held this land; they could grant and sell to whom
they would.
　Of these 5½ hides [the monks of] St. Nicholas of Angers now
hold 3 virgates from Nigel in alms.

0 In ARLESEY Herfast holds 3 virgates and the third part of 1 virgate
from Nigel. Land for 1 plough; it is there.
　Meadow for 1 plough.
Value 17s; as much when acquired; before 1066, 20s.
　2 Freemen held this land; they could sell to whom they would.

5   **LAND OF WILLIAM SPEKE**

In MANSHEAD Hundred

1 M. William Speke holds 4 hides in HOLCOT as one manor and Ralph
Passwater from him. Land for 3 ploughs. In lordship 1 plough.
　5 villagers have 2 ploughs. 8 smallholders and 1 slave.
　A mill, 5s 4d; woodland, 50 pigs.
In total, value 60s; when acquired 20s; before 1066, 40s.
　Alfward Bellrope, Alric's man, held this manor; he could sell
to whom he would.
　This land is in exchange for Toddington which he gave in exchange.

In REDBORNSTOKE Hundred

2 William son of Reginald holds STEPPINGLEY from William Speke.
It answers for 5 hides. Land for 7 ploughs. In lordship 1½ ploughs.
　14 villagers have 5½ ploughs. 2 slaves.
　Meadow for 7 ploughs; woodland, 100 pigs.

uał . iiii . liɓ . Q̣do recep̃꞉ xl . fot . T.R.E꞉ viii . liɓ . Hoc ꟽ

tenuit Almaꞅ hō Alurici de Fliƈteuuite . 7 ibi fueꞅ

.ii . ſochi hōes ej̃ . qui potueꞅ trã ſuã uendẽ cui uolueꞅ.

In Stradlei teñ Hugo de Wiłło *IN FLICTHÃ HVND.*

ii . part̃ . i . uirg̃ . Tra . ē . ii . boɓ . Vał 7 ualuit sẽp . ii . fot.

Hanc trã tenuit Aluric̃ hō Alurici parui . 7 potuit

uendẽ cui uoluit.

ꟽ In Bidehã teñ Radulf̃ 7 Serlo de Ros de Wiłło

iiii . hiđ . una uirg̃ 7 dim̃ miñ . Tra . ē . iiii . caꞅ . In dñio

.ii . caꞅ . 7 vi . uiłłi hñt . ii . caꞅ . Ibi . ii . borđ . 7 ii . ſerui.

7 uñ moliñ . x . fot . Ṗtũ . iiii . caꞅ . Vał . xl . fot . Q̣do

recep̃꞉ xx . fot . T.R.E꞉ xl . fot . Hoc ꟽ tenueꞅ . xi . ſochi.

7 cui uolueꞅ trã ſuã dare 7 uendẽ potueꞅ . Hanc trã

dic̃ Wiłłs ſe habẽ p excãbio de Totingedone.

In Heneuuic . teñ Walter de Wiłło *IN WILGE HVND.*

i . hiđ . Tra . ē . ii . caꞅ . Ibi . ē dim̃ caꞅ . 7 altera c̃ 7 dim̃

poteſt fieri . Vał . x . fot . 7 tñtđ qḍo recep̃ . T.R.E꞉ xx . fot..

Hanc trã tenuit Vlnod hō Vlſi filij Borgret . 7 cui

uoluit dare potuit.

In Wimentone teñ Walteꞅ de Wiłło . iii . uirg̃.

215 a

Tra . ē dim̃ caꞅ . Vał . ii . fot . Q̣do recep̃꞉ x . fot . T.R.E꞉

x . fot . Hanc trã tenuit Leuric̃ hō Borgred . 7 cui uoluit

dare potuit.   *IN BEREFORDE HVND.*

In Chaueleſtorne teñ Wiłłs fili Raineuuardi . de Wiłło

vii . hiđ 7 i . uirg̃ . Tra . ē . vii . caꞅ . In dñio . i . caꞅ . 7 xvi.

uiłłi hñt . vi . caꞅ . Ibi . ii . borđ . 7 i . feru̅ . 7 i . moliñ

de . xiii . fot . 7 iiii . den̄ . p̃tũ . vii . caꞅ . Silua x . porc̃.

Int tot uał . vi . liɓ . Q̣do recep̃꞉ iiii . liɓ . T.R.E꞉ ix . liɓ.

Hanc trã . xii . fochi tenueꞅ . 7 uendẽ potueꞅ cui uolueꞅ.

In total, value £4; when acquired 40s; before 1066 £8.
Aelmer, Aelfric of Flitwick's man, held this manor.
There were 2 Freemen there, his men, who could sell their land
to whom they would.

In FLITT Hundred

3 In STREATLEY Hugh holds two parts of 1 virgate from William.
Land for 2 oxen.
The value is and always was 2s.
Aelfric, Aelfric Small's man, held this land; he could sell to
whom he would.

[In BUCKLOW Hundred]

4 M. In BIDDENHAM Ralph and Serlo of Rots hold 4 hides less 1½ virgates
from William. Land for 4 ploughs. In lordship 2 ploughs.
6 villagers have 2 ploughs. 2 smallholders and 2 slaves.
A mill, 10s; meadow for 4 ploughs.
Value 40s; when acquired 20s; before 1066, 40s.
11 Freemen held this manor; they could grant and sell their land
to whom they would.
William says that he has this land in exchange for Toddington.

In WILLEY Hundred

5 In HINWICK Walter holds 1 hide from William. Land for 2 ploughs;
½ plough there; another 1½ ploughs possible.
Value 10s; as much when acquired; before 1066, 20s.
Wulfnoth, Wulfsi son of Burgred's man, held this land;
he could grant to whom he would.

6 In WYMINGTON Walter holds 3 virgates from William.
Land for ½ plough.   215 a
Value 2s; when acquired 10s; before 1066, 10s.
Leofric, Burgred's man, held this land; he could grant to whom
he would.

In BARFORD Hundred

7 In CHAWSTON William son of Rainward holds 7 hides and 1 virgate
from William. Land for 7 ploughs. In lordship 1 plough.
16 villagers have 6 ploughs. 2 smallholders and 1 slave.
1 mill at 13s 4d; meadow for 7 ploughs; woodland, 10 pigs.
In total, value £6; when acquired £4; before 1066 £9.
12 Freemen held this land; they could sell to whom they would.

De his. vii. hid 7 una uirg. reclam hões Witti spec
.i. acrā p̄ti 7 dim. sup hões Eudonis dapif. 7 hund
testat q̄d ej antecessor habuit. T.R.E. 7 alias. vii.
acs træ reclamat isdē Witts sup quendā hoēm
Hugonis de belcāp. unde ipse desaisit. s̃ antecessor
ej fuit saisitus. De p̄dicta tra reclamat Eudo dapif.
.i. acrā. sup Ruallon hoēm Hugonis de belcamp.

In ead ten Witts gros. dim hid de Witto spec. Tra. ē
dim car. 7 ibi. ē. p̄tū dim car. Ibi. ii. uitti. Vat. v. sot.
Q̄do recep̄. v. sot. T.R.E. x. sot. Hanc trā tenuer. ii.
hões regis. E. 7 cui uoluer uendē potuer.

Ɱ In ROCHESDONE ten Witts spec. viii. hid. 7 iii. uirg.
Tra. ē. viii. car. In dn̄io. iiii. hide 7 iii. uirg. 7 ibi sunt
ii. car. 7 xii. uitti hn̄t. vi. car. Ibi. i. bord. 7 i. seru. 7 un
molin de xxxiii. sot 7 cclx. anguitt. P̄tū. iii. car. Silua
xx. porc. Vat. vii. lib. Q̄do recep̄. l. sot. T.R.E. x. lib.
Hoc Ɱ xii. sochi tenuer. 7 cui uoluer trā suā uendē potuer.

Ɱ In Aisseuuorde tenet   IN BICHELESWADE HVND.
Witts spec. ix. hid p uno Ɱ. Tra. ē. ix. car. In dn̄io. v.
hidæ 7 dimidia. 7 ibi sunt. iii. car. 7 xiii. uitti hn̄t
vi. car. Ibi. ii. bord 7 vi. serui. 7 i. molin de. viii. sot.
p̄tū. ix. car. Vat vii. lib. Q̄do recep̄. similit. T.R.E.
viii. lib. Hoc Ɱ tenuer. xx. sochi. 7 trā suā cui uo
luer dare t uendē potuer. sine licentia dn̄oᵹ suoᵹ.

Ɱ In Sudgiuele teneᵹ IN WICHENESTANESTOV HD.
.ii. franc de Witto spech. v. hid 7 dim uirg. Tra. ē
vii. car. In dn̄io. iiii. car. 7 viii. uitti hn̄t. iii. car.
Ibi. viii. bord. 7 vi. serui. p̄tū. vii. car. Silua. cc.
porc. Vat iiii. lib 7 x. sot. Q̄do recep̄. iiii. lib. T.R.E.
iii. lib. Hoc Ɱ tenuer. xvi. sochi. 7 trā suā cui uo
luer dare 7 uendē potuer.

Of these 7 hides and 1 virgate William Speke's men claim 1½ acres of meadow from Eudo the Steward's men; the Hundred testifies that his predecessor had them before 1066. William also claims another 7 acres of land against a man of Hugh of Beauchamp by whom he was dispossessed; but his predecessor was put in possession. Eudo the Steward claims 1 acre of the said land against Rhiwallon, Hugh of Beauchamp's man.

8   In the same (village) William Gross holds ½ hide from William Speke. Land for ½ plough; it is there.
    Meadow for ½ plough.
    2 villagers.
    Value 5s; when acquired 5s; before 1066, 10s.
    2 of King Edward's men held this land; they could sell to whom they would.

9   M. In ROXTON William Speke holds 8 hides and 3 virgates. Land for 8 ploughs. In lordship 4 hides and 3 virgates; 2 ploughs there.
    12 villagers have 6 ploughs. 1 smallholder and 1 slave.
    A mill at 33s and 260 eels; meadow for 3 ploughs;
      woodland, 20 pigs.
    Value £7; when acquired 50s; before 1066 £10.
    12 Freemen held this manor; they could sell their land to whom they would.

In BIGGLESWADE Hundred
10   M. In EYEWORTH William Speke holds 9 hides as one manor. Land for 9 ploughs. In lordship 5½ hides. 3 ploughs there.
    13 villagers have 6 ploughs. 2 smallholders and 6 slaves.
    1 mill at 8s; meadow for 9 ploughs.
    Value £7; when acquired the same; before 1066 £8.
    20 Freemen held this manor; they could grant or sell their land to whom they would without their lords' permission.

In WIXAMTREE Hundred
11   M. In SOUTHILL 2 Frenchmen hold 5 hides and ½ virgate from William Speke. Land for 7 ploughs. In lordship 4 ploughs.
    8 villagers have 3 ploughs. 8 smallholders and 6 slaves.
    Meadow for 7 ploughs; woodland, 200 pigs.
    Value £4 10s; when acquired £4; before 1066 £3.
    16 Freemen held this manor; they could grant and sell their land to whom they would.

In Stanford. ten̄ Hugo de Witto ſpech . i . hid . Tra . ē

.i . car.7 ibi eſt.7 dim̄ molin̄.v . ſolid.Ibi . ii . ſerui.

p̊tū . i . car̄ . Silua . xx . porc̄ . Val . xv . ſot . Q̊do recep̊:

xx . ſot.7 tn̄td̄ . T.R.E . Hanc tr̄a tenuit Lemar teign̄

M̄ In Wardone ten̄ Witts ſpec . ix . hid de rege . ∫ R.E.

p uno m̄ . Tra . ē . ix . car̄ . In dn̄io . iii . hid 7 dimid̄.7 ibi.ē

una car̄.7 altera poteſt fieri . Ibi xviii . uitti hn̄t

vii . car̄.Ibi . iiii . bord̄.7 iiii . ſerui.7 i . molin̄ . xii . ſot.

P̊tū . vi . car̄ . Val . vi . lib̄.7 tn̄td̄ q̊do recep̄ . T.R.E:

viii . lib̄ . Hoc m̄ tenuer̄ . viii . ſocħi.7 tr̄a ſuā cui

uoluer̄ dare potuer̄.

In Biſtone ten̄ Witts ſpech . iii . uirḡ 7 dim̄ . Tra . ē . i . car̄.

Ibi.ē dim̄ car̄.7 dim̄ poteſt fieri . p̊tū dim̄ car̄ . Val

.x . ſot.7 tn̄td̄ q̊do recep̄ . T.R.E: xx . ſot . Hanc tr̄a

215 b

tenuit Leuuin̄ teign̄ regis.

In Nortgiuete ten̄ Witts ſpec . vi . hid 7 dim̄ p uno m̄.

Tra . ē . vii . car̄ . In dn̄io . iiii . hid.7 ibi ſunt . iii . car̄.7 x . uitti

hn̄t . iiii . car̄ . Ibi . iiii . ſerui.7 dim̄ molin̄ de . xiii . ſolid.

p̊tū . vii . car̄ . Silua . cc . porc̄ . Int totū ual . vi . lib̄.

7 tn̄td̄ q̊do recep̄ . T.R.E viii . lib̄ . Hoc m̄ tenuer̄ . vi . ſocħi.

potuer̄ dare 7 uende cui uoluer̄ . T.R.E.

.XXVI. R TERRA ROBERTI DE TODENI. IN STANBVRGE HD.

M̄ Rotbert de Todeni de rege . ten̄ Eſtodhā.7 Baldric

de Robto . p vi . hid ſe defd̄ . Tra . ē . vi . car̄ . In dn̄io . ii . car̄.

7 x . uitti hn̄t . iiii . car̄ . Ibi un bord̄.7 iiii . ſerui . Silua

c . porc̄ . Val . iiii . lib̄ . Q̊do recep̊: xl . ſot . T.R.E: viii . lib̄.

Hoc m̄ tenuit Oſulf fili̊ Frane . teign̄ regis . E.

In Achelei tenent . ii . milites de Robto . iiii . hid . Tra . ē

viii . car̄ . In dn̄io . iii . car̄.7 iiii . poteſt . ee . Ibi . vii . uitti

12 In STANFORD Hugh holds 1 hide from William Speke. Land for 1 plough; it is there.
 ½ mill, 5s. 2 slaves; meadow for 1 plough; woodland, 20 pigs.
 Value 15s; when acquired 20s; as much before 1066.
 Leofmer, a thane of King Edward's, held this land.

13 M. In (Old) WARDEN William Speke holds 9 hides from the King as one manor. Land for 9 ploughs. In lordship 3½ hides; 1 plough there; a second possible.
 18 villagers have 7 ploughs. 4 smallholders and 4 slaves.
 1 mill, 12s; meadow for 6 ploughs.
 Value £6; as much when acquired; before 1066 £8.
 8 Freemen held this manor; they could grant their land to whom they would.

14 In BEESTON William Speke holds 3½ virgates. Land for 1 plough; ½ plough there; ½ possible.
 Meadow for ½ plough.
 Value 10s; as much when acquired; before 1066, 20s.   215 b
 Young Leofwin, a thane of the King's, held this land.

15 In NORTHILL William Speke holds 6½ hides as one manor.
 Land for 7 ploughs. In lordship 4 hides; 3 ploughs there.
 10 villagers have 4 ploughs.
 4 slaves; ½ mill at 13s; meadow for 7 ploughs; woodland, 200 pigs.
 In total, value £6; as much when acquired; before 1066 £8.
 6 Freemen held this manor; they could grant and sell to whom they would before 1066.

26   LAND OF ROBERT OF TOSNY

In STANBRIDGE Hundred

1 M. Robert of Tosny holds STUDHAM from the King and Baldric from Robert. It answers for 6 hides. Land for 6 ploughs. In lordship 2 ploughs.
 10 villagers have 4 ploughs. 1 smallholder and 4 slaves.
 Woodland, 100 pigs.
 Value £4; when acquired 40s; before 1066 £8.
 Oswulf son of Fran, a thane of King Edward's, held this manor.

[In STODDEN Hundred]

2 In OAKLEY 2 men-at-arms hold 4 hides from Robert. Land for 8 ploughs. In lordship 3 ploughs; a fourth possible.

hñt.IIII.car̄.7 III.borđ.7 v.ſerui.7 I.moliñ.xxvi.ſolid.

7 cc.Anguiłł.p̄tū.IIII.car̄.Vał.IIII.lib̄.Q̇do recep̄:ſimilit.

T.R.E:IIII.lib̄ 7 x.ſoł.Hanc tr̄a tenuit Oſulf teigñ.R.E.

In Toruei tenent.II.milites de Rob̄to IN WILGE HVND.

II.hiđ.7 I.uirg.Tra.ē.IIII.car̄ 7 dim̄.In dñio.II.car̄.

7 III.uiłłi hñt.II.car̄.7 dim̄ car̄ poteſt fieri.Ibi.vI.borđ.

7 II.ſerui.p̄tū.I.car̄.Silua.x.porc̄.Vał.xL.ſoł.Q̇do

recep̄:Lx.ſoł.T.R.E:Lxx.ſoł.Hanc tr̄a tenuit Oſulf p̄dict.

.XXVII TERRA GISLEB̄TI DE GAND. IN DIMID HVND de STANBVRGE.

GISLEBERT de gand ten Edingeberge.p.x.hiđ

ſe defđ.Tra.ē.vII.car̄.In dñio.v.hidæ.7 ibi ſuȷ̄ IIII.

car̄.7 x.uiłłi hñt.IIII.car̄.In totis ualentijs uał.c.ſoł.7 x.

Q̇do recep̄:ſimilit.T.R.E:x.lib̄.Hoc M̄ tenuit Vlf

teigñ.R.E.7 potuit inde facere qđ uoluit.

.XXVI. TERRA ROBERTI DE OILGI. IN WILGE HVND.

ROTBERT de Olgi.ten ȷn Lalega.7 Ricard baſſet de eo

dim̄ hiđ.Tra.ē.II.car̄.Vna m̄ ibi ē.7 alta poteſt fieri.

Ibi.I.uiłłs 7 III.borđ.7 II.ſerui.Silua.xxx.porc̄.Vał

7 ualuit ſēp.xL.ſoł.Hanc tr̄a tenuit Ouiet teigñ.R.E.

7 cui uoluit uende potuit.Hanc clamant hōes Eudonis

p̄ anteceſſorē dñi ſui.cuȷ tras om̄s W.rex ſibi donauit.

In eađ ten Salomon p̄br.I.uirg de Rob̄to de olgi.

Tra.ē.I.car̄.7 ibi eſt.cū uno borđ.Vał 7 ualuit ſēp.x.ſoł.

Hanc tr̄a Aluuiñ tenuit hō Wluui ep̄i.7 uende potuit.

7 villagers have 4 ploughs; 3 smallholders and 5 slaves.
1 mill, 26s and 200 eels; meadow for 4 ploughs.
Value £4; when acquired the same; before 1066 £4 10s.
Oswulf, a thane of King Edward's, held this land.

In WILLEY Hundred

3 In TURVEY 2 men-at-arms hold 2 hides and 1 virgate from Robert.
Land for 4½ ploughs. In lordship 2 ploughs.
   3 villagers have 2 ploughs; ½ plough possible. 6 smallholders
   and 2 slaves.
   Meadow for 1 plough; woodland, 10 pigs.
Value 40s; when acquired 60s; before 1066, 70s.
The said Oswulf held this land.

27   LAND OF GILBERT OF GHENT

In the Half-Hundred of STANBRIDGE

1 Gilbert of Ghent holds EDLESBOROUGH. It answers for 10 hides.
Land for 7 ploughs. In lordship 5 hides; 4 ploughs there.
   10 villagers have 4 ploughs.
Total value 100s 10[d]; when acquired the same; before 1066 £10.
   Ulf, a thane of King Edward's, held this manor; he could do
what he would with it.

28   LAND OF ROBERT D'OILLY

In WILLEY Hundred

1 Robert d'Oilly holds ½ hide in THURLEIGH and Richard Basset from him.
Land for 2 ploughs; 1 now there; a second possible.
   1 villager; 3 smallholders and 2 slaves.
   Woodland, 30 pigs.
The value is and always was 40s.
   Wulfgeat, a thane of King Edward's, held this land; he could sell to
whom he would.
   Eudo's men claim this land through their lord's predecessor, all of
whose lands King William bestowed upon him.

2 In the same (village) Solomon the priest holds 1 virgate from
Robert d'Oilly. Land for 1 plough; it is there, with
   1 smallholder.
The value is and always was 10s.
   Alwin, Bishop Wulfwy's man, held this land; he could sell.

.XXIX. TERRA RANN FR̄IS ILGERIJ. *IN DIM̄ HVND̄ DE BOCHELAI.*

RANNVLF fr̄ Ilgerij ten̄ . v . hid̄ in Pabenehā.7 Robt̄
filius Nigelli de eo . Tra.ē.vi.car̄.In dn̄io.i.car̄.7 alia
poteft fieri.7 ix.uilli hn̄t.ii.car̄.7 aliæ.ii.poffuṅ fieri.
Ibi . ii . bord̄.7 iii . ferui . P̄tū . vi . car̄ . Val . iii . lib̄ . Q̄do
recep̄:´iiii.lib̄ . T.R.E.´vi . lib̄ . Hoc m̄ tenuit Goduin̄
teign̄.R.E.De ifta tra reclamat Rannulf fr̄ Ilgerij
xii.ac̄s træ.fup Gislebtū filiū Salomonis.7 iiii.ac̄s p̄ti
fup Hug de Grentmaifnil.unde Rannulf defaifit eft
injufte.7 hōes de dimid̄ hund̄ dn̄t qd̄ ifta tra quā m̄
teneṅ Hugo 7 Gislebt̄.jacuit ad trā quā tenet Rannulf
fr̄ Ilgerij . T.R.E.

.XXX. TERRA ROBERTI FAFITON. *IN FLICTHĀ HVND̄.*

ROTBERTVS Fafiton ten̄ de rege *FLICTHA* . p̄ v . hid̄ fe defd̄.

215 c

Tra.ē.vi.car̄. In dn̄io . ii . hidæ.7 ibi fuṅ.ii . car̄.Ibi
iii.uilli hn̄t.ii . car̄.7 aliæ . ii . poffunt.ee . Ibi.iii.
bord̄ 7 iiii . ferui . P̄tū . vi . car̄ . Silua . l . porc̄ . Int̄
tot̄ ual.lx.fol.7 tntd̄ qdo recep̄ . T.R.E.´c . fol . Hoc
m̄ tenuit Aluin̄ horim teign̄ regis . E.

.XXXI. TERRA ALVREDI DE LINCOLIA *IN WILGE HVND̄.*

ALVERED̄ de Lincolia 7 Gleu de eo ten̄ in Wimen
tone.iii . hid̄ . Tra.ē.iiii ; car̄. In dn̄io . i . car̄ ;7 alia
poteft fieri.Ibi un uills 7 vi . bord̄.7 iii . ferui . cū . ii . car̄ ;
p̄tū . ii . car̄ ; Ual . xl ; fol . Q̄do recep̄:´l . fol . T.R.E.´
lx . fol . Hoc m̄ tenuit Goduin̄ Franpold ;7 uende
potuit.Cū his . iii ; hidis reclamat Aluered̄ fup Walt
flandr̄ dim̄ hid̄ . de qua injufte defaifiuit eū . ut
hōes de hund̄ inde portaṅ teftimon̄ . qm̄ Antecessor
ej ; T.R.E. inde faifit fuit.7 ifdē Aluered̄ poftea fuit

29   LAND OF RANULF BROTHER OF ILGER

In the Half-Hundred of BUCKLOW

Ranulf brother of Ilger holds 5 hides in PAVENHAM, and Robert son
of Nigel from him. Land for 6 ploughs. In lordship 1 plough;
another possible.
> 9 villagers have 2 ploughs; another 2 possible. 2 smallholders
> and 3 slaves.

Meadow for 6 ploughs.
Value £3; when acquired £4; before 1066 £6.
> Godwin, a thane of King Edward's, held this manor.

Of this land Ranulf brother of Ilger claims 12 acres of land against
Gilbert son of Solomon and 4 acres of meadow against Hugh of
Grandmesnil, of which Ranulf was wrongfully dispossessed; the men
of the Half-Hundred state that before 1066 this land, which Hugh and
Gilbert now hold, lay with the land which Ranulf brother of Ilger holds.

30   LAND OF ROBERT [SON OF] FAFITON

In FLITT Hundred

1   Robert Fafiton holds FLITTON from the King. It answers for 5 hides.
Land for 6 ploughs. In lordship 2 hides; 2 ploughs there.   215 c
> 3 villagers have 2 ploughs; another 2 possible. 3 smallholders
> and 4 slaves.

Meadow for 6 ploughs; woodland, 50 pigs.
In total, value 60s; as much when acquired; before 1066, 100s.
> Alwin Horn, a thane of King Edward's, held this manor.

31   LAND OF ALFRED OF LINCOLN

In WILLEY Hundred

1 M. Alfred of Lincoln holds 3 hides in WYMINGTON, and Glew from him.
Land for 4 ploughs. In lordship 1 plough; another possible.
> 1 villager, 6 smallholders and 3 slaves with 2 ploughs.

Meadow for 2 ploughs.
Value 40s; when acquired 50s; before 1066, 60s.
> Godwin Frambold held this manor; he could sell.

With these 3 hides Alfred claims ½ hide against Walter of Flanders,
of which he wrongfully dispossessed him, as the men of the Hundred
bear witness thereon, since his predecessor was possessed of it before
1066, and Alfred was possessed afterwards. Further, with this land

faifit. Cũ hac tra adhuc reclamat ifdẽ Aluered

fup ep̃m conſtantiensẽ filuã . c. quã habuit ſuus ante

ceſſor . T.R.E. ſed eps defaiſiuit eũ injuſte . ut hões

de hund teſtant.   ſ BVRGE.

XXXII. TERRA WALTERIJ FLANDRENS In dim hvnd de Stan

ⓂWALTERVS Flandrenſis 7 Osbt de eo teñ Totenehov

.p xv . hid ſe defd . T.R.E. Sed poſtq; rex . W. uenit

in Anglia . ñ ſe defd niſi .p. x . hid . 7 hões qui . v . hid

tenuer 7 tenent . oms cſuetudines regis 7 gabl reti

nuer 7 retinent . Tra . ẽ . x . car . In dñio . II . car . 7 xxiI.

uiħi hñt . IIII . car . 7 aliæ . IIII . poſs fieri . Ibi . II . bord

7 IIII . ſerui . Ibi . III . molini de . x . ſol 7 VIII . den . P̃tũ

IIII . car . Silua . CL . porc . Int tot ual VIII . lib . Q̃do

recep. x . lib . T.R.E. xvi . lib . Hoc Ⓜ tenuit Leuenot

teign regis . E. 7 cui uoluit uendẽ potuit.   ſ HVND.

In Mildentone teñ Rainald de Waltero In Stoden

II . hid . Tra . ẽ . III . car . In dñio . ẽ . I . car . 7 II . uiħi hñt

. I . car . 7 alia poteſt fieri . Ibi . I . bord . P̃tũ . II . car.

Val . xx . ſol . 7 tñtd q̃do recep . T . R . E. xxv . ſol . Hanc

tra tenuer . II . ſochi hões Brictric . 7 cui uoluer dare potr.

In Tornei teñ Hugo de Waltero In Wilge hvnd.

. I . hid . Tra . ẽ . II . car . In dñio una . ẽ . 7 VIII . bord 7 uñ

ſeru cũ . I . car . p̃tũ . I . car . Silua . xL . porc . Val . xxx .

ſol . Q̃do recep. x . ſol . T.R.E. xL . ſol . Hanc tram

tenuit Leuenot teign . R . E. 7 cui uoluit uendẽ potuit.

ⓂIn Wadehelle teñ Walter fland de rege . v . hid.

7 unã uirg . 7 II . partes uni uirg . Tra . ẽ . v . car . In dñio

II . hidæ . 7 ibi ſunt . II . car . 7 xiii . uiħi cũ . III . car . Ibi

v . bord . 7 v . ſerui . 7 I . molin de . xxxvi . ſol . 7 VIII . den.

7 cc . Anguiħ . p̃tũ . v . car . Silua . Lx . porc . Val . c . ſol.

215 c

Alfred also claims from the Bishop of Coutances woodland for
100 pigs, which his predecessor previously had before 1066, but the
Bishop wrongfully dispossessed him, as the men of the Hundred testify.

2   **LAND OF WALTER OF FLANDERS**

In the Half-Hundred of STANBRIDGE
M. Walter of Flanders holds TOTTERNHOE and Osbert from him. It
answered for 15 hides before 1066, but after King William came to
England it did not answer, except for 10 hides. The men who
held and hold the 5 hides kept and keep all the King's customary
dues and tribute. Land for 10 ploughs. In lordship 2 ploughs.
     22 villagers have 4 ploughs; another 4 possible.
     2 smallholders and 4 slaves.
     3 mills at 10s 8d; meadow for 4 ploughs; woodland, 150 pigs.
In total, value £8; when acquired £10; before 1066 £16.
     Leofnoth, a thane of King Edward's, held this manor; he could
sell to whom he would.

In STODDEN Hundred
2   In MILTON (Ernest) Reginald holds 2 hides from Walter. Land for 3
ploughs. In lordship 1 plough.
     2 villagers have 1 plough; another possible. 1 smallholder.
     Meadow for 2 ploughs.
Value 20s; as much when acquired; before 1066, 25s.
     2 Freemen, Brictric's men, held this land; they could grant
to whom they would.

In WILLEY Hundred
3   In TURVEY Hugh holds 1 hide from Walter. Land for 2 ploughs.
In lordship 1;
     8 smallholders and 1 slave with 1 plough.
     Meadow for 1 plough; woodland, 40 pigs.
Value 30s; when acquired 10s; before 1066, 40s.
     Leofnoth, a thane of King Edward's, held this land; he could
sell to whom he would.

4 M. In ODELL Walter of Flanders holds 5 hides, 1 virgate and 2 parts
of 1 virgate from the King. Land for 5 ploughs. In lordship 2 hides;
2 ploughs there;
     13 villagers with 3 ploughs. 5 smallholders and 5 slaves.
     1 mill at 36s 8d and 200 eels; meadow for 5 ploughs;
         woodland, 60 pigs.

Q̃do recep̃: viii . lib . T.R.E. x . lib . Hoc ᴍ̃ Leuenot te
nuit teign . R.E. 7 ibid un̄ focħs dim̄ hid̄ habuit . q̃ po
tuit dare cui uo!uit.

ᴍ̃ In Podintone ten̄ Hugo de Waltero . i . hid̄ 7 iiii . uirg.
Tra . ē . v . caŕ . 7 dim̄ . In dn̄io fuŋ . ii . caŕ . 7 iiii . uilli
hn̄t . iii . caŕ . 7 dim̄ . Ibi . ix . bord̄ 7 ii . ferui . p̃tū . i . caŕ .
Silua . xx . porc̄ . Val . iiii . lib̄ 7 x . fol . Q̃do recep̃: l . fol.
7 tn̄td̄ . T.R.E. Hoc ᴍ̃ tenuit Leuenot teign̄ regis . E.

215 d

ᴍ̃ In Wimentone ten̄ Osb̃t de Walterio . iiii . hid̄ ꝑ uno
ᴍ̃ . Tra . ē . v . caŕ . In dn̄io . iii . caŕ . 7 ibi un̄ uilts 7 viii .
bord̄ 7 iiii . ferui . cū . i . caŕ . p̃tū . ii . caŕ . Val . iii . lib̄ .
7 tn̄td̄ q̃do recep̃ . T.R.E. iiii . lib̄ . Hoc ᴍ̃ tenuit Lant
ħo Leuenot teigni regis . 7 ibi un̄ focħs . i . hida̅ habuit .
7 cui uoluit dare potuit.
In ead̄ uilla ten̄ iſd̄ Osb̃t de Walterio dim̄ hid̄ . Tra . ē
dim̄ caŕ . ſ̧ non . ē ibi . Val . ii . fol . Q̃do recep̃: iiii . fol.
T.R.E. x . fol . Hanc tra̅ tenuit Goduin̄ franpalt.
7 cui uoluit dare potuit . Hanc eand̄ reclamat Alured̄
Lincol fup Walteriū Flandrenſem.
In Lalega ten̄ Hugo de Walterio . iii . hid̄ ꝑ uno ᴍ̃
Tra . ē . vii . caŕ . In dn̄io . ii . caŕ . 7 viii . uilli hn̄t . v . caŕ .
Ibi . xii . bord̄ . 7 iii . ferui . Silua . cl . porc̄ . Val . c . fol.
Q̃do recep̃: lx . fol . T.R.E. iiii . lib̄ . Hoc ᴍ̃ tenuit
Leuenot teign̄ regis . E.
In ead̄ ten̄ Raẏnald̄ de Walterio dim̄ hid̄ . Tra . ē
ii . caŕ . In dn̄io . i . caŕ . 7 iiii . bord̄ cū . i . caŕ . Val . xx . fol.
Q̃do recep̃: x . fol . T.R.E. v . fol . Hanc tra̅ tenuit
Ordric ħo Leuenot . 7 uend̄e potuit . IN BICHELESWADE
In Stratone ten̄ . i . hid̄ 7 i . uirg . Tra . ē   ſ HVND.
. i . caŕ 7 dim̄ . 7 una caŕ 7 dim̄ poteſt fieri . Ibi . iii . bord̄ .

Value 100s; when acquired £8; before 1066 £10.
Leofnoth, a thane of King Edward's, held this manor; there also 1
Freeman had ½ hide which he could grant to whom he would.

5 M. In PODINGTON Hugh holds 1 hide and 3 virgates from Walter.
Land for 5½ ploughs. In lordship 2 ploughs.
    4 villagers have 3½ ploughs. 9 smallholders and 2 slaves.
    Meadow for 1 plough; woodland, 20 pigs.
Value £4 10s; when acquired 50s; as much before 1066.
Leofnoth, a thane of King Edward's, held this manor.

6 M. In WYMINGTON Osbert holds 4 hides from Walter as one manor.   215 d
Land for 5 ploughs. In lordship 3 ploughs;
    1 villager, 8 smallholders and 4 slaves with 1 plough.
    Meadow for 2 ploughs.
Value £3; as much when acquired; before 1066 £4.
Lank, a man of Leofnoth's, a thane of King Edward's, held this
manor. 1 Freeman had 1 hide there; he could grant to whom he would.

7   In the same village Osbert also holds ½ hide from Walter.
Land for ½ plough; but it is not there.
Value 2s; when acquired 4s; before 1066, 10s.
    Godwin Frambold held this land; he could grant to whom he would.
Alfred of Lincoln claims this (land) from Walter of Flanders.

8   In THURLEIGH Hugh holds 3 hides from Walter as one manor.
Land for 7 ploughs. In lordship 2 ploughs.
    8 villagers have 5 ploughs. 12 smallholders and 3 slaves.
    Woodland, 150 pigs.
Value 100s; when acquired 60s; before 1066 £4.
Leofnoth, a thane of King Edward's, held this manor.

9   In the same (village) Reginald holds ½ hide from Walter.
Land for 2 ploughs. In lordship 1 plough;
    4 smallholders with 1 plough.
Value 20s; when acquired 10s; before 1066, 5s.
    Ordric, Leofnoth's man, held this land; he could sell.

  In BIGGLESWADE Hundred
10   In STRATTON [.....] holds 1 hide and 1 virgate. Land for 1½
ploughs; 1½ ploughs possible.
    3 smallholders.

P̃tū . i . car̄ . Val̄ . x . fot̃ . 7 sẽp ualuit . Hanc t̃ra tenuit
Leuuin Steign regis . E . 7 dare 7 uende potuit . H̃ jacet
7 jacuit in Langeford M̃ ej̃d Walterii.

In Holme ten̄ Walteri . i . hid . T̃ra . ē . i . car̄ 7 dim̄ . Ibi
ē una car̄ . 7 dim̄ poteſt fieri . Ibi . iii . bord . P̃tū . i . car̄
7 dim̄ . Val̄ xx . fot̃ . Q̃do recep̃ʹ xvi . fot̃ . T.R.E.ʹ xx . fot̃.
Hanc t̃ra tenuer̄ . ii . fochi . 7 potuer̄ dare cui uoluer̄.

In Eſtuuiche ten̄ Hugo . i . uirg̃ de Walterio . T̃ra . ē . ii . bob.
7 ibi funt . Ibi . i . bord . 7 i . molin̄ de xiii . fot̃ . Val̄ 7 ualuit
sẽp xvi . fot̃ . Hanc t̃ra tenuit Leuuin teign regis . E.

M̃ Ipfe Walteri ten̄ *LANGEFORD* . p x . hid fe defd̃ . T̃ra . ē
xvi . car̄ . In dn̄io . iiii . hid̃ 7 i . uirg̃ . 7 ibi fuſ . iiii . car̄ . 7 v.
poteſt fieri . Ibi . xii . uiłłi . vii . bord . v . ferui . cū . ix . car̄.
7 adhuc . ii . poſſ fieri . Ibi . ii . molini . de xxvi . fot̃ . 7 viii . den̄.
p̃tū xvi . car̄ . 7 ii . fot̃ defup plus . De paſtura . vi . folid̃.
7 adhuc paſt̃ . ē ad . ccc . oues . Silua . xvi . porc̃ . Int̃ tot̃
ual̄ xv . lib̃ . 7 x . fot̃ . Q̃do recep̃ʹ x . lib̃ . T.R.E.ʹ xv . lib̃.
Hoc M̃ tenuit Leuuin teign regis . E . 7 ibi un̄ fochs ha
buit . i . hid̃ . 7 cui uoluit dare potuit . *IN WICHESTANESTOV*
In Sudgiuele ten̄ Walteri dim̄ hid̃ filuæ   *[HVND.*
quã Anteceſſor ej̃ tenuit . T.R.E.

In ead̃ uilla ten̄ Alric̃ de Walterio . i . uirg̃ . T̃ra . ē . iiii.
bob . 7 ibi funt . P̃tū . iiii . bob . Val̄ . v . fot̃ . Q̃do recep̃ʹ iii.
folid̃ . T.R.E.ʹ x . fot̃ . Hanc t̃ra tenuit Leuuin teign regis
in uadimonio . T.R.E. S̃ʒ poſtʒ rex . W . ueoit in angliã.
ille ipfe qui inuadiauit hanc t̃ra redemit . 7 Seiher
eã occupauit fup regē . ut hoẽs de hund̃ teſtantur.
In Hanflaue ten̄ Hugo de Walto *[IN CLISTON HVND.*
iii . hid̃ 7 dim̄ . T̃ra . ē . iii . car̄ 7 dim̄ . In dn̄io . i . car̄ . 7 alia
poteſt fieri . Ibi . iiii . uiłłi cū . ii . car̄ . 7 iiii . bord 7 ii . ferui.

Meadow for 1 plough.

Value 10s; it always was.

Leofwin, a thane of King Edward's, held this land; he could grant and sell. It lies and lay in (the lands of) Langford, Walter's manor.

11 In HOLME Walter holds 1 hide. Land for 1½ ploughs; 1 plough there; ½ possible.

3 smallholders.

Meadow for 1½ ploughs.

Value 20s; when acquired 16s; before 1066, 20s.

2 Freemen held this land; they could grant to whom they would.

12 In ASTWICK Hugh holds 1 virgate from Walter. Land for 2 oxen; they are there.

1 smallholder.

1 mill at 13s.

The value is and always was 16s.

Leofwin, a thane of King Edward's, held this land.

13 M. Walter holds LANGFORD himself. It answers for 10 hides.

Land for 16 ploughs. In lordship 4 hides and 1 virgate;

4 ploughs there; a fifth possible.

12 villagers, 7 smallholders and 5 slaves with 9 ploughs;
    a further 2 possible.

2 mills at 26s 8d; meadow for 16 ploughs and 2s over and above;
    from pasture 6s; in addition, pasturage for 300 sheep;
    woodland, 16 pigs.

In total, value £15 10s; when acquired £10; before 1066 £15.

Leofwin, a thane of King Edward's, held this manor. 1 Freeman had 1 hide; he could grant to whom he would.

In WIXAMTREE Hundred

14 In SOUTHILL Walter holds ½ hide of woodland which his predecessor held before 1066.

15 In the same village Alric holds 1 virgate from Walter. Land for 4 oxen; they are there.

Meadow for 4 oxen.

Value 5s; when acquired 3s; before 1066, 10s.

Leofwin, a thane of King Edward's, held this land in pledge before 1066; but after King William came to England, the man who pledged it redeemed this land, and Sihere appropriated it in the King's despite as the men of the Hundred testify.

In CLIFTON Hundred

16 In HENLOW Hugh holds 3½ hides from Walter. Land for 3½ ploughs.

In lordship 1 plough; another possible.

4 villagers with 2 ploughs; 4 smallholders and 2 slaves.

Ptū . iii . car 7 dim . 7 i . moliñ de xxx.iiii . ſol . Int totū ual

lx . ſol . Qdo receṗ: xl . ſol . T . R . E: lxx . ſol . Hanc trā

tenueŕ vi . ſochi . 7 cui uolueŕ trā ſuā dare potueŕ.

.XXXIII. **W**TERRA WALTERIJ FŔIS SEIER *IN RATBORGESTOC HVND.*

Ⱳ̃ ALTERVS FŕSeiheri . ten SEGENEHOV . p x . hid ſe

defd . Tra . ē . x . car . In dñio . iiii . hidæ . 7 ibi . ē una car . 7 ii .

car poſſ fieri . Ibi xxiiii . uilli hñt . vii . car . Ibi . iiii . bord .

7 iii . ſerui . ptū . viii . car . Silua . ccc . porc . 7 de cſuetudine

ſiluæ . x . arietes p annū . Int totū ual . vi . lib . Qdo receṗ:

x . lib . T . R . E: xvi . lib . Hoc Ⱳ̃ tenuit Leuenot teign . R . E.

7 ibi un ſocħs habuit dim hid . 7 cui uoluit uendē potuit.

Ⱳ̃ In SEWILESSOV . ten Hugo   *IN FLICTHA HVND.*

de Walterio . iiii . hid p uno Ⱳ̃ . Tra . ē . x . car . In dñio

ii . car . 7 vi . uilli 7 viii . bord 7 iiii . ſerui . cū . vii . car . 7 viii .

poteſt fieri . Ibi . i . moliñ de . xxvi . den . Ptū . vi . car .

Silua . c . porc . 7 ii . ſol . Int tot ual . viii . lib . Qdo receṗ:

. c . ſolid . T . R . E: xi . lib . Hoc Ⱳ̃ tenuit Leuenot teign

R . E . 7 ibi . iii . ſochi dim hid tenueŕ . 7 cui uolueŕ dare

7 uendē potueŕ . Hanc dim hid ten Hugo de rege . ut dñt

.IIII. **H**TERRA HVGON FLANDR *IN WILGA HVND.* hocs ej.

HVGO Flandrenſis ten de rege in Podintone . ii . hidas

7 unā uirg . Tra . ē . ii . car 7 dim . In dñio dimid hida .

7 una car . 7 iii . uilli hñt . i . car 7 dim . Ibi . vi . bord 7 un

ſeruus . Val . xxx . ſol . 7 tntd qdo receṗ . T . R . E: xl . ſol .

Hanc trā . iiii . ſochi tenueŕ . 7 cui uolueŕ uendē potueŕ.

Ipſe Hugo ten in Haneuuich . i . hid 7 dim de rege . Tra

ē . iii . car . In dñio . ii . car . 7 i . uilli 7 iiii . bord 7 iii . ſerui

cū . i . car . Val xxx . ſol . Qdo receṗ: xx . ſol . T . R . E: xl . ſol.

Hanc trā tenuit Aluuold hō Wluui epi . 7 uendē potuit.

Meadow for 3½ ploughs; 1 mill at 34s.
In total, value 60s; when acquired 40s; before 1066, 70s.
6 Freemen held this land; they could grant their land to
whom they would.

33   LAND OF WALTER BROTHER OF SIHERE   216 a

In REDBORNSTOKE Hundred
1   M. Walter brother of Sihere holds SEGENHOE. It answers for 10 hides.
Land for 10 ploughs. In lordship 4 hides; 1 plough there;
2 ploughs possible.
     24 villagers have 7 ploughs. 4 smallholders and 3 slaves.
     Meadow for 8 ploughs; woodland, 300 pigs; from customary
     woodland dues, 10 rams a year.
In total, value £6; when acquired £10; before 1066 £16.
     Leofnoth, a thane of King Edward's, held this manor. 1 Freeman
had ½ hide; he could sell to whom he would.

In FLITT Hundred
2 M. In SILSOE Hugh holds 4 hides from William as one manor.
Land for 10 ploughs. In lordship 2 ploughs;
     6 villagers, 8 smallholders and 4 slaves with 7 ploughs;
     an eighth possible.
     1 mill at 26d; meadow for 6 ploughs; woodland, 100 pigs
     and 2s too.
In total, value £8; when acquired 100s; before 1066 £11.
     Leofnoth, a thane of King Edward's, held this manor. 3 Freemen
held ½ hide; they could grant and sell to whom they would.
Hugh holds this ½ hide from the King, as his men state.

34   LAND OF HUGH OF FLANDERS

In WILLEY Hundred
1   Hugh of Flanders holds 2 hides and 1 virgate in PODINGTON from
the King. Land for 2½ ploughs. In lordship ½ hide; 1 plough.
     3 villagers have 1½ ploughs. 6 smallholders and 1 slave.
Value 30s; as much when acquired; before 1066, 40s.
     4 Freemen held this land; they could sell to whom they would.

2   Hugh holds 1½ hides in HINWICK himself from the King.
Land for 3 ploughs. In lordship 2 ploughs;
     1 villager, 4 smallholders and 3 slaves with 1 plough.
Value 30s; when acquired 20s; before 1066, 40s.
     Alfwold, Bishop Wulfwy's man, held this land; he could sell.

In Sernebroc ten Robt de Hugone dim hid 7 IIII.
parte uni uirg. Tra. e. I. car. 7 ibi est. 7 un bord 7 un
seruus. ptu. I. car. Val. x. sol. Qdo recep. v. sol. T.R.E.
xx. sol. Hanc tra tenuit Leuric ho abbis de Ramesy.
7 cui uoluit dare potuit.

.XXXV. **H**ᴛᴇRRA HVGON PINCERNÆ *IN STODEN HVND.*
HvGO pincerna ten de rege. In Estone. II. hidas
7 III. uirg. Tra. e. IIII. car. In dnio. I. hid. 7 ibi. II. car.
Ibi. IIII. uilli. 7 un bord 7 un seruus eu, II. car. ptu
.I. car. Silua. cc. porc. Val. xL. sol. Qdo recep. Lxx.
sol. T.R.E. xL. sol. Hoc M tenuit Wig teign. R.E.
7 ibide un sochs dim hid habuit. 7 cui uol dare pot.
In Segresdone ten Hugo. I. uirg. 7 ual xII. den.
T.R.E. II. sol. Hanc tra tenuit Aluuin ho Heialdi com.
7 cui uoluit dare potuit.   *IN STODEN HVND.*

.XXXVI. **S**ᴛᴇRRA SIGARI DE CIOCHES.
SyGARVS de Cioches ten in Estone. II. hid de rege.
Tra. e. v. car. In dnio. II. carucatæ træ. 7 ibi sun, II. car.
7 vI. uilli hnt. III. car. Ibi. xII. bord. 7 II. serui. ptu.
.I. car. Silua. Lx. porc. Val. IIII. lib. Qdo recep. III. lib.
T.R.E. IIII. lib. Hanc tra Wig teign. R.E. tenuit.
7 cui uoluit dare 7 uende potuit.

.XXXVII. **G**ᴛᴇRRA GVNFRIDI DE CIOCHES *IN WILGA HVND.*
GvNFRID de cioches ten jn Haneuuic. I. hid 7 III. uirg.
Tetbald de eo. Tra. e. III. car. In dnio. I. car. 7 II. car
poss fieri. Ibi. III. uilli. Val. xx. sol. Qdo recep. x. sol.
T.R.E. xL. sol. Hanc tra tenuer. II. sochi. 7 cui uoluer
dare 7 uendere potuer.

3 In SHARNBROOK Robert holds ½ hide and the fourth part of 1 virgate
from Hugh. Land for 1 plough; it is there.
1 smallholder; 1 slave.
Meadow for 1 plough.
Value 10s; when acquired 5s; before 1066, 20s.
Leofric, the Abbot of Ramsey's man, held this land; he could grant
to whom he would.

LAND OF HUGH BUTLER

5

In STODDEN Hundred
1 Hugh Butler holds 2 hides and 3 virgates in EASTON from the
King. Land for 4 ploughs. In lordship 1 hide; 2 ploughs there.
4 villagers, 1 smallholder and 1 slave with 2 ploughs.
Meadow for 1 plough; woodland, 200 pigs.
Value 40s; when acquired 70s; before 1066, 40s.
Wig, a thane of King Edward's, held this manor. There also 1
Freeman had ½ hide; he could grant to whom he would.

2 In 'SHIRDON' Hugh holds 1 virgate.
Value 12d; before 1066, 2s.
Alwin, Earl Harold's man, held this land; he could grant to whom he
would.

LAND OF SIGAR OF CHOCQUES

6

In STODDEN Hundred
1 Sigar of Chocques holds 2 hides in EASTON from the King.
Land for 5 ploughs. In lordship 2 carucates of land besides the
2 hides. 2 ploughs there.
6 villagers have 3 ploughs. 12 smallholders and 2 slaves.
Meadow for 1 plough; woodland, 60 pigs.
Value £4; when acquired £3; before 1066 £4.
Wig, a thane of King Edward's, held this land; he could grant and
sell to whom he would.

LAND OF GUNFRID OF CHOCQUES

7

In WILLEY Hundred
1 Gunfrid of Chocques holds 1 hide and 3 virgates in HINWICK, and
Theodbald from him. Land for 3 ploughs. In lordship 1 plough; 2
ploughs possible.
3 villagers.
Value 20s; when acquired 10s; before 1066, 40s.
2 Freemen held this land; they could grant and sell to whom they would.

TERRA RICARDI FILIJ GISLEBTI IN BEREFORD HVND.

.XXXVIII. **R**ICARD fili Gisllebti comitis tēn in Subberie. 1 . uirg
træ . quæ jacet in æccła S Neoti . 7 jacuit T.R.E.

In Wiboldeſtone tenent monachi S Neoti de Ricardo
p̄diĉto . 11 . hid 7 dim uirg . Tra . ē dim car . ſʒ ñ eſt ibi.
Silua . c . porc . Val . xi . ſol . Q̆do recep̄ſimil . T . R . E.
xxi . ſol . H̄ tra jacuit in æccła S Neoti . T.R.E . in elem.

.XXXIX TERRA RICARDI PVNGIANT. IN BICHELESWADE HD

RICARDVS puniant ten de rege jn Daintone
. viii . hid 7 uirg p̄ uno M . Tra . ē . viii . car.

In dñio . iiii . hid 7 1 . uirg . 7 ibi ſunt . iii . car . Ibi . xii.
uilli hn̄t . v . car . 7 11 . bord . 7 iii . ſerui . Silua . lx.
porc . Int totū ual . viii . lib . Q̆do recep̄ vi . lib.
7 tāntd . T.R.E . Hoc M tenuit Stigand Archieps.

In Tamiſeforde ten Robt de Ricardo pg . 11 . hid de
feudo regis . Tra . ē . 11 . car . In dñio . 1 . car . 7 iiii . uilli cū . 1.
car . p̄tū . 1 . car . Val . xxx . ſol . Q̆do recep̄ xx . ſol . T.R.E.
xx . ſol . Hanc tra tenuer . iii . ſochi . 7 cui uoluer dare potuer.

In Sudgiuele ten Ricard pg dim hid ſiluæ IN WICHESTANSTOV
quā tenuit Stigand Archieps T.R.E.　　　　　ſ HVND.

.XL. TERRA WILLI CAMERAR IN MANESHEVE HVND.

WILLELM camerarius ten in Poteſgraue . 1 . hid de
rege . Tra . ē . 1 . car . 7 ibi eſt . p̄tū . 1 . car . Val . xv . ſol . Q̆do
recep̄ ſimilit . T . R . E . xl . ſol . Hanc tra tenuit Morcar pbr
de Lintone . 7 uende potuit.

38   LAND OF RICHARD SON OF COUNT GILBERT   216 b

In BARFORD Hundred

1   Richard son of Count Gilbert holds 1 virgate of land in 'SUDBURY' which lies in (the lands of) St Neot's Church and did so before 1066.

2   In WYBOSTON the monks of St Neot hold 2 hides and ½ virgate from the said Richard. Land for ½ plough, but it is not there.
       Woodland, 100 pigs.
     Value 11s; when acquired the same; before 1066, 21s.
       This land lay in (the lands of) St Neot's Church before 1066, in alms.

39   LAND OF RICHARD POYNANT

In BIGGLESWADE Hundred

1   M. Richard Poynant holds 8 hides and [a?] virgate in DUNTON from the King as one manor. Land for 8 ploughs. In lordship 4 hides and 1 virgate. 3 ploughs there.
       12 villagers have 5 ploughs. 2 smallholders and 3 slaves.
       Woodland, 60 pigs.
     In total, value £8; when acquired £6; as much before 1066.
       Archbishop Stigand held this manor.

2   In TEMPSFORD Robert holds 2 hides, of the King's Holding, from Richard Poynant. Land for 2 ploughs. In lordship 1 plough;
       4 villagers with 1 plough.
       Meadow for 1 plough.
     Value 30s; when acquired 20s; before 1066, 20s.
       3 Freemen held this land; they could grant to whom they would.

In WIXAMTREE Hundred

3   In SOUTHILL Richard Poynant holds ½ hide of woodland which Archbishop Stigand held before 1066.

40   LAND OF WILLIAM THE CHAMBERLAIN

In MANSHEAD Hundred

1   William the Chamberlain holds 1 hide in POTSGROVE from the King. Land for 1 plough; it is there.
       Meadow for 1 plough.
     Value 15s; when acquired the same; before 1066, 40s.
       Morcar the priest of Luton held this land; he could sell.

In Badeleſtone ten Robt de Witto camer dim̄ hid. Tra . ē
dim̄ car̄ . Val . v . ſol . Qᵈo recep̄ ſimilit̄ . T.R.E. vii . lib̄ . Hanc
tr̄a tenuit Morcar p̄or . 7 uende potuit . *IN DIM̄ HVND.*

ⓂIpſe Witts ten̄ Totenehou de rege   ⌐ *DE STANBVRGE.*
ꝑ vii . hid una uirga min̄ ſe defd . Tra . ē . vi . car̄ . In dn̄io
iii . hide 7 iii . uirḡ . 7 ibi . ē una car̄ . Ibi . iiii . uitti hn̄t
iii . car̄ . Ibi . iiii . bord̄ . 7 iiii . ſerui . 7 un̄ molin̄ . iii . ſolid̄ .
P̊tū . iii . car̄ , Silua . xx . porc̄ . Val . l . ſol . Qᵈo recep̄
ſimit . T.R.E. viii . lib̄ . Hoc Ⓜ tenuit Leuuine hō Wallef
comitis . Cū hoc Ⓜ reclamat . W . camerari . ii . hid .
q̄s ej anteceſſor tenuit T.R.E. ſic Hund teſtat̄ . ſed eꝑs
baiocenſis ꝑ uim ei abſtulit . 7 Adelulfo ſuo cam ded̄ .

.XLI.   **TERRA WILLI LOVET.** *IN MANESHEVE HVND.*
ⓂWitts Louet ten̄ in Crauelai de rege . v . hidas .
ꝑ uno Ⓜ . Tra . ē . v . car̄ . In dn̄io . ii . hidæ . 7 ii . car̄ .
7 v . uitti hn̄t . ii . car̄ . 7 tcia poteſt fieri . Ibi . iii . bord̄ .
7 ii . ſerui . 7 ii . molini . x . ſol . p̄tū . v . car̄ . Val xl . ſol .
Qᵈo recep̄ xxx . ſot . T.R.E. c . ſot . Hoc Ⓜ tenuit Grim
bald hō regis . E. 7 cui uoluit dare potuit .   ⌐ *HVND.*

ⓂIpſe Witts ten̄ Flicteuuiche de rege . *IN RABORGESTOV*
ꝑ v . hid ſe defd . Tra . ē . vii . car̄ . In dn̄io . ii . hidæ . 7 ibi
. ii . car̄ . Ibi . iii . uitti hn̄t . iii . car̄ . 7 ii . adhuc poſſuꝗ fieri .
Ibi . vii . bord̄ . 7 un̄ molin̄ . iiii . ſolid̄ . p̄tū . v . car̄ . Silua
c . porc̄ . Val . l . ſol . Qᵈo recep̄ lx . ſol . T.R.E. viii . lib̄ .
Hoc Ⓜ tenuit Aluuin teign̄ regis . E.

.XLII.   **TERRA WILLI**   *IN WILGE HVND.*
Witts ten̄ de rege in Fernadis . ii . hid . Tra . ē . ii . car̄
7 dim̄ . In dn̄io ſunt . ii . car̄ . 7 iii . uitti hn̄t dim̄ car̄ . Ibi . ii .
bord̄ . 7 un̄ ſeruus . p̄tū . i . car̄ . Val . xl . ſol . Qᵈo recep̄
xx . ſol . T.R.E. xl . ſol . Hanc tr̄a tenuer̄ . iii . ſocħi . 7 cui
uoluer̄ dare 7 uendere potuer̄ .

2 In BATTLESDEN Robert holds ½ hide from William the Chamberlain.
Land for ½ plough.
Value 5s; when acquired the same; before 1066 £7 (7s?).
Morcar the priest held this land; he could sell.

In the Half-Hundred of STANBRIDGE

3 M. William holds TOTTERNHOE himself from the King. It answers
for 7 hides less 1 virgate. Land for 6 ploughs. In lordship 3 hides
and 3 virgates. 1 plough there.
4 villagers have 3 ploughs. 4 smallholders and 4 slaves.
1 mill, 3s; meadow for 3 ploughs, woodland, 20 pigs.
Value 50s; when acquired the same; before 1066 £8.
Leofwin, Earl Waltheof's man, held this manor. With this manor
William the Chamberlain claims 2 hides which his predecessor held
before 1066, as the Hundred testifies; but the Bishop of Bayeux
took them away from him by force and gave them to his chamberlain
Aethelwulf.

41   LAND OF WILLIAM LOVETT

In MANSHEAD Hundred

1 M. William Lovett holds 5 hides in (Husborne) CRAWLEY from the King, as
one manor. Land for 5 ploughs. In lordship 2 hides; 2 ploughs there.
5 villagers have 2 ploughs; a third possible. 3 smallholders
and 2 slaves.
2 mills, 10s; meadow for 5 ploughs.
Value 40s; when acquired 30s; before 1066, 100s.
Grimbald, King Edward's man, held this manor; he could grant
to whom he would.

In REDBORNSTOKE Hundred

2 M. William holds FLITWICK himself, from the King. It answers for 5 hides.
Land for 7 ploughs. In lordship 2 hides. 2 ploughs there.
3 villagers have 3 ploughs; a further 2 possible. 7 smallholders.
1 mill, 4s; meadow for 5 ploughs; woodland, 100 pigs.
Value 50s; when acquired 60s; before 1066 £8.
Alwin, a thane of King Edward's, held this manor.

42   LAND OF WILLIAM

In WILLEY Hundred

1 William holds 2 hides in FARNDISH from the King. Land for 2½ ploughs.
In lordship 2 ploughs.
3 villagers have ½ plough. 2 smallholders and 1 slave.
Meadow for 1 plough.
Value 40s; when acquired 20s; before 1066, 40s.
3 Freemen held this land; they could grant and sell to whom they
would.

.XLIII. **H**ENRICVS **TERRA HEN RICI FILII AZOR** *IN WILGA HVND.*

HENRICVS filius Azor in Fernadis teñ de rege
.ı.hid.Tra.ẽ.ı.cař.7 iƀi eſt.7 ıı.uiłłi iƀi ſuɴ.p̃tum
dim cař.Vał 7 ualuit.x.ſoł.T.R.E.xx.ſoł.Hanc
trã.ıı.ſochi teñucř.7 cui uolueř dare potueř.

.XLII. **O**SBERN **TERRA OSBERNI FILII RICARDI** *IN STODENE HVND.*

OSBERN filius Ricardi 7 Hugo hubald de eo teñ in
Eſtone dim hid 7 dim uirg.Tra.ẽ.ı.cař.7 iƀi eſt.
cũ uno ſeruo.P̃tũ.ı.cař.Silua.xx.porc.Vał.x.ſoł.
Q̃do recep̃.ſimił.T.R.E.xıı.ſoł.Hanc trã tenuit
Stori hõ Toſti comitis.7 iƀi q̃dã ſochs dim uirg ha
buit.q̃ dare 7 uende potuit.

In Riſelai teñ Hugo hubald de Osƀto Ricardi filio
dim hid.Tra.ẽ.dim cař.7 iƀi.ẽ cũ uno bord.p̃tũ dim
cař.Vał.v.ſoł.7 ualuit.T.R.E.vııı.ſoł.Hanc trã
tenuit Aluuiñ hõ Stori.7 potuit dare cui uoluit.

In Caiſſot teñ Hugo hubald de Osƀto.ı.uirg.Tra.ẽ.ıı.
boƀ.Vał 7 ualuit.ıı.ſoł.T.R.E.ıııı.ſoł.

Ⅿ **I**pſe hugo teñ de Osƀno Eluendone.p una hid 7 una
uirga ſe defd.Tra.ı.cař 7 dim.7 ſunt iƀi.p̃tũ.ı.cař.
Silua.xxx.porc.Vał 7 ualuit.x.ſoł.T.R.E.xv.ſoł.
Hoc Ⅿ tenuit Aluuiñ hõ Stori.7 cui uoluit dare potuit.

.XLV. **O**SBERN **TERRA OSƀNI FILIJ WALTERIJ.** *IN BICHELESWADE HD.*

Ⅿ **O**SBERN filius Walterij teñ de rege in Bereforde
ııı.hid.p uno Ⅿ.Tra.ẽ.ııı.cař.In dñio.ıı.cař.7 ıııı.
uiłłi hñt.ı.cař.Iƀi.ıı.bord.7 v.ſerui.p̃tũ.ı.cař.
Vał.lx.ſoł.Q̃do recep̃.xl.ſoł.T.R.E.lx.ſoł.Hoc
Ⅿ tenuit Vlmař de Etone teigñ regis.E.

3   **LAND OF HENRY SON OF AZOR**   216 c

In WILLEY Hundred

1   Henry son of Azor holds 1 hide in FARNDISH from the King. Land
for 1 plough; it is there.
2 villagers.
Meadow for ½ plough.
The value is and was 10s; before 1066, 20s.
2 Freemen held this land; they could grant to whom they would.

4   **LAND OF OSBERN SON OF RICHARD**

In STODDEN Hundred

1   Osbern son of Richard holds ½ hide and ½ virgate in EASTON
and Hugh Hubald from him. Land for 1 plough; it is
there, with 1 slave.
Meadow for 1 plough; woodland, 20 pigs.
Value 10s; when acquired the same; before 1066, 12s.
Stori, Earl Tosti's man, held this land. A Freeman had ½ virgate,
which he could grant and sell.

2   In RISELEY Hugh Hubald holds ½ hide from Osbern son of Richard.
Land for ½ plough; it is there, with
1 smallholder.
Meadow for ½ plough.
The value is and was 5s; before 1066, 8s.
Alwin, Stori's man, held this land; he could grant to whom he would.

3   In KEYSOE Hugh Hubald holds 1 virgate from Osbern. Land for 2 oxen.
The value is and was 2s; before 1066, 4s.

4   M.Hugh holds 'ELVEDON' himself from Osbern. It answers for 1 hide
and 1 virgate. Land for 1½ ploughs; they are there.
Meadow for 1 plough; woodland, 34 pigs.
The value is and was 10s; before 1066, 15s.
Alwin, Stori's man, held this manor; he could grant to whom he
would.

5   **LAND OF OSBERN SON OF WALTER**

In BIGGLESWADE Hundred

1   M. Osbern son of Walter holds 3 hides in (Little) BARFORD from the
King as one manor. Land for 3 ploughs. In lordship 2 ploughs.
4 villagers have 1 plough. 2 smallholders and 5 slaves.
Meadow for 1 plough.
Value 60s; when acquired 40s; before 1066, 60s.
Wulfmer of Eaton, a thane of King Edward's, held this manor.

OTERRA OSBERNI PISCATORIS. *In Wilge Hvnd.*

Osbern piſcator ten̄ in Sernebroc de rege dim̄ hiđ.
Tra.ē.ɪ.caȓ.7 ibi.ē.Vnū molin̄.xvɪ.den̄.p̄tū dim̄ caȓ.
Silua.x.porc̄.7 unū uiuariū piſciū.Ibi un̄ uilɫs.7 ɪɪ.
borđ.Vaɫ.xxvɪ.ſoɫ.Qđo recep̄:́x.ſoɫ.T.R.E.́xʟ.ſoɫ.
Hanc trā tenuit Toui Huſcarle regis.E.7 uendē potuit.
Cū iſta tra reclamat iſđ Osb̄t unā uirḡ 7 ɪɪɪɪ.partē
uni uirḡ q̇ tenuit Anteceſſor ej.T.R.E.́ Sed poſtquā
rex.W.in Angliā uenit.ille gablū de hac tra dare
noluit.7 Radulf taillgeboſc gablū dedit 7 p̄ forisfaɕto
ipſam
[terrā sūpſit.7 cuidā ſuo militi tribuit.
In Carlentone ten̄ iſđ Osbn̄ de rege.ɪ.hiđ 7 unā uirḡ
7 dim̄.Tra.ē.ɪɪ.caȓ.In dn̄io.ɪ.caȓ.7 ɪɪ.uilɫi.hn̄t.ɪ.caȓ.
Ibi.ɪɪɪɪ.borđ.p̄tū.ɪɪ.caȓ.Vaɫ 7 ualuit.xx.ſoɫ.T.R.E.
T.R.E.́xʟ.ſoɫ.Hanc trā tenuit Goduin frambolt.
teign̄ regis.E.7 uendē potuit.

TERRA TVRSTINI CAMERAR̄ *In Bvchelai Hvnd.*

Tvrstin̄ camerarius ten̄ de rege in Pabenehā
ɪɪ.hiđ 7 dim̄.p̄ uno ꝏ.Tra.ē.ɪɪɪ.caȓ.In dn̄io.ɪ.
hiđa.7 una caȓ.Ibi.vɪ.uilɫi cū.ɪɪ.caȓ.7 ɪ.borđ.
p̄tū.ɪɪɪ.caȓ.Vaɫ.xʟ.ſoɫ.Qđo recep̄:́ſimiɫ.T.R.E.́
xʟ.v.ſoɫ.Hanc trā tenuit Alſi hō Alli fr̄is ej.7 potuit
In Heneuuic ten̄ Turſtin̄ de rege.ɪ.hiđ.7 ɪɪɪ.uirḡ.
Tra.ē.ɪɪ.caȓ.In dn̄io.ɪ.hiđ 7 ɪ.caȓ.7 ɪɪ.uilɫi cū.ɪ.caȓ.
7 ɪ.borđ.p̄tū.ɪ.caȓ.Vaɫ xxx.ſoɫ.Qđo recep̄:́x.ſoɫ.
T.R.E.́xxx.ſoɫ.Hanc trā tenuit Goduin frābolt
teign̄ regis.E.   *In Wichestanestov Hvnd.*

216 d

In Biſtone ten̄ Turſtin̄ p̄dict dim̄ hiđ de rege.Tra.ē
dim̄ caȓ:ſʒ n̄ ē ibi.P̄tū.ɪ.caȓ.H̄ tra deuaſtata.ē

46   LAND OF OSBERN FISHER

In WILLEY Hundred

1 Osbern Fisher holds ½ hide in SHARNBROOK from the King.
Land for 1 plough; it is there.
A mill, 16d; meadow for ½ plough; woodland, 10 pigs; a fish-pond.
1 villager; 2 smallholders.
Value 26s; when acquired 10s; before 1066, 40s.
Tovi, one of King Edward's Guards, held this land; he could sell.
With this land Osbern also claims 1 virgate and the fourth part of
a virgate which his predecessor held before 1066; but after King
William came to England, he refused to give the tribute of this land,
and Ralph Tallboys gave the tribute, and took over this land as a
forfeiture, and gave it to one of his men-at-arms.

2 In CARLTON Osbern also holds 1 hide and 1½ virgates from the King.
Land for 2 ploughs. In lordship 1 plough.
2 villagers have 1 plough. 4 smallholders.
Meadow for 2 ploughs.
The value is and was 20s; before 1066, 40s.
Godwin Frambold, a thane of King Edward's, held this land; he could
sell.

47   LAND OF THURSTAN THE CHAMBERLAIN

In BUCKLOW Hundred

1 Thurstan the Chamberlain holds 2½ hides in PAVENHAM from the King,
as one manor. Land for 3 ploughs. In lordship 1 hide; 1 plough there;
6 villagers with 2 ploughs; 1 smallholder.
Meadow for 3 ploughs.
Value 40s; when acquired the same; before 1066, 45s.
Alfsi, his brother Alli's man, held this land; he could (sell).

[In WILLEY Hundred]

2 In HINWICK Thurstan holds 1 hide and 3 virgates from the King.
Land for 2 ploughs. In lordship 1 hide; 1 plough there;
2 villagers with 1 plough; 1 smallholder.
Meadow for 1 plough.
Value 30s; when acquired 10s; before 1066, 30s.
Godwin Frambold, a thane of King Edward's, held this land.

In WIXAMTREE Hundred

3 In BEESTON the said Thurstan holds ½ hide from the King.   216 d
Land for ½ plough, but it is not there.
Meadow for 1 plough.

f; q̄do Turſtiñ recep̄;uualebat . x . ſot . T.R.E; xx . ſot.

Hanc tr̄a tenuit Goduin h̄o Toſti comitis . 7 dare potuit.

In Chambeltone teñ Turſtiñ · IN CLISTONE HVND.

de rege . II . hid . 7 IIII . part̄e uni uirḡ min . Tra . ē
una car̄ 7 dim̄ . In dñio . I . hid . 7 I . uirḡ . 7 III . part
uni uirḡ . 7 ibi eſt una car̄ . Ibi . II . uilti 7 uñ bord
h̄nt dim̄ car̄ . p̄tū . I . car̄ . 7 dim̄ . Silua . xx . porc̄.
Vat xxx . ſot . 7 ualuit . T.R.E; xL . ſot . Hanc tr̄a tenuer̄
III . ſochi . 7 cui uoluer̄ dare 7 uende potuer̄.

.XLVII̅ G̅ISLEBERT filius Salomonis teñ Malpteſſelle

TERRA GISLEBTI FILIJ SALOMON. IN CLISTONE HVND.

de rege . p̄ IIII . hid ſe defd in Bedeforde ſcire . Tra . ē
IIII . car̄ . In Herefortſcire ipſa uilla ſe defd p̄ . III .
hid 7 una uirḡ . Tra . ē . III . car̄ . Int totū . VII . car̄ ſuɴ.
In dñio . v . hidæ . 7 III . car̄ . 7 adhuc . II . poſſ fieri . Ibi . v.
uilti h̄nt . II . car̄ . 7 IIII . bord . 7 II . ſerui . P̄tū . VII . car̄ . Silua
.cc . porc̄ . 7 de c̄ſuetudine ſiluæ . x . ſot . Vat 7 ualuit . vI . lib.
T.R.E; x . lib̄ . Hoc m̄ tenuit Leuuiñ cilt teigñ . R.E.
7 in hoc m̄ fuer̄ . IIII . ſochi . II . hid tenuer̄ . 7 cui uoluer̄
uende potuer̄.   IN WILGA HVND.

In Flāmereſhā teñ Gileb̄t vII . hid 7 dim̄ . Tra . ē . vIII.
m̄ car̄ . In dñio . IIII . hide . 7 ibi ſuɴ . III . car̄ . 7 IIII . uilti h̄nt
IIII . car̄ . Ibi . vI . bord . p̄tū . IIII . car̄ . Vat c . ſot . Q̄do recep̄;
xII . lib̄ . 7 tntd T.R.E. Hoc m̄ . vI . ſochi tenuer̄ . 7 uende potuer̄.

.XLIX. A̅LBERTVS Lotherenſis teñ de rege CELGRAVE . p̄ . vIII . hid

TERRA ALBERTI LOTHARIENS IN MANESHEVE HVND.

7 II . partib̄ uni uirḡ ſe defd . Tra . ē . x . car̄ . In dñio . III . caru
catæ træ . 7 ibi ſunt . II . car̄ . Ibi xIII . uilti h̄nt . vIII . car̄ . Ibi
IIII . bord . 7 vI . ſerui . P̄tū . vIII . car̄ . Silua . L . porc̄ . Valet

This land has been laid waste; but when Thurstan acquired it
the value was 10s; before 1066, 20s.
Godwin, Earl Tosti's man, held this land; he could grant.

In CLIFTON Hundred

4   In CAMPTON Thurstan holds 2 hides less the fourth part of 1 virgate
from the King. Land for 1½ ploughs. In lordship 1 hide, 1 virgate
and three parts of a virgate; 1 plough there.
    2 villagers and 1 smallholder have ½ plough.
    Meadow for 1½ ploughs; woodland, 20 pigs.
The value is 30s; before 1066, 40s.
    3 Freemen held this land; they could grant and sell to
whom they would.

48   LAND OF GILBERT SON OF SOLOMON

In CLIFTON Hundred

1   M. Gilbert son of Solomon holds MEPPERSHALL from the King. It answers
for 4 hides in Bedfordshire. Land for 4 ploughs. In Hertfordshire
this village answers for 3 hides and 1 virgate. Land for 3 ploughs.
In total, 7 ploughs. In lordship 5 hides; 3 ploughs there;
a further 2 possible.
    5 villagers have 2 ploughs. 4 smallholders and 2 slaves.
    Meadow for 7 ploughs; woodland, 200 pigs; from the customary
      dues of the woodland, 10s.
The value is and was £6; before 1066 £10.
    Young Leofwin, a thane of King Edward's, held this manor.
    In this manor were 4 Freemen; they held 2 hides; they could sell
to whom they would.

In WILLEY Hundred

2   M. In FELMERSHAM Gilbert holds 7½ hides. Land for 8 ploughs.
In lordship 4 hides; 3 ploughs there.
    4 villagers have 4 ploughs. 6 smallholders.
    Meadow for 4 ploughs.
Value 100s; when acquired £12; as much before 1066.
    6 Freemen held this manor; they could sell.

49   LAND OF ALBERT OF LORRAINE

In MANSHEAD Hundred

1   M. Albert of Lorraine holds CHALGRAVE from the King. It answers for 8
    hides and 2 parts of 1 virgate. Land for 10 ploughs. In lordship 3
    carucates of land; 2 ploughs there.
      13 villagers have 8 ploughs. 4 smallholders and 6 slaves.
      Meadow for 8 ploughs; woodland, 50 pigs.

vii . lib. Qdo recep: vi . lib. 7 tntd T.R.E . Hoc ᴍ̃ tenuit

isdē Albt. T.R.E. 7 cui uoluit dare potuit.　　　⌈HṼND.

ᴍ̃ Ipse Albt ten OTONE . p x . hid se desd. IN RADBERNESTOC

Tra.ē xi.car. In dñio . ii . hidæ . 7 ibi . iii . car. Ibi . xx . uilli

hñt . vii . car . 7 viii . posset fieri. Ibi . vi . serui . ptū . v . car.

Silua . cccc . porc . Val . x . lib . Qdo recep: viii . lib . T.R.E:

x . lib 7 xv . sol . Hoc ᴍ̃ tenuit Almar hō Tosti . 7 uende pot.

In Esseltone ten Albt . iii . hid . Tra . ē . v . car . In dñio una

hida. 7 ibi . ii . car. Ibi . vii . uilti . cū . iii . car . 7 iiii . serui.

ptū . iii . car. Silua . c . porc. Val . xl . sol. Qdo recep: xx .

sol. T.R.E: xlv . sol. Hoc ᴍ̃ fuit 7 est mēbrū de Otone.

Almar tenuit hō Tosti comitis.　IN WILGA HVND

In Sernebroc ten Albt . ii . hid 7 iiii . part uni uirg.

Tra.ē. iii . car. In dñio . i . hida. 7 ibi . ii . car. 7 iiii . uilti cū

una . car. Ibi . iiii . bord. 7 iiii . serui. 7 uñ moliñ . xvi . sol.

ptū . ii . car. Silua . xl . porc. Val . l . sol. Qdo recep:

xxx . sol. T.R.E: lx . sol. Hanc tra tenuit Algar hō Edid

reginæ. 7 cui uoluit dare potuit.

.L. TERRA DAVID DE ARGENT. IN STODENE HVND.

DAVID de Argentomo ten In Riselai . i . hid de rege.

Tra.ē. i . car. sed ibi non.ē. Ibi uñ uilts. 7 iii . bord.

Val . x . sol . Qdo recep: xx . sol . T.R.E: similit. Hanc

tra tenuit Homdai hō Heraldi . 7 cui uoluit uende potuit.

217 a

.LI. TERRA RADVLFI DE INSVLA. IN BICHELESWADE ⌈HVND.

RADVLFVS de insula ten de rege jn Stratone . iiii.

hid. p uno ᴍ̃.Tra . ē . viii . car . Ibi sunt vii . 7 viii . potest

fieri. Ibi . x . uilti 7 ii . bord. ptū. iiii . car. Int totū ual

xii . lib. Qdo recep: iiii . lib. T.R.E: c . sol. Hoc ᴍ̃ tenuit

Stigand archieps.

Value £7; when acquired £6; as much before 1066.
Albert also held this manor before 1066; he could grant to
whom he would.

In REDBORNSTOKE Hundred

2 M. Albert holds WOOTTON himself. It answers for 10 hides.
Land for 11 ploughs. In lordship 2 hides. 3 ploughs there.
20 villagers have 7 ploughs; an eighth possible. 6 slaves.
Meadow for 5 ploughs; woodland, 400 pigs.
Value £10; when acquired £8; before 1066 £10 15s.
Aelmer, Earl Tosti's man, held this manor; he could sell.

3 In SHELTON Albert holds 3 hides. Land for 5 ploughs.
In lordship 1 hide; 2 ploughs there.
7 villagers with 3 ploughs; 4 slaves.
Meadow for 3 ploughs; woodland, 100 pigs.
Value 40s; when acquired 20s; before 1066, 45s.
This manor is and was a member of Wootton. Aelmer,
Earl Tosti's man, held it.

In WILLEY Hundred

4 In SHARNBROOK Albert holds 2 hides and the fourth part of 1
virgate. Land for 3 ploughs. In lordship 1 hide; 2 ploughs there.
4 villagers with 1 plough. 4 smallholders and 4 slaves.
A mill, 16s; meadow for 2 ploughs; woodland, 40 pigs.
Value 50s; when acquired 30s; before 1066, 60s.
Algar, Queen Edith's man, held this land; he could grant
to whom he would.

50   LAND OF DAVID OF ARGENTON

In STODDEN Hundred

1 David of Argenton holds 1 hide in RISELEY from the King.
Land for 1 plough; but it is not there.
1 villager and 3 smallholders.
Value 10s; when acquired 20s; before 1066 the same.
Honday, Earl Harold's man, held this land; he could sell
to whom he would.

51   LAND OF RALPH DE L'ISLE   217 a

In BIGGLESWADE Hundred

1 M. Ralph de L'Isle holds 4 hides in STRATTON from the King as
one manor. Land for 8 ploughs. 7 there; an eighth possible.
10 villagers and 2 smallholders.
Meadow for 4 ploughs.
In total, value £12; when acquired £4; before 1066, 100s.
Archbishop Stigand held this manor.

ⓂIpſe Radulf⁹ teñ Pichelefuuade .p.x. hid ſe defd.

Tra.ē.x.caƀ. In dñio.v. hid 7 dim.7 iii. caƀ ibi ſuɴ.

Ibi.vii.uilli cū.vii.caƀ.7 x.bord.7 iii.ſerui.7 ii.molini

de.xlvii.ſol.p̃tū.x.caƀ.7 v.ſolid de feno. Val.xvii.

liƀ. Q̨do recep̃ꞏ xv.liƀ.T.R.E.x.liƀ. Hoc Ⓜ tenuit

Stigand archieps.7 ibi.ii.ſochi dimid hid habueƀ.

quā dare 7 uende potueƀ.

ⓂIn Holme teñ iſd Radulf⁹.ii.hid.Tra.ē.v.caƀ.7 ibi

ſunt.Ibi.vi.uilli.p̃tū.i.caƀ. Val.xl.ſol. Q̨do recep̃ꞏ

xxx.ſol.T.R.E.ꞌxl.ſol. Hoc ⓂⓂ tenuit Stigandus

arch.7 ibi.iii.ſochi.ii.uirg tre habueƀ.7 uende potueƀ.

In Wardone teñ iſd Radulf⁹ IN WICHESTANESTOV HD.

de rege.i.uirg 7 dim. H̃ tra jacet in Bicheleſuuade.

7 ibi eſt ap̃pciata.7 qui eā.T.R.E. tenuit nec uendere

nec dare potuit ſine licentia ej⁹ qui Bicheleſuuade teñ.

.LII.   GTERRA GOZELINI BRITONIS. IN MANESHEVE HVND.
Ⓜ Gozelin brito teñ de rege in Poteſgraue.vii.hid

7 dim p uno Ⓜ.Tra.ē.vii. caƀ 7 dim.In dñio.iii.hid.

7 ibi ſunt.iii.caƀ.Ibi.iii.uilli hñt.ii.caƀ.7 aliæ.ii.7 dim

pot fieri.Ibi.vi.bord.7 iii.ſerui.P̃tū.v.caƀ.Val.l.

ſol. Q̨do recep̃ꞏc.ſol.T.R.E.ꞌx.liƀ. Hoc ⓂⓂ.iiii.teigni

tenueƀ.7 cui uolueƀ trā ſuā dare 7 uendere potueƀ.

IpſeGozelin teñ Gledelai   IN DIM HVND STANBVRGE.

p.ii.hid 7 dim.Tra.ē.i.caƀ.7 ibi ſunt.iiii.boues.7 uñ

moliñ.xvi.ſol.p̃tū.i. caƀ.Silua.c.porc. Val 7 ualuit

xx.ſol.T.R.E.ꞌxl.ſol.Hanc trā tenuit Wigot uenator

regis.E.7 cui uoluit uende potuit.   ꝔHVND.

.LIII.   JTERRA JVDITÆ COMITISSÆ. IN RADBORGESTOC
Ⓜ Jvdita comitiſſa teñ in Meldone.v.hid.7 i.uirg 7 dim.

7 Moniales de Elneſtou tenent de ea in elemoſina.Tra

ē.v.caƀ.In dñio.ii.caƀ.7 vii.uilli hñt.iii.caƀ.Ibi.ii.

2 M. Ralph holds BIGGLESWADE himself. It answers for 10 hides.
  Land for 10 ploughs. In lordship 5½ hides; 3 ploughs there.
  7 villagers with 7 ploughs; 10 smallholders; 3 slaves.
  2 mills at 47s; meadow for 10 ploughs; 5s from hay.
  Value £17; when acquired £15; before 1066 £10.
  Archbishop Stigand held this manor.   2 Freemen had ½ hide
  which they could grant and sell.

3 M. In HOLME Ralph also holds 2 hides. Land for 5 ploughs; they are there.
  6 villagers.
  Meadow for 1 plough.
  Value 40s; when acquired 30s; before 1066, 40s.
  Archbishop Stigand held this manor. 3 Freemen had 2 virgates
  of land; they could sell.

  In WIXAMTREE Hundred
4   In (Old)WARDEN Ralph also holds 1½ virgates from the King.
  This land lies in Biggleswade; it is assessed there. Before 1066
  the holder could neither sell nor grant without the permission of
  the holder of Biggleswade.

52   LAND OF JOCELYN THE BRETON

  In MANSHEAD Hundred
1 M. Jocelyn the Breton holds 7½ hides in POTSGROVE from the King as one
  manor. Land for 7½ ploughs. In lordship 3 hides; 3 ploughs there.
  3 villagers have 2 ploughs; another 2½ possible.
  6 smallholders and 3 slaves.
  Meadow for 5 ploughs.
  Value 50s; when acquired 100s; before 1066 £10.
  4 thanes held this manor; they could grant and sell their land to
  whom they would.

  In the Half-Hundred of STANBRIDGE
2   Jocelyn holds (Nares) GLADLEY himself for 2½ hides.
  Land for 1 plough; 4 oxen there.
  A mill, 16s; meadow for 1 plough; woodland, 100 pigs.
  The value is and was 20s; before 1066, 40s.
  Wigot, King Edward's Huntsman, held this land; he could sell
  to whom he would.

53   LAND OF COUNTESS JUDITH

  In REDBORNSTOKE Hundred
1 M. Countess Judith holds 5 hides and 1½ virgates in MAULDEN the nuns of
  Elstow hold from her, in alms. Land for 5 ploughs. In lordship 2 ploughs.
  7 villagers have 3 ploughs. 2 slaves.

ſerui.7 ı.moliñ.ııı.ſolid.p̃tũ.v.car̄.Silua.c.porc̄.

Val̄.lx.ſol̄.Q̇do recep̄:ıııı.lib.T.R.E.:vıı.lib.Hoc

m̄ tenuit Aluuold teign regis.E.7 ibi uñ ſochs dim̄ uirḡ

habuit.7 cui uoluit dare potuit.

In Houſtone teñ Hugo de Judita comitiſſa dim̄ hid.

T̃ra.ē.ı.car̄.7 ibi eſt.7 ıı.bord.7 ſilua.xxv.porc̄.Val̄

7 ualuit.x.ſol̄.T.R.E.:xıı.ſol̄.Hanc tr̄a Lepſi tenuit

hō Toſti com̄.7 cui uoluit dare 7 uende potuit.

m̄ Ipſa comitiſſa teñ WINESSAMESTEDE.7 moniales teñ

de ea.p̣ ııı.hid ſe defd̄.T̃ra.vı.car̄.In dñio.ıı.car̄.

Ibi.xı.uiłłi hñt.ıııı.car̄.7 xı.bord.7 ı.ſeru.p̃tũ dim̄

car̄.Val̄.vıı.lib.7 vı.ſol̄.Q̇do recep̄:xl.v.ſol̄.T.R.E.:

x.lib 7 x.ſol̄.Hoc m̄.tenuer̄.vııı.ſochi.7 dare 7 uende

potuer̄.Judita com̄ ded S̃ MARIÆ de Elneſtou in elemo

ſina.ſed ſoca jacuit ſep̄ in Cameſtone.

m̄ ELNESTOV.p̣.ııı.hid 7 dim̄ ſe defd̄.Moniales S̃ MARIÆ

tenent de.J.comit̄.T̃ra.ē.vıı.car̄.In dñio.ıı.car̄.7 xıııı.

uiłłi hñt.v.car̄.Ibi.xı.bord.7 ıııı.ſerui.7 ı.moliñ

de.xxıııı.ſol̄.p̃tũ.ıııı.car̄.Silua.lx.porc̄.Val̄.c.ſol̄.

Q̇do recep̄:xl.ſol̄.T.R.E.:x.lib.Hoc m̄ tenuer̄.ıııı.

ſochi.hōes regis.E.fuer̄.tr̄a ſua dare 7 uende potuer̄.

ſed in Cameſtone jacuit ſep̄ ſoca eoʒ

m̄ CAMESTONE p̣ x.hid ſe defd̄.T̃ra.ē xx.car̄.Comitiſſa

tenet.In dñio.ıı.hide.7 ibi.ıııı.car̄.7 xvııı.uiłłi hñt

xıı.car̄.7 adhuc ıııı.poſſ fieri.Ibi xıı.bord.7 vııı.ſerui.

7 uñ moliñ de.v.ſolid.p̃tũ.xx.car̄.Silua.cc.porc̄.

7 de paſtura.ıı.ſol̄.In totis ualentijs ual xvııı.lib.Q̇do

recep̄:xxıı.lib.T.R.E.:xxx.lib.Hoc m̄ tenuit Guert

comes.7 ibid̄.ıı.teigni.ıı.hid 7 dim̄.7 ı.uirḡ 7 dimid̄

habuer̄.7 cui uoluer̄ dare 7 uende potueruñ.

1 mill, 3s; meadow for 5 ploughs; woodland, 100 pigs.
Value 60s; when acquired £4; before 1066 £7.
 Alfwold, a thane of King Edward's, held this manor. A Freeman
had ½ virgate; he could grant to whom he would.

2 In HOUGHTON (Conquest) Hugh holds ½ hide from Countess Judith.
 Land for 1 plough; it is there.
 2 smallholders.
 Woodland, 25 pigs.
 The value is and was 10s; before 1066, 12s.
 Leofsi, Earl Tosti's man, held this land; he could grant and
sell to whom he would.

3 M. The Countess holds WILSHAMSTEAD herself and the nuns from her.
 It answers for 3 hides. Land for 6 ploughs. In lordship 2 ploughs.
 11 villagers have 4 ploughs. 11 smallholders and 1 slave.
 Meadow for ½ plough.
 Value £7 6s; when acquired 45s; before 1066 £10 10s.
 8 Freemen held this manor; they could grant and sell.
 Countess Judith gave it to St. Mary's of Elstow in alms; but the
jurisdiction always lay in Kempston.

4 M. ELSTOW answers for 3½ hides. The nuns of St. Mary's hold it from
 Countess Judith. Land for 7 ploughs. In lordship 2 ploughs.
 14 villagers have 5 ploughs. 11 smallholders and 4 slaves.
 1 mill at 24s; meadow for 4 ploughs; woodland, 60 pigs.
 Value 100s; when acquired 40s; before 1066 £10.   217 b
 4 Freemen held this manor. They were King Edward's men.
 They could grant and sell their land; but their jurisdiction
always lay in Kempston.

5 M. KEMPSTON answers for 10 hides. Land for 20 ploughs. The Countess
 holds it. In lordship 2 hides. 4 ploughs there.
 18 villagers have 12 ploughs; a further 4 possible.
 12 smallholders and 8 slaves.
 1 mill at 5s; meadow for 20 ploughs; woodland, 200 pigs;
  from pasture 2s.
 Total value £18; when acquired £22; before 1066 £30.
 Earl Gyrth held this manor. There also 2 thanes had 2½ hides
and 1½ virgates; they could grant and sell to whom they would.

In Boleheſtre ten Hugo dim̃ hidā *In Stoden Hvnd.*
de comitiſſa.Tra.ē.1.car̃.7 ibi.ē.cū.11.borđ.Ptū
1111.bob.Silua.xx.porc.Vaɫ.x.ſoɫ.Qdo recep:
v.ſoɫ.T.R.E:xii.ſoɫ.Hanc trā tenuit Almar teign
regis.E.7 dare 7 uende potuit.
In Acheleia.ten Milo criſpin de comit.1.hiđ.Tra.ē
1.car̃ 7 dim̃.Vna car̃.ibi.ē.7 dim̃ poɫ fieri.Ibi.1111.
borđ.7 ptū.1.car̃.Vaɫ 7 ualuit.x.ſoɫ.T.R.E:xx.ſoɫ.
Hanc trā tenuit Goduin hō Heraldi.7 uende potuit.
comitis.
In Blacheſhou ten Osbn *In Dim̃ Hvnd de Bvchelai.*
de comitiſſa.11.hiđ 7 dim̃.Tra.ē.1111.car̃.In dñio.1.car̃.
7 vi.uiɫɫi hñt.111.car̃.Ibi.111.borđ.7 111.ſerui.7 dim̃
molin̄ de.x.ſoɫ.ptū.1.car̃.Silua.c.porc.Vaɫ 7 ua
luit ſep.lx.ſoɫ.Hoc m̃ Leueua tenuit.hō regis.E.
7 uendere 7 dare potuit cui uoluit.
In Brunehā ten Hugo de comit.11.hiđ.Tra.ē.11.car̃.
7 ibi ſunt.7 v.uiɫɫi 7 11.borđ.7 1.molin̄ de.xl.ſoɫ
7 c.anguillis.De feudo qđe comitiſſæ.ē.ſ; ñ jacet in hac
tra.ptū.11.car̃.Vaɫ.xx.ſoɫ.Qdo recep 7.T.R.E:x.ſoɫ.
coin̄
Hanc trā tenuit Goduin hō Heraldi.7 uende potuit.
In Stachedene ten Hugo de comit.1.hiđ.Tra.ē.1.
car̃.7 ibi eſt.7 11.uiɫɫi 7 11.borđ.Silua.xl.porc.
Vaɫ 7 ualuit.x.ſoɫ.T.R.E:xx.ſoɫ.Hanc trā.11.ſochi
hōes regis E.tenuer̃.7 cui uoluer̃ uende potuer̃.
In Falmereſhā ten Giſlebt de comitiſſa *In Wilga Hvnd.*
111.hiđ 7 dim̃.Tra.ē.111.car̃.In dñio.1.car̃.7 11.uiɫɫi
cū.1.car̃.7 alia poɫ fieri.Ibi.1111.borđ.7 unū molin̄
de.x.ſoɫ.Ptū.1.car̃.Vaɫ.111.liɓ.Qdo recep:c.ſoɫ.
7 tntđ.T.R.E.Hanc trā tenuit Alli teign regis.E.

In STODDEN Hundred

6 In BOLNHURST Hugh holds ½ hide from the Countess. Land for 1 plough; it is there, with
    2 smallholders.
    Meadow for 4 oxen; woodland, 20 pigs.
Value 10s; when acquired 5s; before 1066, 12s.
    Aelmer, a thane of King Edward's, held this land; he could grant and sell.

7 In OAKLEY Miles Crispin holds 1 hide from the Countess.
Land for 1½ ploughs; 1 plough there; ½ possible.
    3 smallholders.
    Meadow for 1 plough.
The value is and was 10s; before 1066, 20s.
    Godwin, Earl Harold's man, held this land; he could sell.

In the Half-Hundred of BUCKLOW

8 In BLETSOE Osbern holds 2½ hides from the Countess.
Land for 4 ploughs. In lordship 1 plough.
    6 villagers have 3 ploughs. 3 smallholders and 3 slaves.
    ½ mill at 10s; meadow for 1 plough; woodland, 100 pigs.
The value is and always was 60s.
    Leofeva, King Edward's man, held this manor; she could sell
and grant to whom she would.

9 In BROMHAM Hugh holds 2 hides from the Countess. Land for 2 ploughs; they are there.
    5 villagers and 2 smallholders.
    1 mill at 40s and 100 eels; it is of the Countess' Holding,
        but it does not lie in this land. Meadow for 2 ploughs.
Value 20s; when acquired and before 1066, 10s.
    Godwin, Earl Harold's man, held this land; he could sell.

10 In STAGSDEN Hugh holds 1 hide from the Countess. Land for 1 plough; it is there.
    2 villagers and 2 smallholders.
    Woodland, 40 pigs.
The value is and was 10s; before 1066, 20s.
    2 Freemen, King Edward's men, held this land; they could sell
to whom they would.

In WILLEY Hundred

11 In FELMERSHAM Gilbert holds 3½ hides from the Countess.
Land for 3 ploughs. In lordship 1 plough;
    2 villagers with 1 plough; another possible. 4 smallholders.
    1 mill at 10s; meadow for 1 plough.
Value £3; when acquired 100s; as much before 1066.
    Alli, a thane of King Edward's, held this land.

In Radeuuelle ten̄ Hugo de feudo comitiſſæ. ii. hiđ
7 ii. uirg̃ 7 dim̄. Tra.ē.i.car̄ 7 dim̄.7 ibi ſuɴ̄.Ibi un̄
uiłłs 7 i.borđ 7 un̄ ſeruus.p̃tū.i.car̄.Vał.xx.ſoliđ.
Q̣do recep̃.x.ſoł.T.R.E.xl.ſoł.Hanc tr̄a tenuit
Toui huſcarle regis.E.
Gisleḃt de bloſſeuile ten̄ de comitiſſa Hareuuelle.
p̃ x.hiđ.ſe defđ.Tra.ē.xvi.car.In dn̄io.iii.car̄ poſ̃
fieri.una.ē ibi.7 x.uiłłi cū̄.vii.car̄.7 adhuc.vi.poſ̃
fieri.p̃tū.vi.car.Silua.cc.porc̄.7 un̄ molin̄ de xxxvi.
ſoł 7 viii.den̄.7 cc.anguiłł.Int totū uał.vi.liḃ. Q̣do
recep̃.xvi.liḃ.T.R.E.xx.liḃ.Hoc m̄ tenuer̄.iii.teigni
regis.E.7 cui uoluer̄ uendere potuer̄.
In Sernebroc ten̄ Hugo de comitiſſa.iii.uirg̃ træ.
Tra.ē.i.car̄.7 ibi eſt.Ibi un̄ uiłłs.7 i.borđ.p̃tū.i.car̄.
Vał.x.ſoł.Q̣do recep̃.v.ſoł.T.R.E.xx.ſoł.Hanc
tr̄a tenuit Ouiet hō regis.E.7 potuit dare cui uoluit.

217 c

In HVND de Bereforde ten̄ Osḃn.ii.hiđ 7 iii.uirg̃.
Tra.ē.iii.car̄.In dn̄io.ii.car̄.7 iii.uiłłi cū̄.i.car̄.
Ibi.ii.borđ 7 un̄ ſeru.P̃tū.i.car̄.Silua.cc.porc̄.Vał
xl.ſoł.Q̣do recep̃.x.ſoł.T.R.E.l.ſoł.Hanc tr̄a tenuit
V̓lfech Stirman regis.E.7 uend̄e potuit.
In Potonc ten̄ Hugo de comitiſſa dim̄ uirg̃ træ.Tra
ē.i.car̄.7 ibi.ē.cū̄.i.borđ.Vał 7 ualuit.v.ſoł.T.R.E.
ii.ſoł.Hanc tr̄a tenuit com̄ Toſti.in Potone ſuo m̄.
In Stratone ten̄ Fulcher IN BICHELESWADE HD̄.
de pariſio.iii.uirg̃ 7 dim̄ de comitiſſa.Tra.ē.ii.car̄.
In dn̄io.i.car̄.Ibi un̄ uiłłs 7 v.borđ.p̃tū.i.car̄.
Vał.viii.ſoł.7 ualuit.T.R.E.xx.ſoł.Hanc tr̄a
tenuit Aluuin hō regis.E.7 uendere potuit.

12 In RADWELL Hugh holds 2 hides and 2½ virgates from the Countess' Holding. Land for 1½ ploughs; they are there.
 1 villager, 1 smallholder and 1 slave.
 Meadow for 1 plough.
Value 20s; when acquired 10s; before 1066, 40s.
 Tovi, one of King Edward's Guards, held this land.

13 Gilbert of Blosseville holds HARROLD from the Countess. It answers for 10 hides. Land for 16 ploughs. In lordship 3 ploughs possible; 1 there;
 10 villagers with 7 ploughs; a further 6 possible.
 Meadow for 6 ploughs; woodland, 200 pigs; a mill at 36s 8d
  and 200 eels.
In total, value £6; when acquired £16; before 1066 £20.
 3 thanes of King Edward's held this manor; they could sell
to whom they would.

14 In SHARNBROOK Hugh holds 3 virgates of land from the Countess. Land for 1 plough; it is there.
 1 villager and 1 smallholder.
 Meadow for 1 plough.
Value 10s; when acquired 5s; before 1066, 20s.
 Wulfgeat, King Edward's man, held this land; he could grant
to whom he would.

 In the Hundred of BARFORD
15 Osbern holds 2 hides and 3 virgates. Land for 3 ploughs.   217 c
 In lordship 2 ploughs;
 3 villagers with 1 plough; 2 smallholders and 1 slave.
 Meadow for 1 plough; woodland, 200 pigs.
Value 40s; when acquired 10s; before 1066, 50s.
 Wulfheah, King Edward's steersman, held this land; he could sell.

16 In POTTON Hugh holds ½ virgate of land from the Countess.
Land for 1 plough; it is there, with
 1 smallholder.
The value is and was 5s; before 1066, 2s.
 Earl Tosti held this land in Potton, his manor.

 In BIGGLESWADE Hundred
17 In STRATTON Fulchere of Paris holds 3½ virgates from the Countess.
Land for 2 ploughs. In lordship 1 plough.
 1 villager; 5 smallholders.
 Meadow for 1 plough.
The value is and was 8s; before 1066, 20s.
 Alwin, King Edward's man, held this land; he could sell.

In Holme ten̅ Fulcher̅ de com̅.dim̅ hid̅.Tra dim̅
car̅.7 ibi.e̅ dim̅ car̅.p̅tu̅ dim̅ car̅.Ibi un̅ uil̅ls.
Val̅ 7 ualuit.vii.fol̅.T.R.E.ʹx.fol̅.Hanc tr̅a
tenuit Aluuin̅ ho̅ regis.E.7 dare 7 uende̅ potuit.
In ead̅ tene͛s.ii.hoȇs de comitiſſa.i.uirg̅.Tra.ii.
bob̅.7 ibi funt.Val̅ 7 ualuit se̅p.v.fol̅.Hanc tr̅a
tenuit Goduin̅ ho̅ regis.E.7 uende̅ potuit.

(H)
(t) Ipfa comitiſſa Judita *IN DIM̅ HD̅ DE WENESLAI.*
ten̅ *POTONE*.p x.hid̅ fe defd̅.Tra.e̅.xii.car̅.
ˑIn dn̅io.iii.hide 7 dim̅.7 ibi funt.iii.car̅.Ibi.xviii,
uil̅li 7 ii.fochi cu̅.viii.car̅.7 ix ͫͣ.pot fieri.Ibi
xiii.bord̅ 7 iii.ferui.7 i.molin̅.v.folido₴.p̅tu̅
xii.car̅.Paftura ad pec uillæ.Int totu̅ ual̅.xii.lib̅.
Qdo recep̅.ʹc.fol̅.T.R.E.ʹxiii.lib̅.Hoc M̅ tenuit
rex EDW.7 fuit com̅ Tofti.Ibid̅ fuer̅.iiii.fochi
qui habuer̅.i.hid̅ 7 i.uirg.7 cui uoluer̅ dare potuer̅.

In Sudtone ten̅
Aluuin de Jud̅ com
.i.hid̅.Tra.e̅.i.car.
Ibi st̅.iii.bord.
7 pt̅ i.ii.car.
Val̅.viii.fol̅b.
Sex fochi tenuer̅
; dꝛe 7 uende potuer̅.
In Sudtone ten̅ Torchil.i.hid̅ 7 dim̅.Tra.e̅.i.car̅ 7 dim̅.
Vna car̅ ibi.e̅.7 dim̅ pot fieri.Ibi.iiii.bord̅.P̅tu̅.i.car̅
7 dim̅.7 xvi.den̅.Val̅ x.fol̅.Qdo recep̅.ʹviii.fol̅.T.R.E.ʹ
xx.fol̅.Hanc tr̅a.iii.fochi tenuer̅.7 uende̅ potuer̅.
In ead̅ ten̅ Leuegar dim̅ hid̅.Tra.e̅ dim̅ car̅.7 ibi eft.
P̅tu̅ dim̅ car̅.7 xii.den̅.Val̅.v.fol̅.Qdo recep̅.ʹ7 T.R.E.ʹ
x.fol̅.Ifte ꝙ nc̅ tenet tenuit.ho̅ regis fuit.7 uende̅ pot̅.
In ead̅ ten̅ Rob̅t.iii.uirg 7 dim̅.Tra.e̅.i.car̅.ſ̨ n̅ fu͛s
Ibi.iii.nifi.ii.boues.P̅tu̅.i.car̅.Val̅.viii.fol̅.7 ualuit.T.R.E.ʹ
bord.
x.fol̅.Hanc tr̅a.ii.fochi tenuer̅.7 uende̅ potuer̅.

18   In **HOLME** Fulchere holds ½ hide from the Countess.
Land for ½ plough; ½ plough there.
   Meadow for ½ plough.
   1 villager.
The value is and was 7s; before 1066, 10s.
Alwin, King Edward's man, held this land; he could grant and sell.

19   In the same (village) 2 men hold 1 virgate from the Countess.
Land for 2 oxen; they are there.
The value is and always was 5s.
Godwin, King Edward's man, held this land; he could sell.

   In the Half-Hundred of **WENSLOW**
20   M. Countess Judith holds **POTTON** herself. It answers for 10 hides.
Land for 12 ploughs. In lordship 3½ hides; 3 ploughs there.
   18 villagers and 2 Freemen with 8 ploughs; a ninth possible.
   13 smallholders and 3 slaves.
   1 mill, 5s; meadow for 12 ploughs; pasture for the village livestock.
In total, value £12; when acquired 100s; before 1066 £13.
King Edward held this manor; it was Earl Tosti's.
There were 4 Freemen who had 1 hide and 1 virgate; they could grant
to whom they would.

21   In **SUTTON** Thorkell holds 1½ hides. Land for 1½ ploughs; 1 plough
there; ½ possible.
   4 smallholders.
Meadow for 1½ ploughs, and 16d too.
Value 10s; when acquired 8s; before 1066, 20s.
   3 Freemen held this land; they could sell.

22   In **SUTTON** Alwin holds 1 hide from Countess Judith.
Land for 1 plough.
   3 smallholders.
   Meadow for 2 ploughs.
Value 8s.
   6 Freemen held it; they could grant and sell.

23   In the same (village) Leofgar holds ½ hide. Land for ½ plough;
it is there.
   Meadow for ½ plough and 12d.
Value 5s; when acquired and before 1066, 10s.
   The present holder held it; he was the King's man; he could sell.

24   In the same (village) Robert holds 3½ virgates. Land for 1 plough,
but there are only 2 oxen.
   3 smallholders.
   Meadow for 1 plough.
The value is and was 8s; before 1066, 10s.
   2 Freemen held this land; they could sell.

In ead teneꝗ Sueting 7 Roḃt.ı.uirg̈ træ 7 dimiđ.

Tra.ıııı.boḃ.7 ibi funt.Ptū.ı.car.7 uñ borđ.Val.ıııı.

fol 7 ualuit.T.R.E. v. fol. Hanc trā Eduuard tenuit.

hō Aḃḃis S̃ Albani.7 uendere potuit IN DIM HVND

In Sudtone ten Turḃt.ıı.hiđ de comitiffa.Tra.ē

ıı.car.In dñio.ı.car.7 ıııı.borđ cū.ı.car.ptū.ıı.car.

Val 7 ualuit.xx.fol.T.R.E.xxv.fol.Hanc trā.ıı.fochi

tenueī.7 uendē potueī.

In ead ten Goduin.ııı.uirg̈ de comitiffa.Tra.ē.ı.car.

fed m̃ non.ē.Val.ııı.fol.Q̈do recep:vı.fol.T.R.E.x.fol.

Hanc trā Vlmar tenuit hō Ordui.7 uende potuit.

In ead ten Ederic dim hiđ.Tra.ē dim car.7 ibi.ē.cū

uno uitto.ptū dim car.Val 7 ualuit.v.fol.T.R.E.x.

fol.Ifte q̃ tenct tenuit. hō regis fuit.7 uendē potuit.

217 d

M In Hatelai.ten Jud comitiffa.ııı.hiđ 7 ıı.uirg 7 dim ꝑ uno

M.Tra.ē.vı.car 7 dim.In dñio.ı.hiđ 7 dim uirg.7 ibi.ıı.car.

Ibi.vııı.uitti.cū.ıııı.car 7 dim.Ibi.vııı.borđ.7 ptū.ıı.car.

Silua.ıııı.porc.Val.vı.liḃ.7 v.fol.Q̈do recep:c.fol.T.R.E.

vı.liḃ.Hoc M Tofti com tenuit.7 jacet in Potone M ꝓpo

comitiffæ.7 ibi q̃dā fochs unā uirg habuit.potuit

dare 7 uendere.7 ad alterū dñm recedere.

M Rannulf fr Ilgerij ten de comitiffa Euretone.ꝑ.v.

hiđ fe defđ.Tra.ē.v.car.Ibi funt.ıı.car.7 ııı.poffuꝗ

fieri.Ibi.ıııı.uitti.7 v.borđ.ptū.ı.car.Val.ııı.liḃ.

Q̈do recep:c.fol.7 tntđ.T.R.E.Hoc M com Tofti tenuit.7 ja

cuit in Potone M ꝓpo comitiffæ. IN HVND DE WICHESTANESTOV.

In Sudgiuele ten Hugo de comitiffa.ı.hiđ.Tra.ē.ıı.car.7 ibi

25 In the same (village) Sweeting and Robert hold 1½ virgates of land. Land for 4 oxen; they are there.
   Meadow for 1 plough.
   1 smallholder.
   The value is and was 4s; before 1066, 5s.
   Edward, the Abbot of St. Alban's man, held this land; he could sell.

In the same Half-Hundred
26 In SUTTON Thorbert holds 2 hides from the Countess.
Land for 2 ploughs. In lordship 1 plough;
   4 smallholders with 1 plough.
   Meadow for 2 ploughs.
   The value is and was 20s; before 1066, 25s;
   2 Freemen held this land; they could sell.

27 In the same (village) Godwin holds 3 virgates from the Countess. Land for 1 plough, but it is not there now.
Value 3s; when acquired 6s; before 1066, 10s.
   Wulfmer, Ordwy's man, held this land; he could sell.

28 In the same (village) Edric holds ½ hide. Land for ½ plough; it is there, with
   1 villager.
   Meadow for ½ plough.
   The value is and was 5s; before 1066, 10s.
   Its holder held it; he was the King's man; he could sell.

29 M. In (Cockayne) HATLEY Countess Judith holds 3 hides and 2½ virgates as one manor. Land for 6½ ploughs. In lordship 1 hide   217 d
and ½ virgate; 2 ploughs there.
   8 villagers with 4½ ploughs. 8 smallholders.
   Meadow for 2 ploughs; woodland, 4 pigs.
Value £6 5s; when acquired 100s; before 1066 £6.
   Earl Tosti held this manor. It lies in Potton, the Countess'
own manor. A Freeman had 1 virgate; he could grant and sell, and withdraw to another lord.

30 M. Ranulf brother of Ilger holds EVERTON from the Countess. It answers for 5 hides. Land for 5 ploughs; 2 ploughs there; 3 possible.
   4 villagers; 5 smallholders.
   Meadow for 1 plough.
Value £3; when acquired 100s; as much before 1066.
   Earl Tosti held this manor. It lay in Potton, the Countess' own manor.

In the Hundred of WIXAMTREE
31 In SOUTHILL Hugh holds 1 hide from the Countess. Land for 2 ploughs; they are there.

funt.Ibi.iii.uilli.7 iii.borđ.7 un̄ ſeru.p̄tū.ii.car.Silua
lx.porč.Val.xxx.ſol.Q̨do recep.xl.ſol.T.R.E.lx.ſol.
Hanc trā tenuit Tuſſa hō comitis Wallef.7 uende potuit.

In Hergentone ten̄ canonici,de Bedeforde de comitiſſa. .iiii.hidas
Tra.e.iii.car.7 ibi ſunt.7 vi.uilli 7 iiii.borđ.p̄tū.ii.car.
Val.xxx.ſol.Q̨do recep.xx.ſol.T.R.E.xl.ſol.Hanc trā
tenuit Azelin hō comitis Toſti.n̄ potuit neq̨ uende dare ſine
licentia illius qui cameſtone ꝏ com̄ tenuit.

In Chernetone ten̄ Hugo de comitiſſa.iii.hiđ 7 unā uirg
7 tcia par̄ uni uirg.Tra.e.iiii.car.7 ibi ſunt.Ibi ſunt
xii.uilli.7 iii.borđ 7 iii.ſerui.P̄tū.i.car.Val.xl.ſol.Q̨do
recep.xx.ſol.T.R.E.xl.ſol.Hanc trā tenuit Azelin hō
Toſti com̄.n̄ potuit dare ɫ uende ſine licentia ej q̄ Cameſton

In Cochepol ten̄ Hugo de comitiſſa.i.uirg træ. ʃtenuit.
H̄ tra.xxx.den ual 7 ualuit ſēp.Hanc tenuit Wluuin
hō regis.E.7 cui uoluit uendere potuit.

In Blunhā.ten̄ abb̄ S̄ Edmundi dim̄ hiđ de comitiſſa.
Tra.e.i.car.7 ibi eſt.p̄tū.i.car.Val.xx.ſol.Q̨do recep.
x.ſol.T.R.E.xx.ſol.Hanc trā hō.R.E.tenuit.7 uende pot.

In Cliſtone ten̄ Aluuin de comitiſſa In Clistone Hvnđ.
.i.hiđ.Tra.e dim̄ car.7 ibi eſt.p̄tū dim̄ car.Val 7 ualuit
v.ſol.T.R.E.x.ſol.Hanc trā Vluric hō regis.E.tenuit.
7 uendere potuit.   ʃHvnđ.

.LIIII.   Terra Vxoris Hvgon̄ De Grent maiſnil In Radborgestoch
          Adeliz vxor. H. de grentemaiſnil ten̄ de rege dim̄ hiđ in Eſeltone.Tra.e dim̄
car.7 ibi.e.p̄tū dim̄ car.Silua.vi.porč.Ibi un̄ borđ.
Val.vi.ſol.7 ualuit.T.R.E.x.ſol.Hanc trā tenuit Goduin
hō Guert comitis.7 cui uoluit dare potuit.

3 villagers; 3 smallholders and 1 slave.
Meadow for 2 ploughs; woodland, 60 pigs.
Value 30s; when acquired 40s; before 1066, 60s.
Tuffa, Earl Waltheof's man, held this land; he could sell.

32 In HARROWDEN the Canons of Bedford hold 3 hides from the Countess.
Land for 3 ploughs; they are there.
6 villagers and 4 smallholders.
Meadow for 2 ploughs.
Value 30s; when acquired 20s; before 1066, 40s.
Azelin, Earl Tosti's man, held this land; he could neither grant nor sell
without the permission of the holder of the Earl's manor of Kempston.

33 In CARDINGTON Hugh holds 3 hides and 1 virgate and the third part
of 1 virgate from the Countess. Land for 4 ploughs; they are there.
12 villagers, 3 smallholders and 3 slaves.
Meadow for 1 plough.
Value 40s; when acquired 20s; before 1066, 40s.
Azelin, Earl Tosti's man, held this land; he could not grant or
sell without the permission of the holder of Kempston.

34 In COPLE Hugh holds 1 virgate of land from the Countess.
The value of this land is and always was 30d.
Wulfwin, King Edward's man, held it; he could sell to whom he would.

35 In BLUNHAM the Abbot of St. Edmund's holds ½ hide from the Countess.
Land for 1 plough; it is there.
Meadow for 1 plough.
Value 20s; when acquired 10s; before 1066, 20s.
A man of King Edward's held this land; he could sell.

In CLIFTON Hundred
36 In CLIFTON Alwin holds 1 hide from the Countess. Land for ½ plough;
it is there.
Meadow for ½ plough.
The value is and was 5s; before 1066, 10s.
Wulfric, King Edward's man, held this land; he could sell.

54   **LAND OF HUGH OF GRANDMESNIL'S WIFE**

In REDBORNSTOKE Hundred
1 Adelaide, wife of Hugh of Grandmesnil, holds ½ hide in SHELTON
from the King. Land for ½ plough; it is there.
Meadow for ½ plough; woodland, 6 pigs.
1 smallholder.
The value is and was 6s; before 1066, 10s.
Godwin, Earl Gyrth's man, held this land; he could grant
to whom he would.

In Ouſtone ten Ernald de Adeliz.IIII.hid 7 dim ꝑ uno ꝳ.
Tra.ē.VI.caꝛ.In dñio.II.caꝛ.7 XI.uiłłi 7 VII.bord cū.III.
caꝛ 7 dim.7 adhuc dim pot fieri.Ibi.III.ſerui.P̃tū.II.caꝛ.
Silua.CC.XXV.poꝛ.De hac tra ten uñ ſochs.I.hid.Vał.IIII.lib.
Q̨do recep̃꞉LX.ſoł.T.R.E꞉VIII.lib.Hoc ꝳ tenueꝛ.III.ſochi.
qui trā ſuā dare 7 uendere uolueꝛ.In hac ead reclamat
Adeliz p̃dicta dim uirg.7 XXX.acs int ſiluā 7 planū ſup
Hugonē dc belcāp.7 hões de hund portaꝗ̃ teſtimoniū
qd h̄ terra jacuit T.R.E.cū alia tra q̨ ten Adeliz.7 ille qui
hanc trā tenuit potuit dare uel uende cui uoluit.Ḥanc
trā Radulf⁹injuſte occupauit.qdo uicecomes fuit.
ꝳ Ipſa Adeliz ten Cerlentone. *IN WICHESTANESTOV HD.*
ꝑ X.hid.ſe defd.Tra.ē.X.caꝛ.In dñio.V.hid.7 ibi.II.caꝛ.
7 adhuc.III.poſſuꝗ̃ fieri.Ibi.XVI.uiłłi 7 IX.bord cū.V.caꝛ.
Ibi.II.ſerui.7 uñ moliñ.XXX.ſoł.p̃tū.X.caꝛ.Silua.XVI.
porc.Int totū uał.X.lib.Q̨do recep̃꞉VIII.lib.T.R.E꞉XII.
lib.Hoc ꝳ tenuit rex Edw.7 fuit Toſti comitis.H̄ tra
fuit Berew de potone T.R.E.ita qd null inde ſeparare

⌐ꝳ Juditæ comit¬   ⌐potuit.

218a
ꝳ In Mildentone ten Iuo dapifer *de gent* hugon *IN STODEN HVND.*
III.hid 7 unā uirg ꝑ uno ꝳ.Tra.ē.IIII.caꝛ.In dñio.II.caꝛ.
7 VIII.uiłłi cū.II.caꝛ.Ibi uñ ſeruus.7 I.moliñ.XX.ſolidoꝛ.
p̃tū.II.caꝛ.Silua.XL.porc.Vał.LX.ſoł.7 ualuit.T.R.E꞉
IIII.lib.Hoc ꝳ tenuit Goduin hō Borret.7 uende potuit.

.LV. Azelina femina Radulfi tallgeboſc ten de rege **TERRA VXORIS RADVLFI TAILLEB** *IN MANESHEVE HD.*
in Badeleſdone.I.hid 7 dim.Tra.ē caꝛ 7 dim.Vna ibi.ē
7 dim poteſt fieri.Ibi.II.uiłłi 7 uñ bord.p̃tū.I.caꝛ.Vał
7 ualuit.XX.ſoł.T.R.E꞉XL.ſoł.Hanc trā tenueꝛ.II.
ſochi.Anſchill 7 Aluuin.7 cui uolueꝛ uende potueꝛ.

2   In HOUGHTON (Conquest) Arnold holds 4½ hides from Adelaide,
as one manor. Land for 6 ploughs. In lordship 2 ploughs.
  11 villagers and 7 smallholders with 3½ ploughs;
      a further ½ possible. 3 slaves.
  Meadow for 2 ploughs; woodland, 225 pigs.
  1 Freeman holds 1 hide of this land.
Value £4; when acquired 60s; before 1066 £8.
  3 Freemen held this manor; they could grant and sell their land.
  In the same (village) the said Adelaide claims from Hugh of
Beauchamp ½ virgate and 30 acres of wood and open land.
The men of the Hundred bear witness that before 1066 this land
lay with the other land which Adelaide holds, and the holder of
this land could grant or sell to whom he would. Ralph Tallboys
appropriated this land wrongfully, when he was Sheriff.

    In WIXAMTREE Hundred
3   M. Adelaide holds CHALTON herself. It answers for 10 hides. Land for 10
ploughs. In lordship 5 hides; 2 ploughs there; a further 3 possible.
  16 villagers and 9 smallholders with 5 ploughs.
  2 slaves; 1 mill, 30s; meadow for 10 ploughs; woodland, 16 pigs.
In total, value £10; when acquired £8; before 1066 £12.
  King Edward held this manor; it was Earl Tosti's. This land
was an outlier of Potton, Countess Judith's manor, before 1066,
so that no one could separate it from it.

    In STODDEN Hundred   218 a
4   M. In MILTON (Ernest) Ivo, Hugh of Grandmesnil's Steward, holds 3 hides
and 1 virgate as one manor. Land for 4 ploughs. In lordship 2 ploughs;
  8 villagers with 2 ploughs.
  1 slave; 1 mill, 20s; meadow for 2 ploughs; woodland, 40 pigs.
The value is and was 60s; before 1066 £4.
  Godwin, Burgred's man, held this manor; he could sell.

55   **LAND OF RALPH TALLBOYS' WIFE**

    In MANSHEAD Hundred
1   Azelina, wife of Ralph Tallboys, holds 1½ hides in BATTLESDEN
from the King. Land for 1½ ploughs; 1 there; ½ possible.
  2 villagers and 1 smallholder.
  Meadow for 1 plough.
The value is and was 20s; before 1066, 40s.
  2 Freemen, Askell and Alwin, held this land; they could sell
to whom they would.

ꝏ Ipſa Azelina teñ Hocheleia . p̄ x . hiđ ſe defđ . T̃ra

ē . viii . car̃ . In dñio . v . hidæ . 7 ibi ſunt . ii . car̃ . Ibi xiii .

uiłłi 7 xi . borđ cũ . vi . car̃ . p̃tũ . iiii . car̃ . Silua . c . porc̃.

Int̃ tot̃ ual̃ 7 ualuit . viii . liƀ . T.R.E.ʹ xii . liƀ . Hoc ꝏ tenuit

Anſchilł . T.R.E . 7 uendē potuit . IN FLICTHA HVND̃.

In Cainou teñ Turſtin de Azelina . i . hiđ . T̃ra . ē . ii . car̃.

Iu dñio . i . 7 uñ uiłłs h̃t aliã . Ibi . iii . borđ . 7 p̃tũ . i . car̃.

7 Silua . c . porc̃ . Val̃ . xx . ſol̃ . Q̃do recep̃ ʹ x . ſol̃ . T.R.E.ʹ

xx . ſol̃ . Hanc tr̃a tenuit Vluric ſoch regis . E . 7 cui uoluit

dare 7 uendere potuit . IN BEREFORDE HVND̃.

In Wiboldeſtone teñ Judichel . v . uirg̃ 7 dim̃ de Azelina

T̃ra . ē . i . car̃ . 7 ibi . ē . cũ uno uiłło 7 ii . borđ . p̃tũ dim̃ car̃.

Val̃ . x . ſol̃ . Q̃do recep̃ ʹ v . ſol̃ . T.R.E.ʹ xxx . ſol̃ . Hanc tr̃a te

nuit Almar h̃o Vlmari . 7 potuit uendē 7 dare cui uoluit.

In Aieuuorde teñ Brodo . i . hiđ IN BICHELESWADE HVND̃.

de Azelina . T̃ra . ē . i . car̃ . 7 ibi . ē . cũ uno borđ p̃tũ . i . car̃.

Val̃ 7 ualuit ſēp . x . ſol̃ . H̃ tr̃a . ē de maritagio . Hanc te

nuit iſđ Brodo . 7 cui uoluit uendē potuit . ┌ HVND̃.

ꝏ In Hatelai teñ Azelina de maritagio IN WENESLAI

ſuo . v . hiđ 7 una uirg̃ 7 dim̃ . T̃ra . ē . viii . car̃ . In dñio . i . hiđ

7 i . uirg̃ . 7 ibi . ii . car̃ . Ibi . viii . uiłłi 7 iiii . borđ . cũ . vi . car̃.

Ibi . uñ ſerũ 7 i . moliñ . xviii . ſolidoꝛ . p̃tũ . ii . car̃ . Silua

iiii . porc̃ . 7 de redđ . iii . ſol̃ . Int̃ tot̃ ual̃ . vi . liƀ . Q̃do re

cepit ʹ c . ſol̃ . T.R.E.ʹ vi . liƀ . Hoc ꝏ tenuit Vlmar teigñ

2   M.   Azelina holds HOCKLIFFE herself.   It answers for 10 hides.
Land for 8 ploughs.   In lordship 5 hides; 2 ploughs there.
13 villagers and 11 smallholders with 6 ploughs.
Meadow for 4 ploughs; woodland, 100 pigs.
In total, the value is and was £8; before 1066 £12.
Askell held this manor before 1066; he could sell.

In FLITT Hundred
3   In CAINHOE Thurstan holds 1 hide from Azelina.   Land for 2 ploughs.
In lordship 1.
1 villager has the other.   3 smallholders.
Meadow for 1 plough; woodland, 100 pigs.
Value 20s; when acquired 10s; before 1066, 20s.
Wulfric, a Freeman of King Edward's, held this land; he could
grant and sell to whom he would.

In BARFORD Hundred
4   In WYBOSTON Iudichael holds 5½ virgates from Azelina.
Land for 1 plough; it is there, with
1 villager and 2 smallholders.
Meadow for ½ plough.
Value 10s; when acquired 5s; before 1066, 30s.
Aelmer, Wulfmer's man, held this land; he could sell and grant
to whom he would.

In BIGGLESWADE Hundred
5   In EYEWORTH Brodo holds 1 hide from Azelina.   Land for 1 plough;
it is there, with
1 smallholder.
Meadow for 1 plough.
The value is and always was 10s.
This land is of her marriage portion.   Brodo also held this land;
he could sell to whom he would.

In WENSLOW Hundred
6   M.   In (Cockayne) HATLEY Azelina holds 5 hides and 1½ virgates of her
marriage portion.   Land for 8 ploughs.   In lordship 1 hide
and 1 virgate; 2 ploughs there.
8 villagers and 4 smallholders with 6 ploughs.   1 slave.
1 mill, 18s; meadow for 2 ploughs; woodland, 4 pigs;
and from its payments 3s.
In total, value £6; when acquired 100s; before 1066 £6.

regis.E.7 ibi fuer̄ ii.ſochi hōes ej.ii.uirg 7 dim̄ habuer̄.

7 cui uoluer̄ dare 7 uendē potuer̄. IN WICHESTANESTOV

In Stanford ten̄ Rogeri.ii.hid̄ de Azelina.   ʃ HVND.

7 h̄ eſt de ſuo maritagio.Tra.ē.ii.car̄.In dn̄io.i.car̄.7 ii.uilli

7 un̄ bord̄ cū.i.car̄.p̄tū.ii.car̄.Silua.xxx.porc̄.7 i.molin̄

xiii.ſol 7 iiii.den.Val.lx.ſol.Q̄do recep̄.xx.ſol.T.R.E.

lx.ſol.Hanc tr̄a tenuer̄.ii.ſochi.7 cui uoluer̄ dare potuer̄,

In Wardone ten̄ Walter monach dimid̄ hid̄ de Azelina.

7 h̄ eſt de ſuo maritagio.Tra.ē dim̄ car̄.ſ; n̄ eſt ibi.Vn̄ bord̄

ibi eſt.p̄tū dim̄ car̄.Silua.xl.porc̄.Val.x.ſol.Q̄do re

cep̄.7 T.R.E.xx.ſol.Hanc tr̄a tenuit Goding hō Edrici

calui.7 cui uoluit dare potuit. IN CLISTONE HVND.

In Haneſlauue ten̄ Widrus.i.hid̄ 7 iii.uirg de Azelina.

Tra.ē.ii.car̄.7 ibi ſunt.Duo uilli.7 ii.bord̄.7 ii.ſerui.p̄tū

ii.car̄.Val.xxx.ſol.Q̄do recep̄.xx.ſol.T.R.E.xxx.ſol.

Hanc tr̄a tenuit Anſchill.7 fuit Bereuuiche de Stodfald

T.R.E.Hanc tr̄a clam̄ Hugo de belcāp ſup Azelinā.dicep̄S

eā habere injuſte.nec ejus dotē unquā fuiſſe.

In ead̄ uilla ten̄ Bernard.i.hid̄ de Azelina.Tra.ē.i.car̄.

7 ibi.ē.7 iii.uilli.p̄tū.i.car̄.Val 7 ualuit.xxiii.ſol.T.R.E.

xxviii.ſol.Hanc tr̄a tenuer̄.ii.ſochi hōes Anſchilli.7 cui

uoluer̄ dare potuer̄.

In Chicheſana ten.iii.ſochi.iii.hid̄ de Aželina.de dote

ſua.Tra.ē.ii.car̄.Vna.ē ibi.7 alia poteſt fieri.p̄tū.ii.car̄.

Silua.xx.porc̄.Val 7 ualuit.xx.ſol.T.R.E.xxv.ſol.

Hoc ꝏ tenuer̄.iiii.ſochi.7 cui uoluer̄ dare ⁊ uendē potuer̄.

Wulfmer, a thane of King Edward's, held this manor. 2 Freemen, his men, were there; they had 2½ virgates; they could grant and sell to whom they would.

In WIXAMTREE Hundred

7 In STANFORD Roger holds 2 hides from Azelina. It is of her marriage portion. Land for 2 ploughs. In lordship 1 plough;
    2 villagers and 1 smallholder with 1 plough.
    Meadow for 2 ploughs; woodland, 30 pigs; 1 mill, 13s 4d.
    Value 60s; when acquired 20s; before 1066, 60s.
    2 Freemen held this land; they could grant to whom they would.

8 In (Old) WARDEN Walter the monk holds ½ hide from Azelina. It is of her marriage portion. Land for ½ plough; but it is not there.
    1 smallholder.
    Meadow for ½ plough; woodland, 40 pigs.
    Value 10s; when acquired and before 1066, 20s.
    Goding, Edric the Bald's man, held this land; he could grant to whom he would.

In CLIFTON Hundred

9 In HENLOW Widder holds 1 hide and 3 virgates from Azelina.
    Land for 2 ploughs; they are there.
    2 villagers, 2 smallholders and 2 slaves.
    Meadow for 2 ploughs.
    Value 30s; when acquired 20s; before 1066, 30s.
    Askell held this land. It was an outlier of Stotfold before 1066.
    Hugh of Beauchamp claims this land from Azelina, stating that she has it wrongfully, and that it was never in her dowry.

10 In the same village Bernard holds 1 hide from Azelina.
    Land for 1 plough; it is there.
    3 villagers.
    Meadow for 1 plough.
    The value is and was 23s; before 1066, 28s.
    2 Freemen, Askell's men, held this land; they could grant to whom they would.

11 In CHICKSANDS 3 Freemen hold 3 hides from Azelina, of her dowry.
    Land for 2 ploughs; 1 there; another possible.
    Meadow for 2 ploughs; woodland, 20 pigs.
    The value is and was 20s; before 1066, 25s.
    4 Freemen held this manor; they could grant and sell to whom they would.

Ín eađ uilla teñ Walterı.ı.hiđ de Azelina.7 ħ eſt de ej
maritagio.Tra.ē.ı.caŕ.7 ibi eſt.p̃tū.ı.caŕ.Silua.L.
porē.7 ı.moliñ de.x.ſoł.Va _ ·· ·· ~~.ſoł.T.R.E.´
xxx.ſoł.Hanc tŕā tenuit Sueteman.ħō Vlmerı ᴜᴜ
Etone.7 cui uoluit dare potuit.

Ín Standone teñ Engeler.ıı.hiđ 7 dim̄ de Azelina.
Tŕa.ē.ıı.caŕ 7 dim̄.In dñio.ıı.caŕ.7 ııı.borđ cū dim̄ caŕ.
Ibi.ıı.ſerui.p̃tū.ıı.caŕ 7 dim̄.Vał Lx.ſoł.Q̨do recep̃´
xL.ſoł.T.R.E.´ıııı.lib̃.Hanc tŕā tenuit Vlmaŕ de Etone
teigñ.R.E.7 ibi.v.ſocħi hōēs ejđ Vlmari fueŕ.7 dare
7 uendē potueŕ cui uolueŕ.

.LVI. TERRA BVRG̃SIV̆ DE BEDEF̄. *IN DIM̄ HVND̄ DE BOCHELAI.*
Ín *BIDEHA´* teñ Oſgaŕ de bedeford.ı.uirg̃ træ de rege.
Tra.ē.ıı.bob꒓.Vał 7 ualuit sēp.ıı.ſoł.Ipſe qui nc̄ tenet
tenuit T.R.E.7 potuit dare cui uoluit.

Ín eađ uilla teñ Goduiñ burgenſis de rege.ı.hiđ 7 ıııı.
part̃ uni̮ uirg̃.Tra.ē.ı.caŕ.7 ibi eſt.p̃tū.ı.caŕ.Valet
7 ualuit sēp.x.ſoł.Dimidiā hidā de hac tra iſte qui nc̄
teñ tenuit.T.R.E.quā potuit dare cui uoluit.Dimidiā
u̇ hidā 7 ıııı.part̃ uni̮ uirg̃ emit poſtꝙ rex.W.in anglia
uenit.ſꝫ nec rᴜgi nec alicui inde ſeruitiū fecit.nec
de ea liberatorem habuit.Suꝑ eunđ hōēm reclamat
Wiłłs ſpecħ.ı.uirg̃ 7 ıııı.part̃ uni̮ uirg̃.quæ ſibi libata
fuit 7 poſtea ꝑdidit.

Ín eađ uilla teñ Orduui burgenſis de rege.ı.hiđ.7 ııı.
part̃ dimidiæ hiđ.Tŕa.ē.ı.caŕ.7 ibi.ē.Ibi.ıı.uiłłi.
7 ı.borđ.p̃tū.ı.caŕ.Vał 7 ualuit sēp.x.ſoł.Dim̄ hiđ 7 ıııı.part̃.ı.uirg̃

12 In the same village Walter holds 1 hide from Azelina. It is of 218 b
her marriage portion. Land for 1 plough; it is there.
   Meadow for 1 plough; woodland, 50 pigs; 1 mill at 10s.
The value is and was 20s; before 1066, 30s.
   Sweetman, Wulfmer of Eaton's man, held this land; he could
grant to whom he would.

13 In STONDON Engelhere holds 2½ hides from Azelina.
Land for 2½ ploughs. In lordship 2 ploughs;
   3 smallholders with ½ plough.
   2 slaves; meadow for 2½ ploughs.
Value 60s; when acquired 40s; before 1066 £4.
   Wulfmer of Eaton, a thane of King Edward's, held this land. 5
Freemen, this Wulfmer's men, were there; they could grant and sell
to whom they would.

56   LAND OF THE BURGESSES OF BEDFORD

   In the Half-Hundred of BUCKLOW
1 In BIDDENHAM Oscar of Bedford holds 1 virgate of land from the King.
Land for 2 oxen.
The value is and always was 2s.
   Its present holder held it before 1066; he could grant
to whom he would.

2 In the same village the burgess Godwin holds 1 hide and the fourth
part of 1 virgate from the King. Land for 1 plough; it is there.
   Meadow for 1 plough.
The value is and always was 10s.
   Before 1066 the present holder held ½ hide of this land which he
could grant to whom he would. But he bought ½ hide and the fourth
part of 1 virgate after King William came to England, but he did not
do service for it to the King or to anyone else; and he did not have a
deliverer for it. William Speke also claims from him 1 virgate and the
fourth part of 1 virgate, which was delivered to him; but he lost it later.

3 In the same village the burgess Ordwy holds 1 hide and the third
part of ½ hide from the King. Land for 1 plough; it is there.
   2 villagers and 1 smallholder.
   Meadow for 1 plough.
The value is and always was 10s.

de hac t̃ra tenuit T.R.E. isdē qui n̄c tenet. 7 potuit dare cui uoluit. Vnā uirg̃ ů in uadimonio tenuit T.R.E. 7 adhuc tenet. ut hoēs de hoc hund testantur. Idem ipse emit. I. uirg̃. 7 IIII. part̃ uni⁹ uirg̃ postq̄ rex W. in Anglia uenit. 7 nec regi nec alicui seruitiū redd.

In ead uilla ten̄ Vlmar⁹ burgensis de rege. II. partes unius uirg̃. T̃ra. ē. I. boui. Val 7 ualuit sēp. XII. den̄. Istemet tenuit. T.R.E. 7 potuit dare cui uoluit.

IN WILGA HVND.

In Heneuuich ten̄ Eduuard⁹ dim̄ hid de rege. T̃ra. ē dim̄ car̃. Ibi. II. boues sunt. 7 I. bord. Val 7 ualuit v. sol. T.R.E. x. sol. Hanc t̃rā tenuit pat̃ huj⁹ hōis. 7 uende potuit. T.R.E. Hanc rex. W. in elemosina eid concessit. unde 7 breuē regis hт̄. 7 testimon̄ de hund.

In Scernebroc ten̄ Almar⁹ dim̄ uirg̃ de rege. T̃ra. ē dim̄ car̃. s; ibi non. ē. Val 7 ualuit. II. sol. T.R.E. .v. sol. Hanc t̃rā pat̃ ejd⁹ hōis tenuit. 7 rex. W. ei p̱ breuē suū reddidit.

IN WICHESTANESTOV HD.

In Bistone ten̄ Godmund⁹ de rege. III. uirg̃. T̃ra. III. bob⁹ 7 ibi sunt. P̃tū. III. bob⁹. Val 7 ualuit. v. sol. T.R.E. x. sol. Istemet tenuit. T.R.E. 7 cui uoluit uende potuit.

IN CLISTONE HD.

In Hanslau ten̄ Alric⁹ de rege. I. uirg̃. T̃ra. ē. II. bob⁹. 7 ibi sunt. p̃tū. II. bobz. Val 7 ualuit semp̱. II. sol. Istemet tenuit T.R.E. 7 uendere potuit.

In Alricesei ten̄ q̄dā p̃bendari⁹ regis. Vlsi. duas partes uni⁹ uirg̃ de rege.

Before 1066 the present holder held ½ hide and the fourth part of 1 virgate of this land; he could grant to whom he would. But he held 1 virgate in pledge before 1066 and still holds it, as the men of this Hundred testify. He also bought 1 virgate and the fourth part of 1 virgate after King William came to England; he does not pay service to the King or to anyone.

4 In the same village the burgess Wulfmer holds 2 parts of 1 virgate from the King. Land for 1 ox.
The value is and always was 12d.
He held it himself before 1066; he could grant to whom he would.

In WILLEY Hundred
5 In HINWICK Edward holds ½ hide from the King.
Land for ½ plough. 2 oxen there.
1 smallholder.
The value is and was 5s; before 1066, 10s.
Before 1066 his father held this land; he could sell.
King William assigned it to him, in alms, for which he has the King's writ and the witness of the Hundred.

6 In SHARNBROOK Aelmer holds ½ virgate from the King.
Land for ½ plough; but it is not here.
The value is and was 2s; before 1066, 5s.
His father held this land. King William returned it to him through his writ.

In WIXAMTREE Hundred
7 In BEESTON Godmund holds 3 virgates from the King.
Land for 3 oxen; they are there.
Meadow for 3 oxen.
The value is and was 5s; before 1066, 10s.
He held it himself before 1066; he could sell to whom he would.

In CLIFTON Hundred
8 In HENLOW Alric holds 1 virgate from the King.
Land for 2 oxen; they are there.
Meadow for 2 oxen.
The value is and always was 2s.
He held it himself before 1066; he could sell.

9 In ARLESEY a prebendary of the King, Wulfsi, holds 2 parts of 1 virgate from the King.

TERRA PPOSITOȝ 7 ELEMOSINAR̃ IN MANESHEVE REGIS THVND.

In Euresot tenet Herbt p̃fect regis dimidiā hidā.

7 In Woberne.iii.uirg̃ træ.7 in Potesgraue.i.hid.

Has.iii.tras ten in miniſterio regis.quæ n̄ jacuer̃ ibi
T.R.E.fed ex quo Radulf uicecom̃ fuit.dicit fe eas h̃a tallgebofc.
buiſſe p conceſſionē regis.Ibi.ē un̄ uiłłs.Int tot uał
vi.soł.Qdo recep.'xx.soł.T.R.E.'fimilit.Hanc trā
v.fochi regis.E.tenuer̃.7 cui uoluer̃ uende potuer̃.

In ead Potesgraua ten q̃dā equari regis dim̃ hid.
Tra.ē dim̃ car̃.7 ibi eſt.Vał 7 ualuit.v.soł.T.R.E.'
x.soł.Hanc trā tenuit Ofuui h̃o comitis Tofti.7 cui
uoluit dare potuit.

.I. In Preſtelai ten p̃fect regis.i.hid.Tra.ē.i.car̃.Ibi
un̄ uiłłs.P̃tū.i.car̃.Silua.xx.porc̃.Vał.v.soł.Qdo
recep.'x.soł.T.R.E.'xxx.soł.Hanc trā tenuer̃.iiii.teigni.
7 cui uoluer̃ dare 7 uende potuer̃. IN RATBORGESTOC HD.

.II. In Meldone ten q̃dā p̃fect regis dimid hid.Tra.ē dim̃
car̃.7 ibi eſt.cū.ii^b.'uiłłis.p̃tū dim̃ car̃.Vał 7 ualuit
iii.soł.T.R.E.'x.soł.Hanc trā.ii.fochi regis.E.tenuer̃.
7 cui uoluer̃ dare potuer̃. IN BICHELESWADE HVND.

.III. In Tamiseforde ten Aluuin p̃fect.i.hidā.7 iiii.part
unius uirg̃.Tra.ē.i.car̃.7 ibi eſt.cū.iii.uiłłis.p̃tū
dim̃ car̃.Vał 7 ualuit.xx.soł.T.R.E.'xxvii.soł.Hanc
trā tenuer̃.vi.fochi.7 cui uoluer̃ uende potuer̃.

.IIII. In Edeuuorde ten Aluuin p̃fect regis.ii.hid 7 dim̃.
Tra.ē.ii.car̃.7 ibi funt.cū.ii.uiłłis.Vał 7 ualuit sep
xxx.soł.Hoc M̃ tenuit Branting h̃o regis.E.7 uende

.V. In Holme ten Aluuin p̃fect regis.i.hid   potuit.
7 dim̃.Tra.ē car̃ 7 dim̃.Ibi eſt.i.car̃.7 dim̃ poteſt

7] LAND OF THE KING'S REEVES, [BEADLES] AND ALMSMEN 218 c

In MANSHEAD Hundred

1 In EVERSHOLT Herbert, a reeve of the King's, holds ½ hide;
in WOBURN 3 virgates of land; in POTSGROVE 1 hide. He holds
these three lands in the King's Administration; they did not lie
there before 1066, but since Ralph Tallboys was Sheriff; he states.
that he has had them by the King's assent.
 1 villager.
In total, value 6s; when acquired 20s; before 1066 the same.
 5 Freemen of King Edward's held this land; they could sell
to whom they would.

2 Also in POTSGROVE a groom of the King's holds ½ hide.
Land for ½ plough; it is there.
The value is and was 5s; before 1066, 10s.
Oswy, Earl Tosti's man, held this land; he could grant
to whom he would.

3 i In PRIESTLEY a reeve of the King's holds 1 hide. Land for 1 plough.
 1 villager.
Meadow for 1 plough; woodland, 20 pigs.
Value 5s; when acquired 10s; before 1066, 30s.
 4 thanes held this land; they could grant and sell to whom they would.

In REDBORNSTOKE Hundred

3 ii In MAULDEN a reeve of the King's holds ½ hide. Land for ½ plough;
it is there, with
 2 villagers.
Meadow for ½ plough.
The value is and was 3s; before 1066, 10s.
 2 Freemen of King Edward's held this land; they could grant
to whom they would.

In BIGGLESWADE Hundred

3 iii In TEMPSFORD Alwin the reeve holds 1 hide and the fourth part
of 1 virgate. Land for 1 plough; it is there, with
 3 villagers.
Meadow for ½ plough.
The value is and was 20s; before 1066, 27s.
 6 Freemen held this land; they could sell to whom they would.

3 iv In EDWORTH Alwin, a reeve of the King's, holds 2½ hides.
Land for 2 ploughs; they are there, with
 2 villagers.
The value is and always was 30s.
 Branting, King Edward's man, held this manor; he could sell.

3 v In HOLME Alwin, a reeve of the King's, holds 1½ hides.
Land for 1½ ploughs; 1 plough there; ½ possible.

fieri . Ibi . ii . uitti . Val 7 ualuit sep . xx . fol . Hanc tra

tenuer Aluric 7 Lemar bedelli . 7 uendere potuer.

.VI. In Sudtone ten Aluuin . i . uirg 7 dim . Val 7 ualuit

iiii . fol . T.R.E. v . fol . Hanc tram . ii . fochi tenuer.

7 cui uoluer dare 7 uendere potuer.

Has . vi . terras appofuit Rad talgebofc in minifte

rio regis . qdo uicecomes fuit . n eni fuer ibi . T.R.E.

Qui eas nc habcν . cceffione regis tenent . fic dnt.

In Stradlei ten pfect de hund IN FLICTHA HVND.

ii . part uni uirg ad op regis . quæ m jacent in Lintone

co regis . fed n jacuer ibi . T.R.E . Bondi ftalr appofuit

in hoc co . 7 Radulf talgebofc appofitas ibi inuenit.

Tra . e dim car . Val 7 ualuit . v . fol . T.R.E. x . fol.

Hanc tra tenuit Vlmar pbr . 7 cui uoluit dare potuit.

In Sudtone ten Aluuin . i . hid . IN WENESLAI HVND.

In dnio . i . car . 7 iii . bord cu . i . car . ptu . ii . car . 7 xii.

den . Val 7 ualuit . xx . fol . T.R.E. x . fol . De hac

tra iftemet tenuit . iii . uirg . 7 qda Eduuard . i . uirg.

potuer dare 7 uende cui uoluer . IN WILGE HVND.

In Carlentone ten Chellct . iii . uirg 7 dim . Tra . e ad

una car . 7 ibi eft cu . ii . uittis 7 iii . bord . ptu . i . car.

Val . x . fol . Qdo recep . duas ores . T.R.E. x . fol.

De hac tra tenuit iftemet . i . uirg . ho fuit Edid reginæ

7 cui uoluit dare potuit . Duas uirg u 7 dim occupauit.

unde nec libatore nec aduocatu inuenit . qua tra

tenuit Alli tcign . E . regis.

In Wimentone teneς . v . frs cu matre fua . iii . uirg de du.

218 d

Tra . e . i . car . f; n eft ibi . Val . iii . fol . T.R.E. xv . fol . Hanc

tra tenuit Lant pat eoʒ . 7 dare 7 uende potuit.

2 villagers.
The value is and always was 20s.
Aelfric and Leofmer, beadles, held this land; they could sell.

3 vi In SUTTON Alwin holds 1½ virgates.
The value is and was 4s; before 1066, 5s.
2 Freemen held this land; they could grant and sell to whom
they would.

Ralph Tallboys put these six lands in the King's Administration when he was
Sheriff, for they were not there before 1066.
The present holders hold them by the King's assent, as they state.

In FLITT Hundred
4 In STREATLEY the reeve of the Hundred holds 2 parts of 1 virgate
for the King's work. They now lie in (the lands of) the King's
manor of Luton, but they did not lie there before 1066. Bondi
the Constable put them in this manor and Ralph Tallboys found
them put there. Land for ½ plough.
The value is and was 5s; before 1066, 10s.
Wulfmer the priest held this land; he could grant to whom he would.

In WENSLOW Hundred
5 In SUTTON Alwin holds 1 hide; In lordship 1 plough;
3 smallholders with 1 plough.
Meadow for 2 ploughs and 12d too.
The value is and was 20s; before 1066, 10s.
He held 3 virgates of this land himself; one Edward, 1 virgate;
they could grant and sell to whom they would.

In WILLEY Hundred
6 In CARLTON Ketelbert holds 3½ virgates. Land for 1 plough;
it is there, with
2 villagers and 3 smallholders.
Meadow for 1 plough.
Value 10s; when acquired 2 *ora*; before 1066, 10s.
He held 1 virgate of this land himself; he was Queen Edith's man;
he could grant to whom he would. However, he appropriated 2½
virgates for which he found neither deliverer nor patron. Alli, a
thane of King Edward's, held this land.

7 In WYMINGTON 5 brothers with their mother hold 3 virgates from
(her) dowry. Land for 1 plough; but it is not there. 218 d
Value 3s; before 1066, 15s.
Their father, Lank, held this land; he could grant and sell.

In Coldentone teñ Alric Wintremelc *IN BEREFORD HĎ.*
dim hiđ de rege.Tra.ē dim car̄.7 ibi eſt.p̄tū.iii.bob.
Val 7 ualuit sēp.v.ſol.Iſte qui nc̄ teñ tenuit.T.R.E.
hō regis.E.fuit.7 potuit dare cui uoluit.Quā poſtea
canonicis S̃ Pauli ſub.W.rege dedit.7 ut poſt morte
ſuā habent omīno c̄ceſſit. *IN WICHESTANESTOV HĎ.*
In Stanford teñ Alric de regę.iiii.part uni uirg̃.
Tra.ē dimiđ boui.7 ibi ē ſemibos.Val 7 ualuit.xii.deñ.
Iſdē ten qui tenuit.T.R.E.7 potuit dare cui uoluit.
In eađ uilla teñ Ordui 7 iiii.part uni uirg̃.Tra.iii.bob.
7 ibi ſuꝯ.p̄tū.iii.bob.Val 7 ualuit sēp.iiii.ſol.Iſtemet
tenuit T.R.E.hō regis fuit.7 cui uoluit uende potuit.
In Biſtone teñ Aluuin.i.uirg̃ 7 dim.Tra.ē dim car̄.
Ibi.ii.borđ.Val.xii.deñ.Q̇do receꝑ.iiii.ſol.T.R.E.
.x.ſol.H̃ tra appoſita.ē in miniſterio regis.ubi non
fuit.T.R.E.ſʒ dot qui eā tenuit 7 dare 7 uende potuit.
In Weſcota.teñ Ordui.i.uirg̃ *IN RADBVRNESTOC HĎ*
de rege.Tra.ē dim car̄.Ibi ſunt.v.boues.cū.i.borđ
7 i.ſeruo.Val 7 ualuit.v.ſol.T.R.E.x.ſol.Iſtemet tc̄
tenuit.hō regis fuit.7 uende potuit. *IN STODEN HVND*
In Dene teneꝯ.xi.ſochi Willi regis.vii.uirg̃ træ
7 iiii.parte uni uirg̃.Tra.ē.iii.car̄ 7 dim.7 ibi ſunt.
Val 7 ualuit sēp.xxx.ſol.Hanc tra tenuer̄.T.R.E.idē ipſi
qui nc̄ teneꝯ ſochi.7 cui uoluer̄ dare potuer̄.Hanc tra
appoſuit Rad in miniſterio regis.ubi non fuit.T.R.E.
In eađ uilla teñ Goduuidere de Bedeford dim uirg̃
de rege.7 ual 7 ualuit sēp.xii.deñ.Iſtemet tenuit
T.R.E.7 potuit inde facere qđ uoluit.

In BARFORD Hundred

8 In GOLDINGTON Alric Wintermilk holds ½ hide from the King.
Land for ½ plough; it is there.
   Meadow for 3 oxen.
The value is and always was 5s.
   The present holder held it before 1066; he was King Edward's
man; he could grant to whom he would. Later he gave it to the
Canons of St. Paul's under King William, and assented that they
should have it altogether after his death.

In WIXAMTREE Hundred

9 In STANFORD Alric holds 4 parts of 1 virgate from the King.
Land for ½ ox; half an ox is there.
The value is and was 12d.
   The present holder held it before 1066; he could grant
to whom he would.

10 In the same village Ordwy holds 4 parts of 1 virgate.
Land for 3 oxen; they are there.
   Meadow for 3 oxen.
The value is and always was 4s.
   He held it himself before 1066; he was the King's man;
he could sell to whom he would.

11 In BEESTON Alwin holds 1½ virgates. Land for ½ plough.
   2 smallholders.
Value 12d; when acquired 4s; before 1066, 10s.
   This land was put in the King's Administration, where it was
not before 1066; but Dot who held it could both grant and sell.

In REDBORNSTOKE Hundred

12 In 'WESTCOTTS' Ordwy holds 1 virgate from the King.
Land for ½ plough; 5 oxen there, with
   1 smallholder and 1 slave.
The value is and was 5s; before 1066, 10s.
   He held it himself then; he was the King's man; he could sell.

In STODDEN Hundred

13 In DEAN 11 Freemen of King William's hold 7 virgates of land and
the fourth part of 1 virgate. Land for 3½ ploughs; they are there.
The value is and always was 30s.
   The same Freemen who now hold this land also held it before
1066; they could grant to whom they would.
   Ralph put this land in the King's Administration, where it
was not before 1066.

14 In the same village Godwy Dear of Bedford holds ½ virgate
from the King.
The value is and always was 12d.
   He held it himself before 1066; he could do what he would with it.

In Hanefeld teñ Saiet . i . uirg de ſoca regis . Tra . ē
dim caŕ . 7 ibi . ē . Val 7 ualuit . v . ſol . T.R.E.'x . ſol.
Iſtemet tc tenuit . 7 potuit inde facere qđ uoluit.
In eođ Stoden hunđ teñ Turgot 7 mat ej de rege
dim hiđ . Tra . ē . i . caŕ . 7 ibi eſt . cū uno uillo 7 ii . borđ.
Silua . iiii . porc . Val 7 ualuit . x . ſol . T.R.E.'xii . ſol.
Hanc trā tenuit pat huj Turgoti . teigñ regis fuit.
7 trā ſuā dare 7 uende potuit.
In Mildentone teñ qđā bedell regis dim uirg de
rege . Tra . ē . ii . bob . Val 7 ualuit . xii . deñ . Hanc trā
tenuit pat ej qui nc tenet . 7 cui uoluit dare potuit.
In Brimehā teñ Oſiet . i . uirg IN DIM HD DE BVCHELAI.
7 ii . part uni uirg . Tra . ē . i . caŕ . 7 ibi . ē . p̃tū dim caŕ.
Val . x . ſol . T.R.E.'v . ſol . Iſtemet tc tenuit . 7 dare potuit.
In·Toruei teñ Aluuin de rege tciā parte IN WILGE HD.
de dim hida . Tra . ē . ii . bob . 7 ibi ſunt . Val 7 ualuit . iii . ſol.
Iſtemet tenuit . T.R.E. 7 potuit facere de ea qđ uoluit.   ※
In eođ hunđ teñ Oſiet regis p̃fect dim hiđ de rege.
Tra . ē dim caŕ . 7 ibi eſt . Val 7 ualuit ſep . iii . ſol . Hanc
trā tenuit . i . ſochs . T.R.E . que rex . W . cū tra hac p̃dicto
p̃fecto cōmdauit . ut quādiu uiueret uictū 7 ueſtitū ei
In Wimtone . teñ Turchill de rege . i . hidā . / ̃ pberet.
Tra . ē . i . caŕ . 7 ibi . ē . Val 7 ualuit . v . ſol . T.R.E.'x . ſol.
Iſtemet tc tenuit . 7 cui uoluit uende potuit.
※ Rex û . W . ſibi poſtea in elemoſina cceſſit . unde ‚p anima
                                    regis 7 reginæ
    oñi edđa . ii . feria miſsā pſoluit.

15   In *HANEFELD* Saegeat holds 1 virgate, of the King's jurisdiction.
Land for ½ plough; it is there.
The value is and was 5s; before 1066, 10s.
He held it himself then; he could do what he would with it.

16   Also in the Hundred of STODDEN Thorgot and his mother hold ½ hide
from the King. Land for 1 plough; it is there, with
1 villager and 2 smallholders.
Woodland, 4 pigs.
The value is and was 10s; before 1066, 12s.
This Thorgot's father held this land; he was a thane of the King's;
he could grant and sell his land.

17   In MILTON (Ernest) a beadle of the King's holds ½ virgate from the King.
Land for 2 oxen.
The value is and was 12d.
The present holder's father held this land; he could grant to
whom he would.

In the Half-Hundred of BUCKLOW

18   In BROMHAM Osgeat holds 1 virgate and 2 parts of 1 virgate.
Land for 1 plough; it is there.
Meadow for ½ plough.
Value 10s; before 1066, 5s.
He held it himself then; he could grant.

In WILLEY Hundred

19   In TURVEY Alwin the priest holds the third part of ½ hide from
the King. Land for 2 oxen; they are there.
The value is and was 3s.
He held it himself before 1066; he could do what he would with it.

(continued below, directed by transposition signs to its proper place.)

20   In the same Hundred Osgeat, a reeve of the King's holds ½ hide
from the King. Land for ½ plough; it is there.
The value is and always was 3s.
A Freeman held this land before 1066. King William commended
him to the said reeve with this land, so that as long as lived he should
provide food and clothing for him.

21   In WYMINGTON Thorkell holds 1 hide from the King. Land for 1 plough;
it is there.
The value is and was 5s; before 1066, 10s.
He held it himself then; he could sell to whom he would.

(57,19 continued, directed by transposition signs to its proper place.)

But King William later granted it to him in alms, for which he performed
mass every week on Mondays for the souls of the King and the Queen.

In HERTFORDSHIRE

1   **LAND OF THE KING**   132 b

In the Half-Hundred of HITCHIN ...   132 c

E1   5   King William holds WESTONING. It answers for 5 hides.
Land for 14 ploughs. In lordship 2 hides; 2 ploughs.
16 villagers with 3 smallholders have 5 ploughs;
a further 5 possible.
4 slaves; meadow for 7 ploughs; pasture for the village
livestock; woodland, 400 pigs, and 3s too.
Earl Harold held this manor; it lay and lies in Hitchin (lands);
but the obligations of this manor lay in Bedfordshire before 1066,
in the Hundred of Manshead. It is and always was a manor there;
since 1066 it has not met the King's tax.

13   **LAND OF ST. PAUL'S, LONDON**   136 b

In DACORUM Hundred

E2   1   The Canons of London hold KENSWORTH. It answers for 10 hides.
Land for 10 ploughs. In lordship 5 hides; 2 ploughs there;
a further 3 possible.
8 villagers with 3 smallholders have 2 ploughs; a further 3
possible.
3 slaves; pasture for the livestock; woodland, 100 pigs, and
from the payments of the woodland 2s.
Total value 70s; when acquired 100s; before 1066 as much.
Young Leofwin held this manor from King Edward.

19   **LAND OF ROBERT D'OILLY**   137 d

[In the Half-Hundred of HITCHIN]

E3   2   In POLEHANGER Martell holds ½ hide from Robert d'Oilly.
Land for 1 plough; it is there, with
2 cottagers and 2 slaves.
Meadow for 1 plough; woodland, 2 pigs.
The value is and was 10s; before 1066, 20s.
Aelfric, Earl Waltheof's man, held this land; he could sell.

21   **LAND OF ROBERT OF TOSNY**   138 a

In DACORUM Hundred

E4   2   In BARWYTHE Baldric holds 5 hides from Robert. Land for 3
ploughs. In lordship 2; a third possible.
3 villagers, with a priest and a Frenchman, with 4 smallholders.
Meadow for 1 plough; pasture for the village livestock;
woodland, 100 pigs.
In total, value 40s; when acquired 30s; before 1066, 60s.
Oswulf son of Fran held this land; he could sell to whom he
would.

2   LAND OF THE BISHOP OF LINCOLN   203 d

LEIGHTONSTONE Hundred ...

E5   9   In PERTENHALL Alwin had 1 virgate of land taxable.
Land for ½ plough.

K   This land is situated in Bedfordshire, but it pays tax
and service in Huntingdonshire. The King's officers
claim it for his work.
Value before 1066 and now 5s.
William holds it from Bishop Remigius and ploughs
there, together with his lordship.

13   LAND OF WILLIAM OF WARENNE   205 c

[KIMBOLTON Hundred]

E6   3   S. In SWINESHEAD 3½ hides taxable. Land for 4 ploughs.
Jurisdiction.
Now 1 Freeman, 7 villagers and 5 smallholders.
Meadow, 16 acres; woodland pasture 1 league long and
     4 furlongs wide.
Value 40s.
Eustace holds from William.

19   LAND OF EUSTACE THE SHERIFF   206 a

KIMBOLTON Hundred

E7   11 M. In SWINESHEAD Fursa had ½ hide taxable. Land for ½ plough,
with full jurisdiction.
Now 1 villager.
Meadow, 3 acres; woodland pasture 1 league long and 1
     furlong wide.
Value before 1066, 15s; now 6s.
Ralph holds from Eustace.

D   DECLARATIONS OF THE SWORN MEN   208 a

E8   14   The men of the County testify that King Edward gave   208 b
SWINESHEAD to Earl Siward, with full jurisdiction, and so
Earl Harold had it; moreover that (its men) paid tax in the
Hundred, and went with them against the enemy.

E9   16   Of Alwin Devil's 1 virgate of land in PERTENHALL,
King Edward had the jurisdiction.

ABBREVIATIONS used in the notes.
BCS . . . Birch *Cartularium Saxonicum.* DB . . Domesday Book. DBB . . . Maitland
Domesday Book and Beyond. DG . . . H.C. Darby and G. H. Versey *Domesday Gazetteer.*
EPNS . . . English Place-Name Society Survey (Bedfordshire, unless otherwise indicated).
KCD . . . Kemble *Codex Diplomaticus.* MS . . . Manuscript. OEB . . . G. Tengvik *Old
English Bynames*.* PNDB . . O. von Feilitzen *The Pre-Conquest Personal Names of
Domesday Book*.* VCH . . . Victoria County History, Bedfordshire, Volume 1.
   **Nomina Germanica,* Uppsala, Volumes 3 and 4.

The manuscript is written on leaves, or folios, of parchment (sheepskin), measuring about
15 inches by 11 (38 bv 28 cm), on both sides. On each side, or page, are two columns,
making four to each folio. The folios were numbered in the 17th century, and the four
columns of each are here lettered a,b,c,d. Chapter numbers and titles are in red ink, and
sections are normally distinguished by initial capitals, outlined in red. Many Hundred and
place names are written in capitals, scored through in red, normally represented by Farley
with italic capitals. Farley's principal variants from this convention are, in place names,
neither capitals nor scored in the MS, 23,16; scored, but not in capitals, 24,9; 26,1; 27,1;
40,3; 41,2; in capitals, but not scored, 23,14; and HVND at 2,2, in capitals but not scored
in the MS. Deletion is normally marked by underlining.
   The MS has more minor careless mistakes in Bedfordshire than in many counties,
chiefly the misspelling, omission or repetition of words and occasionally of phrases. The
overall total of hides is however independently confirmed (see note below), and there is
no reason to suppose serious or frequent error in other figures.

BEDFORDSHIRE. *Bedefordscire* in red at the top of each page, over both columns. The
Shire emerged from the district assigned to the maintenance of the Danish army of Bedford
in the late 9th century, but was formally organised later, probably about 1008 (see
Warwicks. 1,6 note). In the 'County Hidage' (Maitland DBB 475), held to have been
drafted not much later, it is entered at 1200 hides; the 1086 hides also total approximately
1200. The external boundary may therefore have been little changed. It was however
artificial in 1086, dividing a dozen manors and parishes, several of which were not reunited
until the 19th century. The gains however roughly balance the losses, and the total surface
area did not greatly differ from that of the modern county, about 300,000 acres.

B   HIDES. The hide was the unit of measurement of land, of productivity, of extent,
or of tax liability, and contained four virgates. Governments tried to standardise
the hide at 120 acres, but incomplete revision left hides of widely different
extent in different areas (see Sussex, Appendix). In Bedfordshire (32,14; 39,3),
as occasionally elsewhere, woodland was sometimes measured by the hide. If the
Bedfordshire hides regularly included all productive land, they might have been
standardised at 120 acres, 1200 of them accounting for a little under half the
total area of the Shire.
BISHOP REMIGIUS. Of Lincoln.
VALUE. *Valet* normally means the sums due to lords from their lands.
100s. DB uses the English currency system, in force until 1971. The pound
contained 20 shillings, each of 12 pence, and the abbreviations £s.d. preserved
the DB terms *librae, solidi, denarii.* DB often lists smaller sums in multiples of
shillings rather than of pounds, as here. 100s means £5.
L 40   LOVETT. Old French *louet,* wolf-cub, OEB 363; distinct from English *Levet* (20,1).
L 50   ARGENTON. Or, less probably, Argentan, OEB 69.
1,1a   HUNDRED. As in some other Shires, the Bedfordshire Hundreds are normally
entered in the same order in each chapter. The order is Manshead and Stanbridge
(interchangeable), Redbornstoke, Stodden, Flitt, Bucklow, Willey, Barford,
Biggleswade, Wenslow, Wixamtree and Clifton. Apart from marginal insertions,
the main variants are ch. 23, where Hugh of Beauchamp's lordship land and his
men's lands are separately listed, and his last four lordship manors (13-16), are also a
separate list, possibly an addition; and ch. 57, also in three successive lists, which
do not however relate to the three categories of the chapter title. See also 48,2;
54,4; 57, notes.

30 HIDES. 47 with those of 1b, 43 without 1c. The commonest figures are multiples of 5 hides, the old English basis for military and other obligations; e.g., Berks., B 10.

LAND FOR . . PLOUGHS. An estimate of the arable, probably earlier than 1066.

MEADOW FOR . . PLOUGHS. For the oxen who pull the plough, reckoned at eight.

DOG DUES. Payments replacing the obligation to feed and kennel the King's hounds.

IVO TALLBOYS increased the payments of the King's three *dominica maneria,* evidently those which had been King Edward's; to each of them his brother Ralph, the Sheriff, added manors which had not been King Edward's. Ivo was a magnate, later Steward to William II, and survived till about 1115. He is chiefly remembered as an outstanding commander in the King's siege of Hereward and the English earls in Ely in 1069, and as an enemy to the monks of Crowland. Ralph acquired most of the numerous manors of Askell of Ware, but exchanged Ware (see Index of Places) with Hugh of Grandmesnil for various Bedfordshire lands. He died before 1086, and most of his lands passed to Hugh of Beauchamp, but some went to his widow, his daughter and his niece, married to Ranulf son of Ilger. His heirs and the two Hughs disputed many items of the inheritance; see ch.23, and also Hertfordshire, especially EB 3, note.

1,1b   **HIDES . . PLACED.** Probably including Eggington, Stanbridge and Billington, not named in DB, since 47 hides is over large for Leighton Buzzard on its own.

1,1c   **BISHOP WULFWY.** Of Dorchester-on-Thames, died 1067; under his successor, Remigius, the see was transferred to Lincoln.

1,2   **MANSHEAD HUNDRED.** Luton was later in Flitt Hundred, but not in DB; it was therefore presumably in Manshead in 1086, probably in Woodcroft Hundred before 1066 (1,4 note). Dunstable was a deserted Roman ruin, not yet resettled.

1,3   **HOUGHTON.** MS clearly *HOVSTONE;* unclear in Farley's print.

1,4   **QUEEN EDITH.** Wife of King Edward, daughter of Earl Godwin.

      WOODCROFT HUNDRED. Otherwise unknown. Evidently merged in Manshead and Stanbridge, both of which were much above the normal size of other Hundreds (1,5 note 'ANOTHER HUNDRED').. The meeting place was presumably *Wodecroft* in Luton, last recorded in 1372, EPNS 160; the Hundred therefore probably included Luton.

      INCREASE IT GAVE HIM. Or possibly 'he gave'.

1,5   **PLACED.** *Apposuit* Accidentally repeated, and deleted.

      5 HIDES. Perhaps those of Caddington.

      ANOTHER HUNDRED. The occasions of transfers from one Hundred to another are rarely noted in DB, though transfers were plainly frequent. EPNS maps later changes, and DB entries point to earlier changes. As in other midland Shires, Bedford's 1200 hides probably originally meant twelve Hundreds, each of 100 hides. There were still twelve Hundreds in 1086, but not of 100 hides each. Three are in several entries termed Half-Hundreds, Stanbridge, Bucklow and Wenslow. By 1086, Wenslow had cut Biggleswade into two separated portions, but the two portions together totalled 100 hides; as in Flitt, compensation after a boundary change is a likely explanation. Precise figures for 1086 cannot be had without close analysis, but a provisional count, to the nearest hide, suggests the main areas of change. Four Hundreds retained their assessment, Stodden and Biggleswade with 100 hides each, Flitt with 97 and Clifton with 99. Five other Hundreds are entered at 501 hides between them, Manshead (167) and Stanbridge (109), both well over their formal rating, with the former Hundred of Woodcroft, and with Redbornstoke (116) and Wixamtree (109). Willey (104) and Barford (93), with the Half-Hundreds of Wenslow (45) and Bucklow (55), total 297 hides, the equivalent of three Hundreds. The grand total of these hides, 1194, is virtually unchanged, but the internal boundaries had evidently been drastically rearranged; beyond the obvious inference that the larger part of Woodcroft was assigned to Manshead and Stanbridge, there is no evident explanation of the nature, date or purpose of these changes. It is possible that analysis of landholding in and before 1066 may suggest some of the reasons.

2,2   **HOLDING.** *De fedo,* MS error for *de feudo,* meaning the Bishop's entire Holding. *In feudo* is occasionally used in DB for land held by a special grant, sometimes for life, see Sussex 11,8 note.

2,3   **FREEMEN.** See Appendix.

2,5   **BEFORE 1066.** Farley *TR..; TRE* is legible beneath a MS blot.

2,6   **BUCKLOW.** The MS is blotted. Read *Boch[el]ai..Stach[eden]e...p[ot].* See 3,4 note.

      7 SMALLHOLDERS. MS *vii;* Farley, in error, *vi.*

2,8 WIMUND. Probably of Tessel, see 23,37.
     ALFWOLD. See 15,2.
2,9 VILLAGERS. As a general term, including Freemen and smallholders.
3,3 5 PLOUGHS. The MS is difficult to read; probably *v car*.
3,4 BEFORE 1066. MS blotted, facing 2,6. Read *[T]RE...v. [so]chi*, and, in 3,5, *d[api]fer*.
     The stop after *v*, before *[so]chi*, is clear in the MS.
3,6 EASTON. See *Inquisitio Eliensis* 66a, columns 1-2 (ed. Hamilton p.166) *in comitatu Huntedonie Spalduuic...7 Ber. Estou, Estune, Bercheham* (In Huntingdonshire Spaldwick and the outliers (Long) Stow, Easton and Barham). The places adjoin each other; see Hunts., Appendix. See also Hunts. D 19 'The County testifies that the third part of ½ hide which lies in Easton (*Estone*) and pays tax in Bedfordshire belongs to Spaldwick, the Abbot of Ely's manor'; Eustace had annexed it in 1071. Spaldwick was in Hunts., but Easton paid tax in Bedfordshire. The eleven entries for Easton total 9½ hides. It may have been a ten-hide manor, the other half-hide being a portion of the Spaldwick outlier which Eustace had not annexed.
     In 1881 Airy emended *Estone* to *Westen*, wasteland, and therefore located it on 'the high clay table of Little Staughton', which was 'one of a series of *Westens*', including Westoning, similarly emended. In 1904 Round (VCH 213-215) properly rejected this etymology (with which he parallelled Airy's derivation of *Segresdone* (Shirdon) from 'sacristan') and the consequent location; he suggested the obvious Easton, noting that William of Warenne's Honour of Kimbolton later retained 1 hide of Easton, where in 1086 he had held over 2 hides (Bedfordshire, 17,4-7). But the identification with Little Staughton was repeated by EPNS 20 in 1926, adding 'sic', and by DG, without qualification.
     The Domesday manor was clearly larger than the later parish. In proportion to the acreage, ploughs and assessed ploughs were both four times as numerous as in the neighbouring parishes of Staughton, which include the DB manors of Dillington and Perry. Easton therefore probably included part of Great Staughton, now in Hunts., and all or part of Little Staughton, now in Beds. It might have consisted of scattered portions, but since such separate outliers are normally individually recorded in Beds., it is here mapped as a single area, with uncertain bounds, separated from Tilsworth by the Honour and former Hundred of Kimbolton, in Hunts.
3,8 BLEADON. The Bishop of Coutances also exchanged Tyringham and Clifton (Raynes) (Bucks. 5,10; 18...145 b,c) for *Bledone*. The only place named in DB with the same or similar spelling (Old English *bleo dun*, 'blue', or coloured, hill) is Bleadon in Somerset, with which VCH identified it, followed by DG. But Bleadon was held by the Bishop of Winchester before and after 1066 (Somerset 2,3... 87 d), whereas all the lands which the Bishop of Coutances received had been held by men of the King, except Tyringham, held by two thanes, one of them a man of Earl Waltheof, whose lands fell to the King on his execution, the other without a named lord. *Bledone* should therefore be a manor formerly held by the King or his men. There are two main alternative possibilities, either a variant spelling of Blewbury or Blewburton (*bleo byrig dune*) (EPNS Berks 151-2), a manor of King Edward's and King William's (Berks. 1,5... 56 d), or a lost place. Since the lands which the Bishop received lay close together, about the junction of Beds., Bucks., and Northants., DB may have omitted a King's manor in this area. Elsewhere the text occasionally refers to a manor not listed in the Survey.

3,9 NEWTON BROMSHOLD. See also Northants.

4	LAND OF THE BISHOP OF COUTANCES	220 c

     20 From the Bishop himself William holds 2 hides less ½ virgate in   220 d
        NEWTON (Bromshold). Land for 2 ploughs. In lordship 2 ploughs;
        8 villagers and 6 smallholders with 2 ploughs.
        Woodland 2 furlongs long and 1 furlong wide.
        The value was 20s; now 40s.
        Azor held it before 1066.
     The whole parish is now in Northants.; DB enters only a small part in Beds.

3,10 4 HIDES. Possibly in Chellington, not named in DB, but held by Geoffrey's heirs, VCH 225.
3,11 TURVEY. MS *Tornai* for *Torvai;* so also 24,23 and 32,3.

3,17　RUSHDEN. See also 22,2 and Northants.

[35]　　　　　LAND OF WILLIAM PEVEREL　　　　　225 d
[In HIGHAM Hundred]
1a William Peverel holds HIGHAM (Ferrers)...
1b In RUSHDEN 6 hides. Land for 12 ploughs.
　　19 Freemen have them.
　　A mill at 10s; meadow,30 acres. ...
1g [Countess] Gytha held it, with full jurisdiction.
　　The Freemen of Rushden, Irchester and Raunds were Burgred's men; for this
　　reason Bishop Geoffrey (of Coutances) claims their homage *(hominationem)*.
Beds. 3,17 had been held by one of Burgred's men, Beds. 22,2 by one of Countess
Gytha's, who was William Peverel's predecessor elsewhere. Rushden is now wholly in
Northants. See also 32,5 and 42,1 (Podington and Farndish).
OXEN. *Terra bobus* (dative), but *pratum bouum* (genitive).

4,2　WILLIAM'S FATHER. Evidently one of the Normans who held from King Edward
　　before 1066.
4,3　PIGS. *Porc* accidentally repeated, but not deleted.
4,5　VALUE...6s. MS *vi sol;* the *i* is thinner and fainter than the *v,* but is clear and distinct;
　　Farley, in error, *v sol.*
6　　ST. EDMUND'S. Bury St. Edmunds.
6,1　ORDWY held more land in Biddenham, 56,3.
　　BOROUGH REEVE. Rarely recorded in DB.
6,2　KINWICK. EPNS 109.
7,1　STANWICK. See also Northants.

6　　LAND OF ST. PETER'S OF PETERBOROUGH ...　　221 b
17 The Church itself holds 1 hide and 1 virgate of land in STANWICK.　221 c
　　Land for 3 ploughs. In lordship 2 ploughs, with 1 slave;
　　　　8 villagers and 4 smallholders with 1 plough and 2 oxen.
　　　　A mill at 20s; meadow 8 acres.
　　　　The value was 40s; now 100s.
Two-thirds of Stanwick was in Beds. in 1086; it is now all in Northants.
PLOUGH IRON. Primarily for plough-shares; from the woodland, where the fuel was;
iron was forged more easily there than by hauling timber to the village.

8,9　VALUE. Added in smaller lettering.
10,1　CARUCATE. Not the *carucata* of the Danish Shires. Here equivalent to 'Land for 1
　　plough', as in the Exon. DB and other comparable records. In the Home Counties,
　　used of lordship land, probably exempt from the King's tax. See Hunts., B 18; B 21
　　and Hurstingstone Hundred entries, where additional 'Land for ploughs' and *carucatae*
　　are equated with each other, but distinguished from *inland* in 6,19. Interlinear
　　corrections there and in Middlesex 24,1 (where the note, from line 2, *carucatae,* onward,
　　should be deleted) suggest that DB was itself in some doubt as to when *carucae,*
　　ploughs, and when *carucatae* should be written for the abbreviated *car.*
12,1　CADDINGTON. See also Herts.

13　　　　　LAND OF ST. PAUL'S, LONDON　　　　　136 b
　In DACORUM Hundred...
2　The Canons hold CADDINGTON themselves. It answers for 10 hides.
　　Land for 10 ploughs. In lordship 4 hides; 1 plough there;
　　　a further 3 possible.
　　　　22 villagers have 6 ploughs. 5 smallholders; 2 slaves.
　　　　Pasture for the livestock; woodland, 100 pigs and 2s too.
　　　　Total value 110s; when acquired £6; before 1066 as much.
　　　　(Young) Leofwin held this manor from King Edward.
The parish of Caddington was not reunited until 1897, when the Hertfordshire portion,
together with the adjoining parish of Kensworth, also held by Leofwin (E 2), was
transferred to Bedfordshire.
　About 1053 (KCD 920) Leofwin's father, Edwin of Caddington, bequeathed
Watford, where Leofwin held Bushey (Herts.33,2), to St. Alban's, and 'to my son
Leofwin' Sundon, Caddington, Streatley (Beds. 24,18), (Cockayne) Hatley, *Pirian,*
Putnoe and Barley (Herts. 29,1). DB enters other 1066 lay holders for Sundon, Hatley

and Putnoe, and Leofwin's lands at Beeston and Meppershall are not named in his father's will. A few years later 'Leofwin of Caddington' was one of the witnesses to Oswulf's grant of Studham to St. Albans (Beds. 26,1 note). He was a King's thane, possibly identical with Leofwin, Earl Harold's man, in Herts.

13,1   BIDDENHAM. Added in the margin.

14   ERNWIN. MS *Ernui* for *Ernuuin.*

14,1   ERNWIN THE PRIEST. He also held in Notts., Lincs., and the future Lancashire.

     PLOUGH. Half a plough there, but no inhabitants mentioned, as in several smaller Bedfordshire holdings. '½ plough possible' omitted.

15   COUNT EUSTACE. Of Boulogne, brother-in-law of King Edward.

15,2   ALFWOLD. *Adeloldus,* Aethelwold. But he is plainly identical with *Aluuoldus,* Alfwold of Stevington (2,8), and therefore with Alfwold of 15,1; 4-7.

15,6   PLOUGHS. 'Land for 5 ploughs' omitted.

16,2   BATTLESDEN. In all, 11 hides; with its neighbour, Chalgrave, 9 hides, a total of 20 hides.

16,5   DUNTON. *Domtone,* MS error for *Donitone.*

16,9   MILL 3s 3d. The abbreviation above *iii solid* is *[tri]um.*

17   WILLIAM OF WARENNE. A prominent magnate, created Earl of Surrey by William II; died 1088.

     DELIVERER. The *liberator* handed over land on the King's behalf, and freed it from other claims.

17,2   TILBROOK. Now in Huntingdonshire.

     SO THAT. The cumbersome phrase is unusual. Very many Freemen and others in DB are said to have had the right, before 1066, to 'withdraw', either without qualification, sometimes equated with *alodium,* 'freehold', or 'to another lord'. Here, as commonly in Beds., they are not said to have been subject to any lord. Normally, the Commissioners, or their clerk, transcribed the phrase without comment; the wording suggests that on this occasion they asked 'the men of the Hundred' to explain its meaning.

     HUGH (OF) BEAUCHAMP...RALPH TALLBOYS. See 1,1a note, Ivo Tallboys, and 23,7 note.

17,3   KIMBOLTON. Formerly a Hundred, in 1086 the centre of William of Warenne's Honour, in Huntingdonshire, jutting into Bedfordshire between Tilbrook and Easton. *Hanefelde* evidently lay close to the Shire boundary in this area.

     OBLIGATIONS. *Warras, werian,* defend, guard, be wary of; probably including both the King's *geld* and liability for military service. Not to be confused with *Waras,* Ware in Hertfordshire (23,7ff.), probably a plural of *waer.* weir, EPNS Herts. 206.

17,4   ASKELL. Of Ware, see 1,1a Ivo Tallboys and 23,7 notes.

     COLMWORTH. See 23,38.

     SHERIFFDOM. Since in 1086 each Shire had its Sheriff *(vicecomes),* but only two had an Earl *(comes),* DB often uses *vicecomitatus* for *comitatus,* county.

17,5   COMMENDED. An unusually explicit definition of *commendatio;* see 23,17; 57,20.

17,7   GODRIC. Possibly a MS error for *homo Godrici vicecomitis,* a man of Godric the Sheriff; see 23,25.

18,1   BOSCOMBE. In Wiltshire. He was William's predecessor in other counties.

20,1   WULFWARD. Wulfward White, a magnate of King Edward's, Arnulf's predecessor in several other counties.

     LEOFED. *Levet,* perhaps *Leofede,* PNDB 322 *(Luvede);* or *Levid, quedam femina* (Essex 30,44...62 a), see PNDB 312; or a misspelling of *Leviet* (Leofgeat).

20,2   EDWARD WHITE. *Uuit* is a frequent byname, used by a number of different unrelated people. But since Edward held from Arnulf, he may have been a relative of Wulfward, (20,1); if so, his is a rare instance of an Old English family name. It is however possible that the interlinear correction was added against the wrong name, intended for Wulfward.

     THE 3 ABOVE. Those of 21,12.

     LISOIS. Of Moutiers. His courage and initiative forced the passage of the Aire in William's campaign against York in 1069, Ordericus 4,7.

22,1   TILSWORTH. MS *Pileworde* mistakes Old English 'thorn' (Th) for P; the return which DB here transcribed was therefore written by a clerk familiar with Old English letters.

22,2   MALET. Normally a byname. The personal name was perhaps omitted.

     COUNTESS GYTHA. Widow of Earl Ralph of Hereford, William Peverel's predecessor elsewhere; different from her namesake, wife of Earl Godwin and mother of King Harold.

23,1	KEYSOE. See also Hunts.	
	13 LAND OF WILLIAM OF WARENNE...	205 c
	2 S. In KEYSOE Aellic, 3 virgates of land taxable. Land for 6 oxen. Jurisdiction. 1 Freeman and 7 smallholders. Meadow, 4 acres; woodland pasture 50 acres.	
	29 LAND OF THE KING'S THANES...	207 c
	LEIGHTONSTONE Hundred	
	2 In KEYSOE Alwin had 1 virgate of land taxable, with full jurisdiction. Land for 2 oxen. It lies in Bedfordshire, but it pays tax in Huntingdonshire. Now he holds it himself from the King and has 1 villager, with 2 oxen in a plough. Value before 1066, 16d; now the same.	

DB reports a total of 5 hides and 1 virgate of Keysoe in Bedfordshire; it may be that the record omitted a statement that William of Warenne's 3 virgates also 'lay in Bedfordshire'. It is probably that the Huntingdonshire taxable hide lay in the north of the manor, adjoining Pertenhall (E 9).

23,5 CHAINHALLE. VCH 237 suggests Channel's End (TL 11 57), apparently on the similarity of the modern name, but queries it because Channel's End is in Barford Hundred; and is followed by DG, without the query. EPNS map gives it as an alternative name for Ravensden, but omits it from its text. Presumably the editors (Mawer and Stenton, in 1926) had some evidence to support this identification; but the relevant EPNS records were lost or destroyed during the war. Its position in the text places it in Bucklow Hundred, which Ravensden adjoins.

23,7 GOLDINGTON HIGHFIELDS. 2½ miles north-west of Goldington, separated from it by Putnoe.

WARE. Ralph received in all (see Index of Places) 22 hides and 3 virgates in exchange for Ware, assessed at 24 hides; but their combined value was much less than the value of Ware. See 1,1a Ivo Tallboys, note.

23,15 AKI. Achi,here and in 23,38, may be a mistake for Aschil, but since Hugh held much land that had not been Askell's, Aki may be a separate person.

23,16 WHEN ACQUIRED. i.e., by Hugh.

23,17 COMMENDED. See 17,5 and 57,20 notes.

23,22 THERE WAS 1 FREEMAN. MS fuerunt for fuit ('were' for 'was'); see 23,53.

23,27 BLETSOE. Here and in 53,8 in Bucklow. Geographically, in 1086, Bletsoe should have been in Willey, Radwell in Bucklow, with the Ouse as Hundred boundary. The anomaly may be the result of a transfer, see 1,5 note.

23,31 OSBERN. MS Osbert for Osbern, see 23,27; 44,2; 46,1 notes.

23,36 HIDES. MS car, underlined for deletion, emended to hid(as).

23,48 HOO. In Wootton (49,2), which Aelmer held; EPNS 86.

23,50 IN THE SAME VILLAGE. Repeated 23,51-55.

23,53 HELD. MS tenuit, probably a MS error for tenet, holds, as in 23,22 above.

24,2 FUGLO. MS Suglo, in error, PNDB 256. The text was evidently transcribing a return which used small-letter hooked 's', easily confused with 'f'.

24,5 OATS FROM THE WOODLAND. Presumably from clearings in the woodland.

24,9 THEY ALL. Evidently some names have been omitted, probably of Freemen.

24,11 BROOM. The marginal addition is placed against the wrong Hundred.

24,13 WESTCOTTS. By Wilshamstead, formerly balancing Eastcotts, the parish centred on Cotton End, TL 08 45; EPNS 86 and 91.

PLOUGH IRON. See 8,1 note.

24,15 SMALLHOLDERS and slaves here entered after resources.

24,17 HOLD. The MS omits de and repeats ten(et).

24,18 SOMEONE. Quidem, probably for a word or name illegible in the return transcribed.

MARRIAGE PORTION. DB distinguishes maritagium, provided by the bride's father, from dos, the dowry provided by the husband; see also ch. 55.

24,19 MILTON ERNEST. With this entry, Milton Ernest makes 10 hides, as does Milton Bryan in Manshead Hundred. Milton Ernest is in Stodden; but it is possible that a portion of its lands lay across the Ouse, in Willey, and that the Hundred heading is inserted after, instead of before, the entry, as occasionally in other counties.

	PLOUGH POSSIBLE. The MS probably omitted *pot(est) fieri* after *vill.*
25,1	PASSWATER. French *passe l'eau,* hence English Paslow, Parslow, etc., OEB 386.
25,11	FRENCHMEN. *Franci,* probably for the more usual *francigenae,* rather than 'freemen'.
25,14	THANE OF THE KING'S. The MS probably omitted *E(dwardi)* after *regis.*
26,1	STUDHAM. Granted to St. Albans (KCD 945) shortly before 1066 by Oswulf and his wife, Aethelida. The named witnesses are Bishop Wulfwy, Bondi the Constable, Burgred and his son Edwin, Godric *'tribunus',* Alstan the Sheriff and Leofwin of Caddington (12,1 note). Aethelida had inherited Studham from her first husband Wulfsi. She and Oswald retained its use for their lives, and the Abbot provided timber to build a church in Studham 'in honour of our Lord Jesus Christ and St. Alban'. St. Albans did not acquire the land, presumably because Oswulf lived until the Conquest, and the medieval church was dedicated to the Virgin.
27,1	EDLESBOROUGH. See also Bucks.

22   LAND OF GILBERT OF GHENT   149 d

In YARDLEY Hundred

1 M. Gilbert of Ghent holds EDLESBOROUGH. It answers for 20 hides. Land for 14 ploughs. In lordship 10 hides; 4 ploughs there.

26 villagers with 4 smallholders have 10 ploughs.

10 slaves; 2 mills at 15s 4d; meadow for 4 ploughs; woodland, 400 pigs.

Total value £13; value before 1066 £14.

Ulf, a thane of King Edward's, held this manor; he could sell.

The two thirds of the manor in Bucks. presumably included the village; the Beds. portion would therefore be in the south-east of the modern parish. The village is now all in Bucks.

	10d. MS probably omits *den(arii),* but might intend 110 shillings.
30,1	SON OF FAFITON. So Hunts. 25,1.
	HORN. MS *Horim,* in error; see Middlesex 4,11.
32,5	PODINGTON. See also Northants.

[35]   LAND OF WILLIAM PEVEREL   225 d

1a William Peverel holds Higham (Ferrers)...

1g In PODINGTON ½ hide in jurisdiction *(de soca).*

4 villagers with 1 plough.

See also Beds. 3,17 and 42,1 (Rushden and Farndish).

The larger part of Podington was in Beds., and the whole parish now is.

32,6	PLOUGHS. 'Another plough possible' omitted.
32,10	THANE. MS *Steignus* for *Teignus.*
32,14	½ HIDE OF WOODLAND. Woodland is occasionally measured by the hide elsewhere, e.g. Essex 24, 1-2 (42a); see Sussex, Appendix. The other half of the Southill woodland is entered at 39,3.
35,2	SHIRDON. EPNS 17.
38,1	SUDBURY. EPNS 59.
39,1	VIRGATE. The figure is omitted; 1 virgate completes a 10 hide manor.
40,1	MORCAR. See 1, 2b.
	LUTON. MS *Lintone* for *Luitone,* as also in 57,4; EPNS 156.
40,2	£7. Probably a MS error for *vii sol.*
40,3	PLOUGHS. '2 ploughs possible' omitted.
42,1	FARNDISH. See also Northants.

[35]   LAND OF WILLIAM PEVEREL   225 d

1a William Peverel holds HIGHAM (Ferrers)...

1f In FARNDISH 3 virgates of land in jurisdiction *(de soca).*

Land for 1 plough; 2 Freemen have it.

See also 3,17 and 32,5 (Rushden and Podington). The whole of the parish is now in Beds.

43	THE FIGURE is clear in the MS, smudged in Farley's print.
44,2	OSBERN. MS Osbert for Osbern, as in 23,31; 46,1.
44,4	ELVEDON. EPNS 17.
46,1	A MILL. Resources entered before people, as occasionally elsewhere.
	OSBERN. MS Osbert for Osbern, as in 23 31; 44,2.
	RALPH... GAVE TRIBUTE. Canute is said to have ruled that if a landholder was more than four days overdue with his payments, whoever came forward and paid might have

the land (Heming *Chartularium Ecclesiae Wigorncnsis* 1, 278); VCH 207.

46,2   BEFORE 1066. TRE accidentally repeated in the MS.

47,4   2 HIDES LESS. *et* accidentally inserted in the MS.

48,1   MEPPERSHALL. See also Herts.

> **40**   **LAND OF GILBERT SON OF SOLOMON**   142 a
>
> 1   Gilbert son of Solomon holds MEPPERSHALL. It answers for 3 hides
>   and 1 virgate.
>   3 villagers and 4 cottagers.
>   This land is assessed in Bedfordshire with (his) other land.
>   Leofwin, a thane of King Edward's, held this land.

The manor was divided by the county boundary, and Polehanger, to the north, was in Herts. This area may have been detached; or the eastern end of Stondon and Shillington may have been included in the manor, with a boundary as here mapped, marked uncertain. GILBERT. Elsewhere he held only 30 acres, at Felsted (Essex 73,1...96 b). YOUNG LEOFWIN. See 12,1 note.

48,2   WILLEY HUNDRED. The normal Hundred order is here reversed, perhaps because Meppershall was Gilbert's principal residence. PLOUGHS. '1 plough possible' omitted.

49,1   ALBERT. Chaplain to King Edward and King William.

50,1   HONDAY. PNDB 292.

52,2   GLADLEY. Now in Heath and Reach parish, to which it may correspond. MILL. No population is recorded, as often on small holdings, but rarely on one of this size. The omission may be accidental, as that rectified by a marginal addition in 53,24.

53,8   MAN...SHE. *Homo* here includes woman.

53,15   OSBERN HOLDS. Perhaps Sudbury, with which this holding would make 3 hides, VCH 258, citing *Feudal Aids*, 1,15,33.
10s. The mark over the *x*, shown in Farley as the abbreviation normally written above the 'm' of marginal manor, is more probably a flourish at the end of *recep(it)*.

53,16   POTTON. Entered out of Hundred order. The entry is also contradictory; lands described as 'held in Potton' should not normally include Potton itself. The holding may be a half virgate in Barford, belonging to Potton.

53,17   PLOUGH. Either 1 villagers' plough, or 1 plough possible, omitted.

53,21   SUTTON. Smaller lettering is used, to 56,4.

53,30   EVERTON. See also Hunts.

> **24**   **LAND OF RANULF BROTHER OF ILGER**   207 b
>   TOSELAND Hundred
>
> 1 M.   In EVERTON Ingward had 7 hides taxable. Land for 18 ploughs.
>   Now in lordship 2 ploughs;
>   19 villagers and 12 smallholders who have 9 ploughs.
>   A priest and a church; meadow, 15 acres; underwood, 40 acres.
>   Value before 1066 £10; now £7.
>   Ranulf brother of Ilger holds from the King.

The larger part of the manor was in Hunts., but the parish is now in Beds. The modern parish is however somewhat small for so large a manor, and the Hunts. manor may have included at least the detached part of Tetworth parish, and the strip of Cambridgeshire that divides Tetworth.

53,32   HOLDER OF KEMPSTON. Not named, perhaps because of uncertainty. Kempston (53,5) is entered as held by Tosti's brother Gyrth; it may have passed to him on Tosti's exile in 1065. It is possible that the abbreviation *com* refers to Countess Judith, as 1086 holder of Kempston, but, with one exception (53,3), her name is written as *comit* or *comitissa*, not *com*.

54,1   MEADOW. Resources before people, see 46,1.

54,4   MILTON ERNEST. Out of Hundred order. Not said to be held of Adelaide, but by her husband's steward. It was perhaps intended as a separate chapter, see VCH 260-1.

55,1   WIFE. *Femina*, not implying widow, but interchangeable with *uxor; uxor* is used in the chapter title of Azelina, who was a widow, but in the Landholders' list *femina* is used both of Azelina, and of Adelaide, whose husband was living.

55,2   HOCKLIFFE. Possibly in Stanbridge Half-Hundred, since the parish lies south and west of Watling Street.

55,5	MARRIAGE PORTION. See 24,18 note; compare e.g. 56,11 *de dote*, dowry.
56,3	HIDE. The total and the details of this holding disagree by a fraction of a virgate. Both figures make Biddenham just under 10 hides.
57	REEVES. The Hundred order is here is three consecutive lists, 1-5 (including 3 i-vi grouped together on their own); 6-11; and 12-21. Of the three categories in the chapter title, Reeves are named in 1-5 and 20-21; a Beadle in 17; and an almsman in 19.
	BEADLE. An unpopular lesser official with minor police functions.
57,1	ADMINISTRATION. *Ministerium Regis*. The phrase is unusual. It does not here carry any generalised meaning of 'service' or 'use', but is confined to lands which the King, as in other counties, distributed in small holdings to various beneficiaries, usually former public servants of various kinds.
57,4	REEVE OF THE HUNDRED. Rarely recorded in DB.
	LUTON. *Lintone* for *Luitone;* see 40,1.
	BONDI. One of the few English notables who retained lands and office for some time after 1066. He was probably Sheriff of Bedfordshire, before Ralph Tallboys.
57,5	PLOUGHS. 'Land for 2(?) ploughs' omitted.
57,5	ORA. Literally an ounce. A unit of currency still in use in Scandinavia. Reckoned at either 16d, as probably here, or at 20d.
57,7	LANK. PNDB 309 (rather than the alternative 'Land').
57,8	ST. PAUL'S. Probably of London.
57,9	4 PARTS. So the MS, as in 57,10. The zig-zag abbreviation over *part* normally abbreviates *partes; parte,* with a line above the *e*, is normal for *partem*, with *tam* added above *iiii* to indicate *quartam*. The usage is not however always consistent, and, since Beds. DB has more scribal errors than most counties, a mistake for 'fourth part' is possible.
	HALF OX. The probable meaning is a half share in an ox; the other share is not reported.
57,12	WESTCOTTS. See 24,13.
57,14	GODWY DEAR. OEB 343.
57,20	COMMENDED. See 17,5 note. In this instance, the Freeman was doubtless aged.
E 5	MARGINAL K. For *Klamor*, claim.
E 6	MARGINAL S. For *Soca*, Jurisdiction.

APPENDIX

Associations of Freemen *(sochemanni)* were numerous in Bedfordshire before 1066, except in the extreme south, and on the lands of the King and of English churches. Elsewhere some 600 *sochemanni* held about a third of the land, rising to two thirds in some Hundreds, with an average of over half a hide each, a range from a single acre to nearly two hides. Only a dozen of them held their land individually, but more than half of them in groups of between eight and twenty-four persons. Only a few are said to have held from lords. But by 1086 the total had been reduced to about 100, all of whom held from lords.

Similar groups on a similar scale are reported throughout the east midland Shires, of Cambridge and Northampton, Leicester and Nottingham, and especially Lincoln. Elsewhere these associations survived in greater numbers for some centuries, but freedom from lords is most marked in the Bedfordshire Survey. *Sochemanni* were somewhat less numerous in Derbyshire and Yorkshire, but plentiful in Norfolk and its borders; there however their different and varied status requires discussion in the county volumes. They are also entered in smaller numbers in Kent and Surrey, in Buckinghamshire, Huntingdonshire, Hertfordshire and Middlesex, where the average holding was twice as large as in Bedfordshire; but groups are fewer and smaller in these counties.

Throughout DB, except in East Anglia, the terms *liber homo* and *sochemannus* are mutually exclusive; where one is plentiful, the other is rare or absent. The difference in meaning in Bedford-shire is clearly stated in the Stanford entry (23,9); of four *sochemanni*, three were *liberi*, but the fourth could neither grant nor sell. The *liber homo* was free to sell his land; most *sochemanni* could 'grant or sell', and most of them were therefore also *liberi*.

The terms overlap, but had different meanings. Though DB enters tens of thousands of *sochemanni*, the word is rare and late in earlier documents. Shortly before 1066 King Edward granted to Westminster land at Eversley in Hampshire, held by four named men, including his brewer and one of his guards, described as *mine fre socne men* (Harmer *Anglo-Saxon Writs* 85 = KCD 845). The corresponding DB entry (Hants. 8,1...43 c) reports that *quattuor liberi homines tenuerunt de rege E in alodium*, 'four free men held from King Edward in freehold'. To King Edward they were both 'free' and also *socnemen;* in Hampshire DB uses only *liberi*, and does not use *sochemanni* or *socnemen*. Elsewhere the distinction may often be verbal; DB selects one of two adjectives that describe different rights of the same individual.

The term *sochemannus* clearly derives from *soca,* jurisdiction, and the profits arising therefrom. Several entries describe this jurisdiction. At Wandsworth (Surrey 21,3) 'Six *soche manni* held from King Edward...There were two Halls...it answered for 12 hides'. These were men of substance, with two hides apiece, and also 'free' to sell ('go where they would' in the idiom of the Surrey Survey); the 'Hall' gave them the jurisdiction normal in a manor. But when smaller men lacked halls, their absence was sometimes worthy of remark; in Kent (5,181...11 a), before 1066, two *sochemanni* had held half a yoke *sine aulis et dominiis,* without halls and lordships. Such men, as in Bedfordshire, had no lord but the King, and are sometimes termed *sochemanni regis.* But others also sometimes had some jurisdiction; on one Ramsey holding (Hunts. 6,3) the Abbot had the larger fines, the *sochemanni* the lesser fines. These and other entries argue that the root meaning is a man who exercised jurisdiction and received its profits, not a man subject to jurisdiction; for in the numerous places described as *soca* of northern manors, in their jurisdiction and subject to their halls, the inhabitants are not *sochemanni.* But the right to exercise limited jurisdiction implies exemption from comparable jurisdiction by others, by the Hundred court, or the lord, or both. *Sochemanni* enjoyed a restricted Franchise or Liberty; and many or most were also *liberi,* free to sell. Those who held only a few acres had little occasion for halls and jurisdiction, as in the Kentish entry, but it is probable that they inherited or acquired the exemptions attached to their name. It is also probable that the numerous *liberi homines* who held manors before 1066 also exercised some jurisdiction over their villagers. Both words describe men whose status and average holdings placed them above the villager, though many individuals among them held less land than some villagers. The differences between them are partly of substance, partly of terminology, partly regional; they cannot be seen more clearly until the information from all counties is examined and compared. Because the terms overlap, and sometimes describe the same persons, the *sochemannus,* with his Franchise, is here translated as 'Freeman', the *liber homo* as 'free man'.

It is however clear that the term *sochemannus* was relatively recent in 1066, abundant and long-lived in areas settled by the Danes in the 9th century, infrequent and in decline elsewhere. Since it is found in areas far removed from Danish influence, it is unlikely to describe a status originated by the Danes. It more probably derives from an older status, which was progressively reduced by English rulers of the 10th and 11th centuries, but which throve and prospered in Danish areas, and thereby acquired a new general name.

INDEX OF PERSONS

Familiar modern spellings are given when they exist. Unfamiliar names are usually given in an approximate late 11th century form, avoiding variants that were already obsolescent or pedantic. Spellings that mislead the modern eye are avoided where possible. Two, however, cannot be avoided: they are combined in the name of 'Leofgeat', pronounced 'Leffyet', or 'Levyet'. The definite article is omitted before bynames, except where there is reason to suppose that they described the individual. The chapter numbers of listed landholders are printed in italics.

Thorgot	57,16	William the Chamberlain	40. 1,2b; 3
Thorkell	23,18. 53,21. 57,21	William, Steward of the	3,5; 9
Thurstan the Chamberlain	47	Bishop of Coutances	
Thurstan	3,12. 55,3	William of Cairon	4,2; 6-8. 21,5; 8-9;
Earl Tosti	23,47. 24,14. 44,1.		17. 24,28
	47,3. 49,2-3. 53,2; 16;	William of Eu	18
	20; 29-30; 32-33.	William of Loucelles	23,22-23
	54,3. 57,2	William of Warenne	17. 23,1 note. E 6
Tovi the priest	2,4	William son of Rainward	25,7
Tovi	46,1. 53,12	William son of Reginald	25.2
Tuffa	53,31	William	42. E 5
Ulf	27,1	Wimund of Tessel	23,37-38
Walraven	1,4	Wimund	2,8. 23,24; 33; 38
Walter Giffard	16	Wintermilk, see Alric	
Walter the monk	55,8	Wulfeva	3,5
Walter of Flanders	32. 8,2. 31,1. 32,4	Wulfgeat	23,24. 28,1. 53,14
Walter brother of Sihere	33	Wulfheah, King Edward's	53,15
Walter, see Osbern		steersman	
Walter	18,2. 23,43; 56.	Wulfmer the burgess	56,4
	25,5-6. 55,12	Wulfmer, King Edward's	6,1
Earl Waltheof	6,2. 23,17. 40,3.	priest	
	53,31. E 3	Wulfmer the priest	57,4
Warner	23,30	Wulfmer of Eaton	21,1; 5-6; 9-10;
Wending	23,46		14-15; 17. 45,1.
White, see Edward			55,12-13
Widder	55,9	Wulfmer	53,27. 55,4-6
Wig	35,1. 36,1	Wulfnoth	23,25. 25,5
Wigot, King Edward's	52,2	Wulfric	18,5. 53,36. 55,3
Huntsman		Wulfsi the prebendary	56,9
William Basset	23,26	Wulfsi son of Burgred	25,5
William Froissart	23,20-21	Wulfward Leofed	20,1
William Gross	25,8	Wulfwin	53,34
William Lovett	41	Bishop Wulfwy	1,1c. 16,4. 24,23.
William Peverel	22. 3,17. 32,5.		28,2. 34,2
	42,1 note	Wynsi the Chamberlain	1,1b
William Speke	25. 17,1. 56,2		

Churches and Clergy. Archbishop of Canterbury ... Stigand. Bishop of Bayeux 2. 40,3.
Coutances 3. 31,1. Dorchester ... Wulfwy. Durham 5. Lincoln ... Remigius. Abbess of Barking 11.
Abbot of St. Alban's 23,12. 53,25. (Bury) St.Edmund's 6. 53,35. Peterborough 7. Ely 3,6 note.
Ramsey 8. 19,1. 34,3. Thorney 10. Westminster 9. Canons of Holy Cross of Waltham 5,1-2.
St Paul's of Bedford 13. 53,32; 35. St Paul's of London 12. 57,8. E 2. See also Ansfrid, Osmund.
Church of Houghton Regis 1,3. Leighton Buzzard 4,9. Luton 1,2b. St Nicholas of Angers 24,29.
Monks of St Neot's 38,1-2. See also Walter. Nuns of St Mary's of Elstow 53,1,3-4.
Prebendary, see Wulfsi. Priests, see Alric, Alwin, Ansketel, Ernwin, Leofgeat, Morcar of Luton,
Roger, Saemer, Solomon, Tovi, Wulfmer.

Secular Titles and Occupational Names. Beadle *(bedellus)*... Aelfric, Leofmer.
Chamberlain *(camerarius)* ...Aethelwulf, Thurstan, William, Wynsi. Constable *(stalre)*.. . Asgar,
Bondi. Count *(comes)*...Eustace, Gilbert. Countess *(comitissa)*...Gytha, Judith. Earl *(comes)*..
Algar, Gyrth, Harold, Siwald, Tosti, Waltheof. Queen *(regina)*...Edith. King's Huntsman
(venator regis)...Wigot. Reeve *(prefectus)*...Alwin, Herbert, Osgeat. Sheriff *(vicecomes)*...
Godric. King Edward's Steersman. *(Stirman)*...Wulfheah. Steward *(dapifer)*... Eudo, Ivo, William.
Young *(cilt)*... Leofwin.

INDEX OF PLACES

The name of each place is followed by (i) the initial of its Hundred and its location on the Map in this volume; (ii) its National Grid reference; (iii) chapter and section references in DB. Bracketed figures denote mention in sections dealing with a different place. Unless otherwise stated, the identifications of EPNS and the spellings of the Ordnance Survey are followed for places in England; of OEB for places abroad. The National Grid reference system is explained on all Ordnance Survey maps, and in the Automobile Association Handbooks; the figures reading from left to right are given before those reading from bottom to top of the map. The Bedfordshire Hundreds (see 1,1 note) are Barford (Ba); Biggleswade (Bg); Bucklow Half-Hundred (Bk); Clifton (C); Flitt (F); Manshead (M); Redbornstoke (R); Stanbridge Half-Hundred (Sb); Stodden (Sd); Wenslow Half-Hundred (Ww); Willey (Wy); Wixamtree (Wx). Places entered in Hertfordshire and Huntingdonshire in DB are indexed as (He) and (Hu). Grid references beginning with the figure 9 are in the 100 kilometre grid square SP. All others are in square TL. Approximate locations are printed in italic type. Places mentioned in the notes, but not in DB, are shown on the map by open circles. Unidentified places are shown in DB spelling, in italics.

	Map	Grid	Text		Map	Grid	Text
Ampthill	R 12	03 38	24,10	Clifton	C 2	16 39	4,7. 8,6. 21,17. 24,28. 53,46
Arlesey	C 6	19 36	5,2. 18,6. 24,30. 56,9	Clophill	F 2	08 38	24,14
Apsley Guise	M 3	94 36	23,17	Colmworth	Ba 2	10 58	23,38. (17,4). (23,24)
Astwick	Bg 12	21 38	23,45-47. 32,12	Cople	Wx 6	10 48	23,49-55. 53,34
Great Barford	Ba 9	13 52	23,36-37; 39-40	Cranfield	R 7	95 42	8,1
Little Barford	Bg 1	17 56	8,5. 45,1	Husborne Crawley	M 4	95 36	24,1. 41,1
Barton-in-the-Clay	F 9	08 30	8,2	Cudessane	C		16,8. 23,57
Barwythe	He B	02 14	E 4	Dean	Sd 6	04 67	3,3. 4,1. 17,1. 57,13-14
Battlesden	M 13	96 28	16,2. 40,2. 55,1	Dunstable	M 19	02 21	1,2 note
Bedford	Bk 10	04 49	B. (4,9. 6,1. 13. 53,32. 56 57,14)	Dunton	Bg 6	23 44	16,5. 39,1
Beeston	Wx 7	16 48	21,12-14. 25,14. 47,3. 56,7. 57,11	Easton	Sd 4	13 71	3,6. 4,2. 17,4-7. 23,24. 35,1. 36,1. 44,1
Biddenham	Bk 9	02 50	4,4. 6,1. 13,1-2. 23,28. 25,4. 56,1-4	Eaton Bray	Sb 7	97 20	2,1
				Eaton Socon	Ba 3	16 58	21,1. See Wulfmer.
Biggleswade	Bg 4	18 44	51,2. (51,4)	Edlesborough	Sb 9	97 19	27,1
Billington	Sb 6	94 22	1,1b note	Edworth	Bg 11	22 40	18,4. 57,3 iv
Biscot	F 13	08 23	1,5	Eggington	Sb 3	95 25	1,1b note
'Bleadon'			(3,8; 10-11)	Elstow	R 2	05 47	53,4. (53,1;3)
Bletsoe	Bk 1	02 58	23,27. 53,8	'Elvedon'	Sd 9	06 66	44,4
Blunham	Wx 1	15 51	6,3. 21,11. 53,35	Eversholt	M 6	99 33	2,2. 23,19 57,1
Bolnhurst	Sd 15	08 59	2,4-5. 3,8. 10,1. 53,6	Everton	Ww 2	20 51	53,30
Bromham	Bk 6	01 51	15,1. 23,29. 53,9. 57,18. (23,28)	Eyeworth	Bg 7	24 45	25,10. 55,5
				Farndish	Wy 3	92 63	42,1. 43,1
				Felmersham	Wy 8	99 57	48,2. 53,11
Broom	Wx 10	17 43	24,11	Flitton	F 3	05 35	30,1
Caddington	F 14	06 19	12,1	Flitwick	R 16	03 34	(25,2). 41,2
Cainhoe	F 4	10 36	24,15. 55,3	Nares Gladley	Sb 1	91 27	52,2
Campton	C 3	12 38	16,9.18,7.47,4	Goldington	Ba 10	07 50	4,5. 23,41-43. 57,8
Cardington	Wx 5	08 47	23,10. 53,33	Goldington Highfields	Bk 4	05 53	23,7
Carlton	Wy 13	95 55	2,7. 24,20-21. 46,2. 57,6	Gravenhurst	F 7	11 35	23,21
Chainhalle	Bk 5		23,5-6	Hanefelde	Sd		17,3. 57,15
Chalgrave	M 15	00 27	20,2. 49,1	Harlington	M 11	03 30	24,5
Chalton	Wx 3	14 50	54,3	Harrold	Wy 11	94 56	53,13
Chawston	Ba 5	15 56	21,3.. 23,34. 25,7-8	Harrowden	Wx 4	06 47	14,1. 24,27. 53,32
Chellington	Wy 12	95 55	3,10 note	Cockayne Hatley	Ww 4	25 49	53,29. 55,6
Chicksands	C 1	12 39	4,8. 55,11-12	Haynes	F 1	08 41	23,15
Clapham	Sd 18	03 52	19,1. (19,2)				

'Westcotts'	R 6 07 43	24,13. 57,12.	Woburn	M 5 94 33	16,1. 57,1
Westoning	M 9 02 32	E1	Wootton	R 3 00 45	49,2. (49,3)
Wilden	Ba 4 09 55	2,9	Wyboston	Ba 6 16 56	8,4. 21,2. 23,33
Willington	Wx 2 11 59	23,11. (23,52)			24,24. 38,2. 55,4
Wilshamstead	R 5 06 43	53,3.	Wymington	Wy 2 95 64	25,6. 31,1. 32,6-7.
'Woodcroft'		1,4			57,7;21
Hundred			Yelden	Sd 5 01 66	3,4

Places not named

BARFORD Hundred 53,15. BIGGLESWADE Hundred 24,25. MANSHEAD Hundred 24,2.
STODDEN Hundred 57,16;20.

Places not in Bedfordshire. Indexed above.

Elsewhere in Britain.
BUCKS...Edlesborough.   HERTS...Holwell; Ware, see Askell.   HUNTS...Everton; Kimbolton;
Tilbrook.   KENT...Rochester, see Ansgot.   LINCOLN ...see Alfred.   NORTHANTS...Newton
Bromshold; Rushden; Stanwick.   WILTS...Boscombe, see Alan.
See also Index of Churches.

Outside Britain
Angers...Churches.   Ardres...Arnulf.   Argenton...David.   Aubigny...Nigel.   Bayeux...Bishop.
Beauchamp...Hugh.   Blosseville...Gilbert.   Bolbec...Hugh.   Breuil...Osbert.   Cairon...William.
Chocques...Gunfrid, Sigar.   Coutances...Bishop.   Eu...William.   Flanders...Hugh, Walter.
Ghent...Gilbert.   Grandmesnil...Hugh.   Hesdin...Arnulf.   Ivry...Acard.   Lanquetot...Ralph.
Les Roches...John.   Le Vast...Nigel.   L'Isle...Ralph.   Lorraine...Albert.   Loucelles...William.
Moutiers ...Lisois.   Oilly...Robert.   Paris...Fulchere.   Rots...Serlo.   Tosny...Robert.
Trelly...Geoffrey.   Warenne...William.

SYSTEMS OF REFERENCE TO DOMESDAY BOOK

The manuscript is divided into numbered chapters, and the chapters into sections, usually marked
by large initials and red ink. Farley however did not number the sections. References in the past
have therefore been to the page or column. Several different ways of referring to the same column
have been in use. The commonest are:

(i)	(ii)	(iii)	(iv)	(v)
152a	152	152a	152	152ai
152b	152	152a	152.2	152a2
152c	152b	152b	152b	152bi
152d	152b	152b	152b.2	152b2

The relation between Vinogradoff's notation (i), here followed, and the sections is:

209 a B	- Landholders		213 a 23,10	-	23,18		217 a 51,1	-	53,4
b 1,1	- 1,2b		b 23,18	-	23,27		b 53,4	-	53,14
c 1,3	- 2,3		c 23,27	-	23,40		c 53,15	-	53,28
d 2,3	- 3,3		d 23,40	-	23,52		d 53,29	-	54,3
210 a 3,3	- 3,12		214 a 23,52	-	24,6		218 a 54,4	-	55,11
b 3,13	- 4,6		b 24,6	-	24,17		b 55,12	-	56,9
c 4,7	- 7,1		c 24,17	-	24,27		c 57,1	-	57,7
d 8,1	- 8,9		d 24,27	-	25,6		d 57,7	-	57,21
211 a 9,1	- 14,1		215 a 25,6	-	25,14				
b 15,1	- 16,2		b 25,14	-	30,1				
c 16,2	- 16,9		c 30,1	-	32,5				
d 17,1	- 18,1		d 32,6	-	32,16				
212 a 18,2	- 20,1		216 a 33,1	-	37,1				
b 20,1	- 21,8		b 38,1	-	42,1				
c 21,9	- 22,2		c 43,1	-	47,2				
d 22,2	- 23,10		d 47,3	-	50,1				

BARFORD Hundred
1 'Sudbury'
2 Colmworth
3 Eaton Socon
4 Wilden
5 Chawston
6 Wyboston
7 Roxton
8 Salph
9 Great Barford
10 Goldington

BIGGLESWADE Hundred
1 Little Barford
2 Tempsford
3 'Kinwick'
4 Biggleswade
5 Stratton
6 Dunton
7 Eyeworth
8 Holme
9 Millow
10 Langford
11 Edworth
12 Astwick

BUCKLOW Hundred
1 Bletsoe
2 Pavenham
3 Stevington
4 Goldington Highfields
5 *Chainhalle*
6 Bromham
7 Putnoe
8 Stagsden
9 Biddenham
10 Bedford

CLIFTON Hundred
1 Chicksands
2 Clifton
3 Campton
4 Henlow
5 Meppershall
6 Arlesey
7 Stotfold
8 Stondon
9 Shillington
10 Holwell

FLITT Hundred
1 Haynes
2 Clophill
3 Flitton
4 Cainhoe
5 Pulloxhill
6 Silsoe
7 Gravenhurst
8 Higham Gobion
9 Barton-in-the-Clay
10 Pegsdon
11 Streatley
12 Sundon
13 Biscot
14 Caddington

MANSHEAD Hundred
1 Salford
2 Holcot
3 Apsley Guise
4 Husborne Crawley
5 Woburn
6 Eversholt
7 Priestley
8 Tingrith
9 Westoning
10 Milton Bryan
11 Harlington
12 Potsgrove
13 Battlesden
14 Toddington
15 Chalgrave
16 Hockliffe
17 Houghton Regis
18 Sewell
19 Dunstable
20 Luton

REDBORNSTOKE Hundred
1 Kempston
2 Elstow
3 Wootton
4 Shelton
5 Wilshamstead
6 'Westcotts'
7 Cranfield
8 Marston Moretaine
9 Houghton Conquest
10 Lidlington
11 Millbrook
12 Ampthill
13 Maulden
14 Segenhoe
15 Steppingley
16 Flitwick

STANBRIDGE Hundred
1 Nares Gladley
2 Leighton Buzzard
3 Eggington
4 Stanbridge
5 Tilsworth
6 Billington
7 Eaton Bray
8 Totternhoe
9 Edlesborough
10 Studham

HUNTS
K Kimbolton
P Pertenhall
S Swineshead

HERTS
B Barwythe
H Hitchin
K Kensworth
P Polehanger

STODDEN Hundred
1 Stanwick
2 Shelton
3 Tilbrook
4 Easton
5 Yelden
6 Dean
7 Newton Bromshold
8 Melchbourne
9 'Elvedon'
10 Knotting
11 Riseley
12 Keysoe
13 'Shirdon'
14 Little Staughton
15 Bolnhurst
16 Milton Ernest
17 Oakley
18 Clapham

WENSLOW Hundred
1 Sandy
2 Everton
3 Potton
4 Cockayne Hatley
5 Sutton

WILLEY Hundred
1 Rushden
2 Wymington
3 Farndish
4 Podington
5 Hinwick
6 Sharnbrook
7 Odell
8 Felmersham
9 Radwell
10 Thurleigh
11 Harrold
12 Chellington
13 Carlton
14 Turvey

WIXAMTREE Hundred
1 Blunham
2 Willington
3 Chalton
4 Harrowden
5 Cardington
6 Cople
7 Beeston
8 Northill
9 Old Warden
10 Broom
11 Southill
12 Stanford

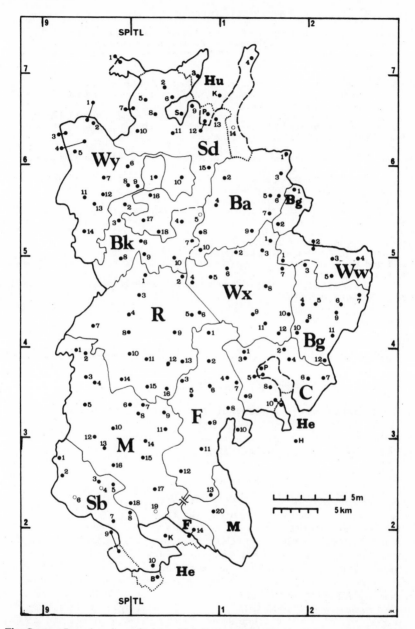

The County Boundary is marked by thick lines, continuous for 1086, dotted for modern boundaries; Hundred boundaries (1086) by thin lines, broken where uncertain.

National Grid 10-kilometre squares are shown on the map border.

Each four-figure square covers one square kilometre, or 247 acres, approximately 2 hides, at 120 acres to the hide.

TECHNICAL TERMS

Many words meaning measurements have to be transliterated. But translation may not dodge other problems by the use of obsolete or made-up words which do not exist in modern English. The translations here used are given in italics. They cannot be exact; they aim at the nearest modern equivalent.

BORDARIUS. Cultivator of inferior status, usually with a little land. *s m a l l h o l d e r*
CARUCA. A plough, with the oxen who pulled it, usually reckoned as 8. *p l o u g h*
CARUCATA. See 10,1 note. *c a r u c a t e*
DOMINIUM. The mastery or dominion of a lord *(dominus)*; including ploughs, land, men, villages, etc., reserved for the lord's use; often concentrated in a *home farm* or *demesne*, a 'Manor Farm' or 'Lordship Farm' *l o r d s h i p*
FEUDUM. See 2,2 note. *H o l d i n g*
FIRMA. Old English *feorm*, provisions due to the King or lord; a sum paid in place of these and of other miscellaneous dues. *r e v e n u e*
GELDUM. The principal royal tax, originally levied during the Danish wars, normally at an equal number of pence on each *hide* of land. *t a x*
HIDE. A unit of land measurement, see B note. *h i d e*
PRAEPOSITUS, PRAEFECTUS. Old English *gerefa*, a royal officer. *r e e v e*
SOCHEMANNUS. See Appendix. *F r e e m a n*
TAINUS, TEGNUS. Person holding land from the King by special grant; formerly used of the King's ministers and military companions. *t h a n e*
T.R.E. *tempore regis Edwardi*, in King Edward's time. *b e f o r e 1 0 6 6*
VILLA. Translating Old English *tun*, town. The later distinction between a small *village* and a large *town* was not yet in use in 1086. *v i l l a g e*
VILLANUS. Member of a *villa*, usually with more land than a *bordarius*. *v i l l a g e r*
VIRGATA. A quarter of a *hide*. *v i r g a t e*

ADDITIONS AND CORRECTIONS to volumes published earlier.

HERTFORDSHIRE

B3 and Index of Persons. *For* Wulfmer of Eton *read* Wulfmer of Eaton.
25,2. *For* [...1½ virgates] *read* [....½ virgate].
Index of Places, Elsewhere in Britain. *For* BUCKINGHAMSHIRE Eton? *read* BEDFORDSHIRE Eaton Socon.

SURREY

1,8. *For* in-going *read* death duty. *Delete* note; *substitute* DEATH DUTY. *Releva*, payable by the heir, normally to the King.
2,1 note. The *Domesday Monachorum* of Canterbury (ed. D C. Douglas 1944), written about 1100, reproduces much of the Kentish DB material. One list of revenues ends with the Archbishop's manors in Surrey, Middlesex, and Sussex. (p.10 folio 5v) = transcript p. 99). The Surrey entries are *Croindene de firma xxx lib & xl sol archiepiscopo. Gablum xxxiiii sol & vii d. De quodam theine xx sol. Mortelace & Heisa de firma lvi lib & xl sol archiepiscopo. Gablum lxxiiii sol & iii d.* The DM *firma* is slightly more than the DB *valet* of Croydon, but less than the *valet* of Mortlake, with Hayes (Middlesex). Under Tarring (Sussex 2 and 2,9 notes) is listed *Buresto viii lib*, evidently Burstow (TQ 31 41) EPNS Surrey 286.

MIDDLESEX

2,1-2 note. *Domesday Monachorum* enters Hayes with Mortlake (Surrey) and continues with Harrow *Herges de firma liiii lib & xx sol archiepiscopo & xxx porcos. Gablum lx & vii sol.* The *firma* is slightly less than the DB *valet*.